Strategies for Effective Desegregation

Strategies for Effective Desegregation

Lessons from Research

Willis D. Hawley
Vanderbilt University

Robert L. Crain
The Johns Hopkins University
and The Rand Corporation

Christine H. Rossell
Boston University

Mark A. Smylie
Vanderbilt University

Ricardo R. Fernández
University of Wisconsin,
Milwaukee

Janet W. Schofield
University of Pittsburgh

Rachel Tompkins
The Children's Defense Fund

William T. Trent
The Johns Hopkins University

Marilyn S. Zlotnik
Vanderbilt University

LexingtonBooks
D.C. Heath and Company
Lexington, Massachusetts
Toronto

Library of Congress Cataloging in Publication Data
Main entry under title:

Strategies for effective desegregation.

    Bibliography: p.
    Includes index.
    1. School integration—United States—Addresses, essays, lectures.
I. Hawley, Willis D.
LC214.5.S73 1982   370.19′342   82–47968
ISBN 0–669–05722–3

Published simultaneously in Canada

Printed in the United States of America

Clothbound International Standard Book Number: 0–669–05722–3

Paperbound International Standard Book Number: 06376–2

Library of Congress Catalog Card Number: 82–47968

Contents

Preface and Acknowledgments

Against the background of continuing public debate about busing and changes in state and federal policies, school systems throughout the country go about the business of racial desegregation. To say that the issue of desegregation is socially and politically divisive is to state the obvious. The conflict over school desegregation has been fired by an enormous amount of misinformation about what happens in desegregating communities and by beliefs that desegregation substantially complicates the already difficult job of ensuring quality public education for the nation's children.

This book seeks to clarify the national experience with school desegregation and to identify a number of ways to maximize the potential benefits and reduce the possible costs of desegregation. The book is the work of several authors, but it is based on the efforts of many others. It is a synthesis of existing research and commentary and in that sense is the work of hundreds of writers. More directly, the book derives from two extensive projects that have involved numerous persons in addition to those listed as authors of this book.

The first of these projects is the National Review Panel on School Desegregation Research. The panel, funded primarily by The Ford Foundation, has produced several books and articles which have sought to identify what is known and not known about desegregation. Panel members are Willis D. Hawley and Betsy Levin (chairs), Mark A. Chesler, Robert L. Crain, Edgar G. Epps, John B. McConahay, James M. McPartland, Gary Orfield, Peter Roos, Christine H. Rossell, William L. Taylor, and Mark G. Yudof. Chapters 1 and 9, which discuss assumptions about the overall consequences of desegregation, are primarily the work of Willis D. Hawley with the assistance of Mark A. Smylie. These chapters draw heavily on the work of the panel and the research of other scholars, including some of the coauthors of this book.

Chapters 3 to 8 identify a number of strategies that appear to be effective ways of developing and implementing desegregation plans. These chapters present a revised version of the summary book of the project, *Assessment of Current Knowledge about the Effectiveness of School Desegregation Strategies,* funded by the National Institute of Education and the United States Office for Civil Rights (Contract No. NIE–R–79–0034). The listed authors of this book drafted or revised significant portions of that summary book. Other members of the study team for that project were Carol Andersen, C. Anthony Broh, Rita E.

Mahard, John B. McConahay, William Sampson, Charles B. Vergon, and Ben Williams. This project benefited from the advice of a distinguished panel of scholars and practitioners who made suggestions and comments on every aspect of the study from the project design to the final report. The members of the advisory board were Mary Berry, Fred Burke, Norman Chachkin, Francis Keppel, Hernan LaFontaine, Sharon Robinson, Peter Roos, and Franklin Wilson.

The authors are grateful to several project participants who reviewed drafts of that study and made substantial suggestions. The contributions of Janet Eyler, Thomas Carter, Rosie Feinberg, Jayjia Hsia, Lorenza Schmidt, and Susana Navarro are especially acknowledged. Marilyn Zlotnik served as coordinator of the project.

We are indebted to Ralph Bohrson and Edward Meade of the Ford Foundation who advised and supported the work of the National Review Panel on School Desegregation Research. We are also grateful for the thoughtful advice of Oscar Uribe, Mary von Euler, and Ron Henderson who in their roles as project officers at The National Institute of Education (NIE) monitored much of the work reflected in these pages. Janice Potker of the United States Office for Civil Rights was helpful in coordinating our efforts with that agency.

Sheila Peters helped identify and organize much of the information, and Bonnie Moore cheerfully typed, retyped, and edited the final manuscript. To all these people, we are very grateful.

Although many contributed to this book, both directly and indirectly, the authors take full responsibility for any errors or omissions. Of course, the views set forth here do not necessarily represent those of The Ford Foundation or the United States Department of Education.

Strategies for Effective Desegregation

1

The Context: Facts and Fantasy about the Consequences of Desegregation

Faded Dreams

The moral imperative and great hopes that gave momentum to desegregation in the late 1960s and early 1970s seem to have been replaced by a combination of pessimism and pragmatism. The faith that children of all races and ethnic backgrounds learning side by side would bring about an end to prejudice and substantially reduce social inequities appears to have given way to a new conviction that the noble experiment has failed.

Belief in the failure of school desegregation has begun to dominate national thought and captivate the development of related national, state, and local policies. Examples abound. In November 1978 voters in the state of Washington approved Initiative 350 limiting the discretion of local school systems to assign and transport students to achieve racial balance among schools even if they wish to do so voluntarily. In 1979 California voters approved Proposition One prohibiting state-ordered desegregation unless intentional discrimination is established. Several local school systems, including Denver and Norfolk, have recently proposed at least partial abandonment of mandatory desegregation. During 1980 to 1981, nineteen separate bills were introduced in the United States Congress to prohibit the Department of Education, the Justice Department, or the federal courts from promoting or requiring mandatory student assignments or busing as strategies to achieve school desegregation. In addition, the Education and Justice Departments under the Reagan administration have publicly opposed mandatory strategies to reduce racial isolation in the public schools.

These initiatives appear to be motivated, at least in part, by a growing belief that school desegregation, as it has been pursued, has not been and cannot be in the best interests of children and communities. Few people argue that intentional efforts to keep minority children from attending school with white children should be tolerated. However, it is widely thought that we have tried our best but that the costs of imposing desegregation on unwilling communities generally outweigh the benefits.

The New Mythology

A new mythology has replaced the old convictions about the promises of school desegregation. The specific assumptions that make up this new mythology of school desegregation include the following propositions:

1. Desegregation has not substantially reduced racial isolation, nor has it effectively created unitary school systems. An extension of this assumption is that desegregation has induced substantial white flight and, therefore, has actually increased racial separation.
2. Desegregation can be achieved without mandatory student assignment and busing to schools, largely through voluntary choice.
3. Desegregation disrupts schools and undermines the quality of education available to students of all races.
4. Desegregation leads to interracial conflict in schools and thus disrupts the educational process and increases racial prejudices.
5. Desegregation results in conflict at the community level that undermines race relations, disrupts social peace, and reduces public support for public education,

Although these beliefs are widely held, the new mythology does not jibe with available evidence from education and social-science research. It distorts the national experience with school desegregation. It ignores positive outcomes that are associated with the national experience and denies the possibility that school desegregation can promote both equity and quality in public education.

The old promises and convictions that school desegregation is a panacea for racial, social, and educational equity do not fit the accumulated evidence. It is not reasonable to argue that desegregation will always have positive consequences, nor can it be argued that desegregation will, in itself, totally eliminate inequities that are rooted in historic patterns of prejudice and social injustice. Nonetheless, the case against school desegregation often misrepresents the facts and even those arguments that have some element of truth are invariably overstated. If the assumptions upon which the new mythology rests are not supported by the evidence, they provide no rationale for abandoning desegregation efforts or for pursuing desegregation only where it can be achieved without disruption, conflict, and significant financial costs.

The New Mythology and Findings from the Research on School Desegregation

The research on school desegregation has often been seen as conflicting and inconclusive. To be sure, many important questions cannot be answered with great certainty. But the view that the research provides little insight to the consequences of desegregation appears often to rest on assessments of research that were conducted prior to the mid-1970s. In the last four or five years a substantial number of new studies have appeared. These studies, coupled with more sophisticated analyses of the available evidence, provide a different picture than might be gained by reviewing the earlier literature. Unfortunately, when recent research is introduced, it is by advocates of particular positions who usually distort or oversimplify a study's findings.

This book's assessment of propositions that comprise the new mythology on school desegregation is based on a comprehensive examination of the empirical evidence on the effects of desegregation on children and communities. Much of the evidence upon which the findings are based are noted in this chapter. However, many of the studies involved are described in greater detail, and additional evidence is introduced in the following chapters of this book.

Racial Isolation and White Flight

The first myth is that desegregation has not substantially reduced racial isolation and, in fact, has induced white flight, which actually increases racial separation. Thus there are two ways of assessing trends in racial desegregation. One is to consider the degree of segregation among schools or the number of minority schools in a given district. The second approach focuses on the amount of interracial contact in a school district which is an indicator of both the relative desegregation among schools and the racial mix of the district. While these two measures are different in important ways, they tell roughly the same story (see Clotfelter 1982; Dziuban 1980; and Zoloth 1976a for discussion and comparison of indices).

The Extent of Segregation in Public Schools. Using an index of dissimilarity which examines the extent to which the racial composition of individual schools approximate or deviate from that racial composition of districtwide enrollment, Karl E. Taeuber and Franklin D. Wilson (1979) indicate that between 1968 and 1976 segregation between minority groups and whites declined by 50 percent. Almost all of this decline reflects changes in the levels of segregation among black and white students. Nationwide, Hispanics and Asian and Native Americans have experienced relatively little desegregation although in most areas they were initially less segregated than blacks. It appears that Hispanics, perhaps because of recent immigration to this country, are becoming increasingly segregated, especially in certain areas of the West and Southeast (Noboa 1980).

The greatest progress in desegregation has been in the South where changes have been dramatic and lasting. Indeed, the South is now the least segregated region of the country as far as blacks and whites are concerned (Taeuber and Wilson 1979). However, Abdin Noboa (1980) finds that Hispanics are more segregated in the South then elsewhere. In some cities, Hispanics and blacks are less segregated from each other than before, in part because some school boards have sought to avoid black-white desegregation by classifying Hispanics as white and mixing them with blacks. In general, however, blacks and Hispanics are becoming increasingly segregated from each other (Noboa 1980).

Not surprisingly, racial isolation has been reduced most extensively when courts have ordered desegregation (see Bullock and Rodgers 1976; Yudof 1981). Desegregation imposed by the United States Office for Civil Rights and state education agencies has also reduced racial isolation substantially. In particular, state education agencies in New Jersey and Pennsylvania have brought about reductions in racial isolation, especially in some smaller communities.

In large urban and county school districts, desegregation progress has been greater under plans that assign students to schools than under plans that rely on voluntary student transfer or choice. Using data collected by the United States Office for Civil Rights, Mark A. Smylie (1982) found that among the nation's largest school districts, those implementing mandatory student assignment plans achieved, on the average, 65 percent of possible racial balance among schools. Those implementing districtwide or metropolitan plans achieved 84 percent of possible balance. However, those districts surveyed that implemented voluntary plans achieved only an average of 18 percent of possible districtwide racial balance. Large districts making the most significant progress under voluntary plans include Kansas City (Missouri), Milwaukee, and San Diego, although this progress was considerably less than that made by most districts implementing mandatory student-reassignment plans.

Indices of racial balance, however, may be reduced while substantial numbers of minority children remain segregated. Although this sometimes occurs because of a well-intentioned effort to achieve desegregation without inducing white flight, the practice is tellingly referred to as *warehousing* by some developers of desegregation plans. In his survey, Smylie (1982) found examples of several districts, including Dallas, Fresno, Los Angeles, Mobile, and Pittsburgh, that implemented partial mandatory student-reassignment plans and increased districtwide levels of racial balance but made only slight progress in reducing numbers of schools with over 90 percent minority enrollment. However, in almost all districts surveyed that implemented voluntary plans, the racial balance achieved was less than that which was achieved in the average district implementing a mandatory plan, and there was virtually no reduction of schools with this minority proportion of enrollment in most districts. Indeed, in some districts, including Flint, Houston, and Philadelphia, the number of minority schools increased upon implementation of voluntary plans.

Despite the fact that progress has been made in many communities across the country, there is still a substantial amount of racial isolation in the nation's schools. In a report to the Subcommittee on Civil and Constitutional Rights of the United States House of Representatives, Gary Orfield (1982) found that in 1980, 63 percent of black students nationwide attended schools that were over half minority and 33 percent attended schools that were 90 to 100 percent minority. That year, 80 percent of all black students in the Northeast attended schools with over half minority enrollment, up 13 percentage points since 1968, and 49 percent attended schools that were over 90 percent minority. Nationwide, the percent of Hispanic students attending schools with over half minority enrollment rose 13 percentage points between 1968 and 1980.

Courts continue to mandate desegregation in communities where the consequences of official action in the past have left school systems segregated. However, the pace of desegregation has slowed, in part because the school systems that engaged in the most obvious forms of *de jure* segregation are more likely to have been the targets of litigation in the past.

What about White Flight? Despite past gains in reducing racial isolation in schools, some observers assert that this ground has been or soon will be lost because of desegregation-induced white flight. As the data already cited suggest, if one measures segregation by either racial-balance measures or racial isolation, this potential reversal did not occur between 1968 and 1980. The late 1960s and early 1970s was the period of greatest desegregation activity, and, most white flight occurs in the period immediately prior to and during the first year of implementation of a comprehensive desegregation plan.

There is no doubt that the proportion of minority students in the public schools, especially in urban school systems, has risen dramatically in the last decade. The extent to which desegregation has caused this change in enrollment is usually overstated. (For a review of the evidence on white flight see Rossell and Hawley 1982 and chapter 3.) The nation is continuing to experience a long-term movement of whites to suburbia that began well before desegregation became an issue. In addition, differences in birth rates among whites and minorities and the immigration of Hispanic and Asian families have contributed to changes in the racial composition of school-age populations. In the absence of desegregation, these conditions result in a 4 to 8 percent annual decline in white-student populations of most northern-city school districts. Nationwide, there has been a decline in the white proportion of students in both public-school systems and private schools, at least through 1978 (Rossell and Hawley 1981).

Whites do flee from desegregation in some cases, especially when their children are bused to minority neighborhoods and when the proportion of minority students in the district exceeds 30 or 35 percent. It is important to note, however, that the greatest amount of white flight occurs before the first year desegregation plans are actually implemented or during the first year of desegregation. This means that most people flee desegregation before they experience it (see Rossell 1978a; Coleman, Kelly, and Moore 1975; Armor 1980; Farley, Richards, and Wurdock 1980; Rossell and Ross 1979).

The long-term effect of desegregation on white flight is more difficult to assess from the available research. In some cases the acceleration of white flight in the implementation year is followed by lower rates of white loss (Coleman, Kelly, and Moore 1975; Rossell 1978a; Ross, Gratton, and Clarke 1981; Morgan and England 1981). Districts less likely to make up their preimplementation- and implementation-year white loss are large-city school districts where blacks comprise more than 35 percent of total enrollment (see Rossell and Ross 1979; Armor 1980).

Most school systems do relatively little that is explicitly aimed at reducing white flight. More could be done. In particular, desegregation plans that are carefully drawn may limit the amount of pupil reassignments and busing time and distance. Furthermore, desegregation plans can encourage residential desegregation and thus reduce the need for busing and eliminate one of the factors that prompts flight (Pearce 1980; Orfield 1981). (For extensive discussion of policy options to reduce white flight, see Rossell and Hawley 1982.) In short, the extent to which the changes in the proportion of minority students in desegregating school systems can be traced to desegregation is almost always overstated.

What about Interracial Contact? It would be possible to reduce racial isolation substantially and not achieve substantial improvements over time in interracial contact. This could not happen, of course, in communities that were legally segregated. In other communities, desegregation strategies that rely on voluntary school selection by whites or that are not comprehensive might result in less white loss and thus more long-term opportunities for interracial contact. Chapter 3 will discuss the relative impact of mandatory and voluntary desegregation plans on white loss and racial isolation.

Suffice it to say that given the evidence as of 1981, desegregation, even considering the most dramatic cases of white loss, does not increase the separation of races in public schools. Such flight has not yet actually reduced the amount of interracial contact over pre-desegregation levels of racial isolation (Rossell 1978a). No school system for which data are now available is more segregated today than it was before desegregation was ordered. In Boston, for example, where substantial flight to suburban and private schools has occurred, there are more opportunities for interracial contact than would have been the case if the schools had not been desegregated.

Experts do differ, however, in their assessments of the effects of desegregation on long-term interracial contact. The disagreements center around three research problems, two of which may not be resolvable. First, some researchers compare interracial contact before desegregation with contact several years after (Ross 1982). This approach, however, fails to take into account the white loss that is occurring in most districts, especially those in the North, West, and Southwest, even when no desegregation plan is adopted or imposed. Second, although racial contact measures may not have fallen below predesegregation levels by 1980, this does not mean that they will not sometime later. The research problem here is that the analyst cannot project a straight-line loss of whites into the future. Plots of the rate of white loss for any given set of school districts show great variations among systems. Some stabilize, some do not, but the rate of white loss declines in almost all systems over time. There is not yet a reliable formula that allows researchers to take into account all the factors that influence white loss so that one could estimate into the future with much certainty.

A third research problem is that one cannot know what would have happened if a school system had been involved in voluntary desegregation as compared to mandatory desegregation. That one can use the experience of a single community to estimate the rate of white loss in another is a very precarious assumption. David J. Armor (1980), for example, has pointed to the San Diego experience to indicate that voluntary plans can achieve reductions in racial isolation and thus more long-term interracial contact than mandatory plans. However, even if one puts aside the fact that San Diego did not achieve much reduction in the racial isolation of minority students through its voluntary plan (Smylie 1982), this district is more multiracial than most communities and has experienced a more rapid rate of population growth than most nonsouthern cities. These two characteristics, among others, make generalizing from the San Diego experience unwarranted.

It seems clear that desegregation has substantially reduced racial separation among schools. There are many fewer schools today that are one race than there were ten to fifteen years ago. However, many schools that are racially mixed end up segregating students within schools by race. The scope of this problem is just now being realized, and several strategies are available for reducing racial isolation within schools (see Cook, Eyler, and Ward 1981). This issue will be examined further in chapter 7.

Desegregation through Voluntary Choice

The second myth is that desegregation can be achieved without mandatory student assignment and busing to schools, largely through voluntary choice. Busing has become a symbol for school desegregation and for many of the problems desegregated school systems currently experience. In other words, busing itself may be less an issue than the actual strategies and policies that take children from segregated neighborhood schools and assign them to schools in different areas of a district in which they comprise a smaller majority or perhaps a minority of the student bodies. Before the validity of this second proposition of the new mythology is directly assessed, a context for that evaluation can be provided by briefly describing the status of busing for desegregation and what is known about its effects on students.

Riding the Bus. In the nation as a whole, more children ride the bus to school today than walk. The number of children who ride the bus under court order is actually quite small. The extent to which busing has become a symbol of opposition to desegregation itself is suggested by the fact that the proportion of students in Los Angeles involved in court-ordered busing between 1978 and 1981 was 4 percent. No one knows for certain what percent of the nation's students ride the bus for desegregation purposes (those students who would not otherwise ride the bus to school), but the number is probably between 3 and 5 percent (see Moody and Ross 1980).

At the same time, busing is essential to substantially reduce the racial isolation in many school districts. In Nashville-Davidson County, for example, a federal district-court judge recently ordered the virtual elimination of busing in kindergarten through fourth grade. Even though every effort was made to desegregate in the absence of busing, 63 percent of kindergarten through fourth-grade classrooms were projected to have less than 10 percent of either black or white students in them in a city in which the population for these grades is about 32 percent black.

The manner in which students get to school does not seem to affect their achievement in or attitudes toward school. The research indicates that students do not seem to be affected by whether they walk, ride the bus, or arrive by car to school (see Davis 1973; Zoloth 1976b; Natkin 1980). Of course, excessively long rides, say of an hour or so each way, could well affect energy and interest in school. Few courts have required rides of such duration. It is also interesting to note that between 1968 and 1978, when most desegregation plans were implemented, the proportion of students being bused more than thirty minutes to school remained the same—about 15 percent (U.S. Bureau of the Census 1979). The issue of busing distance is discussed at greater length in chapter 3.

Carefully designed school-desegregation plans can reduce the time and distance of bus rides and foster the desegregation of housing. In Riverside, California, for example, children were initially bused to more than twenty schools for desegregation. A decade later, childen were bused to only four schools.

Voluntary School Desegregation. Under the best of circumstances, it appears that relatively few whites will voluntarily send their children to predominantly minority schools or to schools in minority neighborhoods. This means that where there are a few minority students in a district, voluntary plans may work because few whites are required to secure racial integration. In districts that are more than 30 to 35 percent minority, even where magnet schools are used, some approximation of districtwide racial balance is seldom achieved without mandating pupil assignments (Rossell 1979). Even in districts that are more than 70 percent white, one cannot be assured that voluntary plans will work (Larson 1980). Their success seems to depend on numerous factors such as the relative socioeconomic status of minorities and the extent of residential segregation.

Almost all school systems first seek to desegregate without requiring reassignment and busing of students. There is a very extensive record of court action documenting the relative ineffectiveness of every sort of plan based on voluntary choice by parents (see Vergon 1981). Indeed, the evidence on large school districts and those with large minority proportions of student enrollment is clear: voluntary strategies do not begin to achieve the levels of desegregation that are achieved through mandatory student assignments and busing to schools (see Foster 1973; Royster, Blatzell, and Simmons 1979; Rossell 1979).

In a case-survey analysis of desegregation plans implemented in fifty-two large school districts, David C. Morgan and Robert E. England (1981) conclude that voluntary strategies of open enrollment and free transfers have little effect on reducing racial isolation among schools. In another recent study, Smylie (1982) found that voluntary plans implemented by large districts with sizable minority populations achieved minimal changes in racial balance among schools and eliminated few schools with over 90 percent minority enrollment. As noted previously, this survey identified several districts in which numbers of schools with this proportion of minority enrollment increased upon implementation of voluntary plans.

Obviously, it would be desirable to achieve desegregation voluntarily and without requiring busing. Such volunteerism should be encouraged even in the face of discouraging evidence that it will have much effect. However, the evidence is very strong that student reassignments and busing are required in many cities along with voluntary strategies if racial isolation is to be substantially reduced.

The Quality of Education

The third myth is that desegregation disrupts schools and undermines the quality of education available to students of all races. When one speaks of a school's education quality, one usually refers to its ability to foster academic achievement. The available evidence suggests that school desegregation, overall, improves the academic achievement of minority students and, at least, does not impede the academic progress of whites. There are three bodies of evidence that inform this finding: case studies, national assessment, and input-output studies.

Case Studies. These studies examine quantitative evidence of academic achievement in schools or school systems undergoing desegregation. In 1978 Robert L. Crain and Rita E. Mahard (1978a) reviewed the studies of particular communities that have implemented explicit desegregation plans. Of seventy-three studies they found forty in which desegregation had a positive effect on black achievement, twenty-one with little or no effect, and only twelve with a negative effect. Ronald A. Krol (1978) independently analyzed fifty-five studies, using a statistical technique called metaanalysis, and came to basically the same conclusions as Crain and Mahard. Studies of the effects of desegregation over time (more than one year) showed more positive outcomes than did studies of the first year of desegregation (see also MacQueen and Coulson 1978).

A 1981 analysis by Crain and Mahard of ninety-three case studies confirms the positive effects of desegregation in the early years and extends the findings to Hispanic students. This study also indicates that one reason that the research has provided somewhat ambiguous signals in the past is that methodologically weak studies appear to yield more negative results than strong studies. Eighty-six percent of the studies with the strongest methodology revealed positive impacts but only 34 percent of the weakest studies showed positive outcomes. Preliminary results of a study by Paul Wortman (1981) and his associates also reveal a positive relationship between minority achievement and desegregation.

Results of the National Assessment of Educational Progress. It is often assumed that desegregation is a major cause of the widely publicized declines in test scores over the last several years. However, not only are the aggregate declines overstated in most cases, but the relationship between desegregation and achievement appears to be the reverse of what many seem to believe. The director of the national assessment recently compared trends in the performance of blacks and whites in the Southeast, the most thoroughly desegregated region of the country, with performance trends in other regions (Forbes 1981). This analysis indicates that changes over the last several years in performance were generally more positive for southeastern students, especially blacks, than for students in other regions. The most recent data on reading performance confirm the continuing progress of southeastern youngsters, both black and white. This progress is resulting, generally, in a narrowing of the historic differences in the performance of southern students and those from other regions. The assessment staff also sought to determine whether these changes were attributable to migration from North to South and concluded that this was not the explanation (see also National Assessment of Educational Progress 1981).

As an aside, one may consider the reanalysis of the national assessment data by Nancy W. Burton and Lyle V. Jones (1982) which shows that during the 1970s the difference in average achievement levels between the nation's black and white youth has become smaller. When achievement for white students declined, achievement for blacks declined less; when whites improved, blacks improved more. Declines in black/white achievement differences were found at both age nine and age thirteen in math, science, reading, writing, and social studies.

The relative gains in achievement among the nation's youth and particularly those of southeastern students is not conclusive evidence that desegregation improves achievement. However, it does turn on its head the widely held assumption that declines in test scores are the consequence of desegregation.

Input-Output Studies. A third source of evidence on the effects of desegregation on achievement are input-output studies, such as the first Coleman report, that correlate school characteristics, including the racial compositions of schools, with test scores across districts (Coleman et al. 1966). However, these studies are generally not concerned with how or when schools came to have a particular mix. R. Gary Bridge, Charles Judd, and Peter R. Moock (1979) completed a careful assessment of the major input-output studies of minority academic achievement. They found, with the exception of one study which dealt with students not desegregated until the junior-high level, that blacks' test performance is higher in predominantly white schools. Another input-output study by Crain and Mahard (1978b) examined data from the National Longitudinal Study (NLS) of the high school class of 1972 and found that in the North, black achievement tends to increase as the proportion of white students in school increases. In the South, attending predominantly white schools does not significantly affect the achievement of black students. Crain and Mahard suggest that the reason for this regional difference may be that the majority of the seniors tested in the southern schools had attended segregated schools most of their lives. In a later analysis of these data, Mahard and Crain (1980) found that Hispanics who attended racially mixed schools had higher achievement-test scores than those who attended segregated schools when students' social backgrounds were controlled.

The most common types of evidence used to judge educational quality suggest that desegregation enhances rather than diminishes the academic achievement of minorities, especially when children are desegregated at an early grade. Moreover, desegregation does not seem to impair, and may even facilitate, the achievement of white students. Why this occurs is not clear. Based on reports from observers around the country, it appears that desegregation often leads to curricular changes, more teacher training, and new programs that have positive influences on student learning and academic performance.

Interracial Conflict

The fourth myth is that school desegregation leads to interracial conflict in schools and thus disrupts the education process and increases racial prejudices. There is never any interracial conflict in segregated schools, and some interracial conflict does occur in desegregated schools. Overall, however, levels of disruption and disorder are usually short lived. Desegregation can lead to improved race relations among the students involved with almost any significant effort to foster interracial contact by school systems.

Desegregated schools experience greater conflict than segregated schools when schools are first racially mixed. Some of this conflict will occur across racial lines. But desegregation does not appear to be a major cause of school violence. Despite the attention the media have given to the violence accompanying the desegregation process, the massive Safe School Study found:

[A] school's being under court order to desegregate is associated with only a slight increase in the amount of student violence when other factors are taken into account. . . . [The statistical analysis] shows further that there is no consistent association between the *number* of students bused and school violence, controlling for other factors. Finally, there is a weak association between student violence and the *recentness* of initial segregation efforts at a school. Together these findings suggest that some violence may be due to the initiation of mandatory desegregation, but that as time goes on and larger numbers of students are bused to achieve racial balance the desegregation process ceases to be a factor (National Institute of Education 1978b, p. 132).

A reanalysis of the Safe School Study by Gary D. Gottfredson and Denise C. Daiger suggests that in junior-high schools, where larger numbers of students are bused to achieve racial balance, there are "slightly higher rates of student victimizations" (1979, p. 171). This study emphasizes, however, that urban schools in general, and especially those located in poverty-striken areas, experience higher rates of victimization and that the contribution desegregation makes to interstudent violence in urban junior-high schools is small, "smaller than the contributions of school administrative and governance styles" (1979, p. 172). In addition, it finds problems of interstudent violence greater only in urban junior-high schools. What apparently occurs is that the desegregation of urban junior-high schools brings together students from different neighborhoods who may have different values at an age when young people are anxious about their identities and peer acceptance. That these factors would contribute to conflict among students is not surprising.

Interracial conflict in schools reflects the class and racial conflicts in the communities of which they are a part. The question is, Can desegregation lead to improvements in levels of interracial tolerance and redirections in discriminatory behavior? The answer clearly is that it can. Simply mixing white and minority students together in schools will not result in better race relations. When schools adopt programs to improve race relations, the desired improvement can occur especially when (1) cooperative interracial contact is provided for both in classrooms and in extracurricular activities, (2) programs are integrated with the rest of the curricula and are continuous, and (3) school and district officials make their support for better race relations clear and known to teachers, students, and parents. Chapter 7 will examine several strategies that have been used to improve race relations in schools.

Conflict at the Community Level

The fifth myth is that school desegregation results in conflict at the community level. This proposition holds that school desegregation has resulted in such social conflict at the community level that it has under-mined race relations and disrupted social peace. A corollary of this prop-osition, which is often buttressed by pointing to white flight, is that desegregation has undermined support for public education.

In some very visible communities, the conflict over desegregation is harsh and bitter, but in most communities it is not. Overall, while the country has desegregated, interracial attitudes and public behavior have changed in positive directions. Communities undergoing desegregation seem to accept it, though often grudgingly, and reflect no continuing patterns of interracial hostility over time. Indeed, interracial hostility in the South, where desegregation has been most extensive, has diminished. Christine H. Rossell (1981a) has summarized evidence available through 1980 from national surveys and the research on community attitudes, most of which has been conducted in school districts experiencing high levels of protest and white flight, and indicates that the following prop-ositions characterize this phase of social change:

1. The reduction in school segregation in the last decade and a half has been followed by a reduction in racial intolerance in both the North and the South.
2. Over time, there appears to be no backlash against the principle of racial integration despite racial confrontations and controversy sur-rounding school desegregation.
3. The prominence of busing as a problem begins to fade by the end of the first year of the implementation of a school-desegregation plan.
4. Although there is increasing support for the principle of racial in-tegration and for racially balanced schools, whites are overwhelm-ingly opposed to busing for racial desegregation of the schools.
5. Both blacks and whites generally overestimate their neighbors' op-position to racial balance in the public schools, and this is important because adult attitudes are influenced by their neighborhood attitu-dinal context.
6. In desegregated school systems, parents who have some children attending public school are more likely to intend to enroll their pre-school children in the public schools than those whose children are all preschool age. In Boston, residents with school-age children in areas affected by the first phase of desegregation were more likely to have a favorable evaluation of desegregation than those without school-age children.
7. Although a few studies show increased prejudice among adults after desegregation, most show no difference or more positive attitudes. None of the studies has been conducted later than the second year

of desegregation, and most are of school districts which experienced violence and controversy.

8. Parents in school districts which experienced violence and controversy continue to have strong fears regarding the quality of education in desegregated schools.

9. In Louisville, one of the few places where follow-up studies were conducted, most whites feel that their relations with blacks are friendly or neutral despite the controversy over desegregation.

10. Both community and parental opinions have a strong influence on children's attitudes toward specific desegregation issues.

The apparently widespread support in the United States Congress for antibusing legislation of various sorts reinforces the idea that desegregation is widely despised and socially divisive. However, the evidence on public attitudes suggests that the opinion is equivocal and that the picture is much more complex than is generally thought. Three recent national surveys indicate that the public mood is different from how the opponents of desegregation picture it (Harris 1981, 1982a, 1982b). In March 1981 Louis Harris reviewed the evidence from a recent national poll and concluded, "Among the public as a whole, there are signs that the long-standing opposition to busing as a means of remedying segregation is beginning to diminish" (1981, p. 1). Among the specific relevant findings of this Harris Poll are the following:

1. A 53 percent majority of adults, blacks and whites, believe that black children would do better "if they all went to school with white children." Only 16 percent think that black children would do worse. Fifty-one percent of whites and 67 percent of blacks think that black children would do better under integrated conditions.

2. Seventy-two percent of whites and 92 percent of blacks simply do not believe the claim that "if black children all went to school with white children, the education of white children would suffer, because black children would hold back the white children."

3. A majority of both black and white respondents nationwide think that most black and white children will be going to school together five years from now. Harris suggests that there is a sense that future desegregation is inevitable.

In addition, Harris (1982b) found that the public opposed, by 55 to 41 percent, a federal law to prohibit the United States Justice Department or the federal courts from ordering busing to achieve school desegregation. More people said they would vote against than for a candidate who supported such legislation (Harris 1982a).

Thus, it is hard to reconcile the evidence with the claim that school desegregation has divided the country. However, it should be stressed that support for desegregation generally does not mean that whites favor busing their own children to desegregated schools if busing to another part of town is involved (Harris 1981). Even here, the picture is more complicated. Parents of children actually involved in desegregation appear to believe that the experience has been satisfactory. The 1981 Harris survey indicated that 85 percent of white parents whose children have been bused reported that their experience had been either very satisfactory or at least partially satisfactory. Only 13 percent reported an unsatisfactory experience. Although this survey is not based on a random sample of parents experiencing desegregation (it is based on a random sample of all citizens), the small proportion of negative responses is significant. Not surprisingly, blacks in the survey were more likely to feel positive about desegregation than were whites. Blacks favoring the busing of their own children if necessary to achieve desegregation outnumber those who oppose busing by a two-to-one margin. Of those blacks actually involved in busing, 95 percent reported a ''very'' or ''partially satisfactory'' experience.

Indeed, the research on attitudes toward desegregation generally indicates that parents whose children attend desegregated schools have more positive attitudes toward and are more supportive of desegregation than parents who have not experienced it (see, for example, Abney 1976; Serow and Solomon 1979; Schweitzer and Griffore 1981). Chapter 9 will try to explain why the available social-science evidence tells such a different story than the story one reads in the media or hears told in the halls of Congress and state legislatures.

The New Mythology and the Future of School Desegregation

The set of beliefs or myths that sustained the advocates of school desegregation were based on high hopes that the racial integration of children would end racial discrimination and the social inequities that are its products. These hopes were not realized. Prejudice and social-class bias run deep, and the problems of securing equal educational opportunity have as much and perhaps more to do with changing educational practices in schools than with changing attitudes.

The great expectations that comprise the old mythology of school desegregation were undermined not only by the reality of limited success but by the unremitting attacks on the public schools by liberal reformers seeking to motivate and justify change, especially change imposed by higher levels of government. The success, limited though it has been, of desegregation and other federal programs promoting equal educational opportunity gave rise in the late 1970s to concerted attacks on the federal role in education from political conservatives. These attacks focused on desegregation as a symbol of federal intrusion and were fueled by the movement of desegregation to the North and West during the mid- and late 1970s.

Efforts to substantially change public policies require a philosophical or ideological case, and the need gave birth to what this chapter has called the *new mythology*. The new mythology is largely unsubstantiated by the facts and in several ways is contradicted by the available evidence. Contrary evidence has not impeded the rate at which the new mythology has become part of the so-called truth about public schools that apparently is believed by much of the public and by most politicians at least so far as the votes of the latter reflect their beliefs.

The importance of the new mythology is, of course, that it sustains the attack on desegregation. In addition, the new mythology, in arguing that past efforts to provide equal educational opportunity have failed, has contributed to the idea that desegregation cannot work and that it is time to refocus national attention on quality rather than equity in education. In other words, the new mythology creates a context that not only encourages resistance to initial desegregation but discourages school systems from seeking to make desegregation more effective. If one believed in the new mythology, one might seek to withdraw from commitments to provide quality integrated education in the nation's schools. That, of course, is precisely the path on which the United States Congress marched during its 1981–82 sessions.

If, however, one accepts the evidence that desegregation, overall, has had positive consequences for children and that its costs have been overstated, one can move away from the question, Does desegregation work? to the question, How can we increase the benefits and decrease the costs of desegregation? This chapter sets the stage for movement to the second question. Chapters 3 to 8 identify a number of ways that school systems can enhance the effectiveness of school desegregation and, in so doing, improve the quality of education in and public support for the public schools.

2 Identifying Strategies for Effective School Desegregation

Until recently, most research on school desegregation has focused on whether desegregation has worked or been effective overall. This research usually provides limited information on the policies or practices that might account for the effects of desegregation and thus offers little guidance to policymakers, educators, and parents. For example, knowing that school desegregation, more often than not, has been associated with improved test scores among minority students is important to the debate over school desegregation, but in itself it does not provide guidance about how to enhance the academic achievement of students in desegregating schools. One needs to know why and how such gains have come about.

Chapters 3 through 8 identify several strategies that seem to be effective in helping attain one or more goals of desegregation. These chapters synthesize data and expert opinion from several different sources in an attempt to provide some guides to actions that seem likely to enhance educational equity and quality in desegregating and desegregated schools.

The Goals of Desegregation

Desegregation has many different objectives, depending on which court order or plan one reviews or to whom one talks in any given community. Thus, the effectiveness of a strategy depends on the goal one has in mind. Some strategies help attain some goals and not others. Moreover, some strategies, but not many, facilitate the achievement of some goals while impeding the attainment of another. The strategies identified and discussed in this book relate to the attainment of one or more of the following possible outcomes of desegregation:

1. Reducing racial isolation among and within schools
2. Avoiding resegregation among and within schools
3. Improving race relations among students
4. Improving educational quality and student academic performance
5. Promoting positive public reaction to desegregation that includes avoiding overt opposition to desegregation, increasing levels of racial and ethnic tolerance, and building support for schools.

These goals do not all derive from constitutional principles. They are widely held values that policymakers, including judges, frequently seek to secure in the process of desegregation. It is assumed that the most effective strategy will be one that maximizes each of the different goals simultaneously. However, few policies or practices do that, and some strategies force one to emphasize one goal over others. When the available evidence illuminates the nature of such trade-offs, that information is presented. The discussion does not assume the primacy of one goal over another. Such choices properly belong to policymakers not to researchers.

The Structure and Purpose of the Discussion of Strategies

The strategies discussed in the next six chapters relate to four key steps to securing effective desegregation. The first step in desegregation is the choice and design of the pupil-assignment plan to reduce racial isolation and, to the greatest extent possible, achieve or set the stage for achieving other goals of desegregation. A second step is to encourage the desegregation of housing so as to minimize the need for pupil reassignment. Third, the effectiveness of desegregation depends importantly on the development of strategies to inform, prepare, and involve the community and especially parents and to build support for and promote compliance with the goals of the desegregation plan. Finally, desegregation requires changes in the things school systems do. In order to enhance the benefits of school desegregation for students, school systems need to implement strategies relating to (1) the organization of school systems at the district level to provide continuing support for desegregation; (2) structural, curricular, and personnel changes within schools; and (3) more effective in-service training for teachers and administrators.

Many of the proposals set forth in this book seem quite unsurprising. If many of the ideas presented here are intuitively sensible, so much the better. The fact is, however, that most desegregated school systems seem not to be doing many of the things that hold promise for improving the effectiveness of desegregation. Clearly, some of the strategies presented have political implications, and some are financially costly. However, such explanations for why these ideas are not more widely implemented do not account for the infrequency with which school systems adopt comprehensive approaches to desegregation that embody relevant strategies such as those suggested in the pages that follow.

Sources of Evidence

This presentation of desegregation strategies is based largely on the central but not the only book of a two-year project funded by the National Institute of Education and the United States Office for Civil Rights entitled *Assessment of Current Knowledge about the Effectiveness of School Desegregation Strategies*. The components of that project include: (1) a synthesis of research findings on effective desegregation strategies from which much of this book is derived; (2) a comprehensive review of the empirical research; (3) a review of the qualitative literature on school desegregation, including studies surveying the opinions of practitioners and policymakers; (4) a longitudinal analysis of ten key court cases on school desegregation; (5) interviews with local and national experts on school desegregation; (6) a review of actions by state governments and interviews with state officials; (7) an agenda for future research to determine the effectiveness of school desegregation strategies; (8) the design of a multicommunity study to determine the factors that account for the effectiveness of school desegregation; (9) a guide to resources that those charged with implementing desegregation might find helpful; and (10) an extensive bibliography of books, articles, papers, documents, and reports that deal with strategies related to the general goals of school desegregation.

The proposals and strategies presented in this book are based on evidence derived from a variety of sources that include:

1. Quantitative studies that employ various types of statistical techniques to demonstrate a relationship between two or more variables. This literature ranges from case studies of particular schools to large national surveys. More than six hundred quantitative studies were reviewed.

2. Qualitative literature that ranges from systematic ethnographic studies of classrooms and schools to reports about national trends or specific situations by informed observers. About six hundred pieces of qualitative literature were examined.

3. Surveys of opinion and consensus articles that are the products of conferences or surveys and reflect perceived agreement about the effectiveness of different desegregation strategies. Four sources of such data were identified and studied.

4. Court documents. Each of ten key school-desegregation cases were examined for evidence or expert opinion on different strategies.

5. Interviews with 135 local and national experts. The local experts were from seventeen local districts across the country that have been involved in significant desegregation activity, in successful or significant practices or changes in desegregation strategies, and with potential generalizability of lessons learned at an individual site. These experts included school board members, superintendents and other administrators, teachers, journalists, attorneys, and federal and

state officials who have worked closely with desegregation in individual districts. Ninety-four local experts were interviewed. Forty national experts with extensive experience and national recognition for their expertise were selected by the advisory board and the entire project team. Most national experts were researchers, consultants, federal education administrators, or heads of federal desegregation-assistance centers. Further information about the interviews is contained in the appendix.

Synthesizing the Information Collected

To be useful, the extensive information collected and reviewed had to be summarized or synthesized into relatively straightforward conclusions. Variation in the character and quality of the evidence, both across and within the different sources of information, precluded quantitative approaches to aggregation. Instead, all of the evidence related to a given strategy was assembled, and the study-team member most expert on that strategy prepared a draft summary statement. Different types of evidence were cited in a draft text and identified by source. The statement of the strategy was then rechecked against the relevant data, especially the expert interviews, and revised once again. The draft was further revised and shared with all study-team members, the advisory board, and special consultants on the education of Hispanics and Asian Americans. Subsequent to submission of the study team's report in mid-1981, new research was analyzed and additional illustrative examples from different school systems were identified. This knowledge, current as of September 1982, was included in the manuscript as appropriate.

In reaching its conclusions, the study team relied most heavily on social-science evidence-research whenever the quality of that inquiry allowed. In many cases, however, the evidence needed to answer policy issues faced by those who develop and implement desegregation policies and programs is missing or mixed. Expert opinion was very helpful in clarifying many of these uncertainties. There is, moreover, remarkable agreement among the desegregation experts, both local and national, who offered opinions about the effectiveness of particular strategies.

For some suggestions made in these chapters, there is little hard evidence available. The proposals are presented when there is agreement among those experts who commented on the issue involved. In a very few cases in which there was no contrary evidence and the idea was theoretically sensible, unanimous agreement among study-team members, all of whom are experienced researchers of school desegregation, was considered an adequate basis for including a proposal. Although all of the evidence relevant to each strategy is not presented in the narrative of this section, the basis upon which each conclusion was reached is specified.

The discussion of strategies would have been more extensive and specific proposals more detailed had the authors relaxed their concern for consensus within the study team. By requiring consensus among the team members and agreement among experts or the written literature and court opinions, the team reduced the level of specificity and speculation that a handbook of practical advice might be expected to provide. A conscious effort was made to make this presentation both comprehensive and brief.

Making Use of the Analysis

The different sources of information used in this book, taken together, represent the most extensive evidence on the effectiveness of desegregation strategies yet collected. The assumption is that research can help structure the development of desegregation plans and strategies for their implementation. This book attempts to develop practical advice on how to more effectively desegregate public schools. The proposals and strategies identified are not foolproof recipes for effective desegregation; they should not be thought of as hard and fast propositions that will work in all circumstances. Educators, judges, and policymakers will need to adapt most of these ideas to local conditions if the proposals derived from this inquiry are to produce maximum benefits for students and communities.

This book is a source of ideas that will often require adaptation to specific local conditions and that may be inappropriate or unnecessary in many situations. The ideas presented here may also serve as a kind of constraint on behavior in the sense that policies and practices that seem contrary to those that have been found to be effective might be reexamined and their justifications clarified. Similarly, those who seek more effective desegregation may find that they can use the information here to raise issues about the absence of certain policies and practices in their schools and communities. It is important to remember that the evidence supporting the conclusions and suggestions in this book varies in its character and extent. The readers may draw their own conclusions about how certain they can be that any given strategy will be effective in a particular school or school system.

3 Pupil-Assignment Strategies

The primary objective of a pupil-assignment plan is to reduce or eliminate instances of unconstitutional segregation among schools. In general, and depending on the nature and extent of the constitutional violations, school districts are obliged to bring about "the maximum amount of actual desegregation in light of the practicalities of the local situation" (*Green* v. *New Kent County* 1968; *Swann* v. *Charlotte-Mecklenburg County Board of Education* 1971; cited in Vergon 1981 p. 5). A primary criterion for assessing the legal adequacy of a pupil-assignment plan is its effectiveness in eliminating one-race or racially identifiable schools (*Green* 1968). In addition, courts are authorized to use racial ratios as a starting point in formulating or evaluating the effectiveness and legal adequacy of proposed and implemented plans. Although prohibited from requiring school districts to achieve a precise racial mix or balance in each school, orders requiring each building to approximate the racial composition of districtwide enrollment (for example, plus or minus 15 percent) have been at least implicitly upheld by the United States Supreme Court (see *Swann* 1971; *Columbus Board of Education* v. *Penick* 1979; cited in Vergon 1981).

Courts have taken into account, in varying degrees, a number of factors in fashioning remedies for unconstitutional segregation. These include the race, ethnicity, and socioeconomic status of students to be reassigned; former racial compositions and neighborhoods of schools to which students are reassigned; the grades during which they are reassigned; the character and continuity of education programs; the distance and costs of transportation; and housing patterns and residential stability (Vergon 1981).

Choices among types of pupil-assignment strategies and the degree to which school districts and courts address these related factors importantly influence the outcomes of desegregation. Typically, however, school districts and courts place primary emphasis on the logistical and political implications of the assignment process. For example, kindergarten and first-grade students have been excluded from the reassignment process in some school desegregation plans, at least in part, because parents oppose having their youngest children assigned to schools outside their neighborhoods. Other features of assignment plans are often developed for their administrative simplicity. Evidence from research and desegregation experts indicate, however, that the assignment process has not only political and economic implications but also important social and educational implications that judges, lawyers, and school administrators should consider.

This chapter is divided into three sections. The first section discusses different types of strategies to reduce racial isolation among schools. The second addresses a variety of considerations that relate to the development of pupil-assignment strategies. The third section identifies factors that should be considered in the implementation of pupil-assignment plans. In each section, where appropriate, the various political, economic, social, and educational implications of the strategies are identified.[1]

Types of Pupil-Assignment Strategies

Voluntary Plans

Voluntary desegregation plans allow students a choice to attend a desegregated school. A white student is thus free to remain at his or her current segregated school although minority students may transfer to that school at their own request, and a minority student may remain at his or her segregated school although whites may request to transfer to that school. Voluntary plans may be court ordered as in Houston and San Diego or developed by school boards as are the majority-to-minority voluntary transfer plans adopted or proposed by many districts with small minority-student populations. The most common voluntary desegregation strategies include open enrollment or freedom-of-choice policies, voluntary majority-to-minority transfers, and magnet schools.

Open enrollment or freedom-of-choice policies allow students to attend any school in the district they choose, and in most cases, systems will provide transportation for students to attend schools of their choice. Voluntary majority-to-minority transfer programs allow students to choose to attend different schools so long as students transfer from schools in which they are in a racial or ethnic majority to schools in which they will comprise a racial or ethnic minority. Under this type of plan, white students are not permitted to transfer from a majority white school to another majority white school but are allowed to transfer from a majority white school to a school in which, for example, blacks or Hispanics comprise the majority proportion of student enrollment. Systems that adopt magnet-school plans institute various types of educational programs in particular schools in order to attract students of different racial and ethnic groups and thus desegregate those schools.

In general, voluntary desegregation plans are not effective means to reduce districtwide levels of racial isolation except, perhaps, in districts with small minority-student populations. What desegregation occurs under voluntary plans tends to be one-way, that is, minority students comprise the greatest proportion of students volunteering for transfer. White transfers to minority schools are highly unlikely although some whites usually will transfer if the schools involved are magnets or are otherwise exceptional in terms of instructional opportunities or noninstructional activities. For these reasons, although they may promote desegregation in a few schools, voluntary strategies result in little districtwide desegregation and have little impact on desegregating or reducing the numbers of predominantly or racially identifiable minority schools, particularly in districts with large minority proportions of total enrollment.

Evidence. The qualitative and quantitative research indicate the voluntary desegregation plans are relatively ineffective in significantly reducing districtwide racial isolation and eliminating substantial numbers of racially identifiable schools. In a survey of ten key desegregation cases, Charles B. Vergon (1981) indicates that plans predicated on voluntary participation have been proposed at some point in the plans advanced by a very substantial proportion of school districts confronted with a legal obligation to desegregate. However, seldom since the United States Supreme Court's ruling in *Green* v. *New Kent County* (1968) have federal judges or other government officials responsible for evaluating the legal adequacy of a proposed desegregation plan approved one which relies exclusively or even primarily on the voluntary participation of large numbers of students. Vergon found that courts have historically held, with very few exceptions, that voluntary plans tend to be ineffective at least in contrast to the desegregation that otherwise could be achieved by use of reasonably available reassignment techniques.

In an early study of desegregation techniques implemented in thirty-two urban school districts, Gordon Foster (1973) found that voluntary desegregation plans seldom proved effective in reducing racial isolation on a districtwide level. Citing evidence from northern school districts, Foster observed that voluntary plans "more often than not served as a form of state-imposed segregation" (1973, p. 22). The relative ineffectiveness of voluntary plans to achieve significant districtwide desegregation is illustrated in two recent analyses of desegregation plans implemented by large urban and metropolitan school districts. In a case-survey analysis of desegregation techniques implemented in fifty-two large school districts, Morgan and England (1981) conclude that voluntary strategies of open enrollment and free transfers contribute insignificantly to reducing racial isolation among schools. This finding is supported by Smylie (1982) who found that voluntary plans implemented by large districts achieved minimal changes in racial balance among schools and eliminated virtually no schools with 90 to 100 percent minority enrollment. Indeed, this survey identified several districts in which numbers of schools with this proportion of minority enrollment increased upon implementation of voluntary plans.

Rossell (1978c, 1979) attributes the relative ineffectiveness of voluntary plans to a variety of factors. First, few white students opt to transfer to minority schools. Second, the minority students who volunteer to attend white schools tend to be mostly blacks—few Hispanics participate. Third, those blacks who do volunteer to attend white schools tend to be disproportionately secondary-school students. In addition, many of the experts interviewed believe that since students who participate in voluntary desegregation are disproportionately minority, these strategies contribute to two phenomena which are dysfunctional to the long-term goals of desegregation. The disproportionate participation of minority students in voluntary programs creates the impression that school desegregation is a minority problem or a minority concern. Also, under such plans minority students tend to remain the outsiders to be transferred or bused to white schools.

Since they accomplish little reduction in racial isolation and because whites are not reassigned to schools outside their neighborhoods, voluntary plans generally produce less white flight and community protest than mandatory student-assignment plans, at least during implementation years (Morgan and England 1981; Smylie 1982). All studies that have analyzed different categories of districts and plans conclude that mandatory school desegregation has a negative long-term impact on white enrollment in large central-city school districts over 35 percent black (Rossell 1978a; Armor 1980; Coleman 1977; Ross, Gratton, and Clarke 1981; Morgan and England 1981; Smylie 1982). There is some disagreement as to the long-term magnitude of white loss in these districts and whether mandatory plans negatively affect countywide school districts and those with less than 35 percent minority enrollment.[2] These disagreements probably hinge as much on characteristics of the districts sampled, especially how extensive the desegregation, as on methodology.

Another consequence of voluntary plans might be to protect bilingual-education programs that could be undermined if limited-English-proficiency (LEP) students are scattered by a mandatory plan among schools that do not have these programs. It is possible that mandatory plans could spread these students across the district to achieve racial and ethnic balance in a manner that their small numbers in any one school makes bilingual-education programs economically impractical.

Examples. Vergon (1981) provides the following example of voluntary desegregation in Charlotte-Mecklenburg County. In 1965 a desegregation plan proposed by this district provided for the establishment of geographic attendance areas and a freedom-of-choice option to students desiring to attend a school other than the one to which they were assigned on the basis of the area of their residence. The plan was approved by the federal district court and affirmed by the fourth United States Circuit Court of Appeals (*Swann* v. *Charlotte-Mecklenburg County Board of Education* 1965). An analysis of the projected impact of the free transfer provision in the first year of implementation led the court to the following conclusion—"all or practically all" of the 396 white students initially assigned to black schools as a result of the geographic zoning exercised their freedom of choice option to transfer out of the formerly black schools, and 91 of 1,955 black students elected to be reassigned from a white school to a black school (*Swann* 1965, p. 668). The plan, nevertheless, was approved by the court under the prevailing interpretation of obligations of school districts to remedy racial isolation.

Three years later in declaring the voluntary plan inadequate in light of intervening legal developments the federal district court observed:

> Freedom of students of both races to transfer freely to schools of their own choice has resulted in resegregation of some schools which were temporarily desegregated. The effect of closing the black inner-city schools and allowing free choice as an overall result tended to perpetuate and promote segregation (*Swann* 1968, p. 1366).

In fall 1981 the Los Angeles Unified School District began implementation of a voluntary plan after abandonment of a 1978 limited mandatory plan that affected students in the fourth through eighth grades. Preliminary data for the first year of that district's voluntary plan reveal that systemwide levels of racial balance declined 10 percent from levels achieved under the limited mandatory plan. According to these data, the number of schools with 90 to 100 percent minority enrollment increased 15 percent although white enrollment in that district's magnet schools increased slightly (Los Angeles Unified School District 1981).[3]

The Denver school district proposed to a federal district court in fall 1981 a freedom-of-choice plan that would allow students in the district to attend any school they chose and would provide a variety of academic magnet schools to draw white students to facilities in minority neighborhoods. During hearings before the court in spring 1982, data were presented that revealed that if students attended schools nearest to their homes under this plan, the district would resegregate in terms of racial balance to a level that would approximate that which was found unconstitutional by federal courts in 1973 to 1975 (Bardwell 1982). According to the nearest school enrollment assumption, numbers of schools whose

racial compositions deviated by at least 15 percent from the racial compositions of districtwide enrollment, the greatest percentage variation
allowed by the court in 1974, would increase from 15 to 70 percent of
all schools in the district.

Magnet-Only Desegregation Plans

In magnet-only desegregation plans, a certain number of schools with
special educational programs or approaches to instruction are designated
magnets to attract students of different racial or ethnic groups to attend
and thus desegregate these schools. In most cases, requirements are established that magnet schools be racially nonidentifiable. These requirements sometimes hold magnets to a more exact approximation of district
racial composition than nonmagnet schools. There are many types of
magnet schools including those for gifted and talented students; those
providing special programs in vocational education, the arts, or science;
and those establishing traditional classroom structures and teaching practices. A campaign is usually initiated to recruit both minority and white
student volunteers to these schools in order to achieve racial quotas and
thus increase desegregation in the school district without placing the
burden solely on minority students as most voluntary plans do.

The effectiveness of magnet-only desegregation plans in achieving
districtwide desegregation depends on a number of factors that include
the size of the minority population in the district, the proportion of schools
in the district that are designated magnets, and the appeals or incentives
programs hold for students and parents, particularly white students and
parents. In other words, the relative effectiveness of magnet-only desegregation plans depends, at least in part, on the degree to which programs
offer benefits to students that outweigh perceived costs of transfer to
different schools in perhaps different neighborhoods.

Generally, magnet-only desegregation plans are comparatively ineffective in districts with large proportions of minority students because
the number of white students required to volunteer to desegregate the
large minority student population is beyond that which can be obtained
through voluntary choice. Magnet plans cannot be evaluated by looking
only at the racial compositions of the magnets themselves. For example,
a district may be able to successfully desegregate those schools it des-
ignates as magnets. However, if those schools comprise only a small
proportion of all schools in the district and if those schools enroll only
a small proportion of the district's student population, the magnets may
have little impact on reducing districtwide levels of racial isolation.

Evidence. In an analysis of eighteen school districts implementing magnet programs under the Emergency School Aid Act, Eugene C. Royster, Catherine Blatzell, and Fran C. Simmons found that "only a limited amount of desegregation can be attributed to magnet schools" (1979, p. i). Enrollment data for these districts, collected from 1968 through 1977, indicate that magnet programs used as the major desegregation strategy achieved only slight districtwide reductions in racial isolation.

In a reanalysis of these data, Rossell (1979) found that in school districts with over 30 percent minority enrollment, magnet-only desegregation plans were not as effective as magnet programs as one component of mandatory plans in achieving substantial levels of districtwide desegregation. Rossell's analysis suggests that magnet-only programs can be effective in districts with less than 30 percent minority enrollment because only small proportions of the white student population, given substantial minority participation, are required to volunteer to desegregate the minority student population. However, in districts with under 30 percent minority enrollment, levels of white volunteerism may be less than sufficient to achieve significant desegregation. In a case analysis of Montgomery County's (Maryland) voluntary desegregation plan, John C. Larson (1980) found that magnet programs had only a modest impact on reducing districtwide levels of racial isolation. The experts interviewed agree that whites are less likely to enroll in magnet schools located in minority neighborhoods than they are if the schools are in white or racially mixed neighborhoods or in commercial areas.

Examples. Vergon (1981) provides the following examples of magnet desegregation plans in Buffalo, Pasadena, and Wilmington/New Castle County. Pursuant to a finding of unconstitutional segregation, the Buffalo public schools proposed the adoption in 1977 of the Buffalo Plan. This voluntary plan utilized ten magnet programs as the primary technique for desegregating selected inner-city, racially identifiable minority schools. Also, it incorporated a voluntary transfer program under which minority students could elect to attend formerly white schools on the periphery of the district. A federal district court approved the plan as a partial remedy and ordered its implementation in the fall of 1977. Although a substantial reduction in the number of elementary students attending racially isolated schools was reported between 1975 and 1977, at least fifteen all-minority schools remained under the plan (*Arthur* v. *Nyquist* 1979). The continued existence of these one-race schools and the implication of data presented in subsequent hearings that the reduction in students attending one-race schools was largely due to school closings suggest that the magnet-school component of the Buffalo Plan was not particularly effective in attracting whites to formerly minority schools. The district court found the magnet component of the plan inadequate to achieve districtwide desegregation and further was disturbed by the inequity of the plan which made reassignment mandatory for substantial numbers of minority students whose buildings were closed while white participation in desegregation via the magnet program was totally voluntary.

Four years after implementation of a 1970 court-ordered desegregation plan requiring mandatory pupil reassignment, the Pasadena school board petitioned the district court for permission to substitute an integrated-zone magnet-school program. The court rejected as unsubstantiated contentions advanced by school-district experts that white enrollment had been precipitously in decline since implementation of the mandatory plan and found evidence introduced regarding the absence of educational benefits or inadequacies of the original mandatory plan neither persuasive nor adequate (*Spangler* v. *Pasadena City Board of Education* 1974). In rejecting Pasadena's proposed magnet plan, the court noted that the district would have had to overcome a number of potentially racially imbalanced schools, something that "other California districts laboring under freedom of choice plans have been less than spectacularly successful in achieving" (*Spangler* 1974, p. 1307). In a footnote to its opinion, the court observed that voluntary plans in San Bernadino and Richmond (California) resulted in limited (11 to 15 percent) black participation and total absence of white involvement (1974, p. 1307). The district court's retention of jurisdiction and rejection of the magnet plan was affirmed by the tenth United States Circuit Court of Appeals, and after the school system appealed, the United States Supreme Court refused to hear the case.

Among the score of proposals advanced to desegregate the Wilmington and New Castle County (Delaware) school districts was one which would have established a system of magnet schools within each of five city-suburban zones of like racial composition. This plan failed to provide for racial controls on enrollment at the magnet schools although it acknowledged that such controls might be included. Nevertheless, a federal district court observed that "the use of [magnet schools] as the sole means of system-wide desegregation is decidedly unpromising" (*Evans* v. *Buchanan* 1976, p. 346). Notice was taken that a similar plan implemented in Houston achieved little success in actually desegregating magnet schools and even increased segregation among some facilities (*Evans* 1976, p. 345).

In Houston, a district with 75 percent minority enrollment and 239 schools in 1980, a voluntary desegregation plan based on magnet schools achieved only 15 percent of possible systemwide racial balance that year. Under this voluntary plan, the number of schools with 90 to 100 percent minority enrollment increased by 11 percent, and the proportion of minority students in the district attending those schools rose by 4 percent between 1978 and 1980. Seattle attempted to desegregate its system with magnet schools in 1977 but found the program prohibitively expensive. After one year the Seattle Board of Education voted to switch to a mandatory student-assignment desegregation plan. The experience of San Diego has been mixed, but magnet schools offering remedial, compensatory, or bilingual programs apparently have done little to attract white students.

Racine (Wisconsin), Tacoma (Washington), and Montclair (New Jersey) have been able to successfully desegregate their school systems with magnet programs. Both the Racine and Tacoma school districts were less than 25 percent minority in 1978, and Montclair, which was 45 percent minority that year, instituted special programs in the majority of its ten (in 1978) schools.

Magnet schools are a central component of the Milwaukee plan and seem to have been attractive to a large number of parents in that city. The United States Commission on Civil Rights (1979) reported that as of fall 1978, the third year of the magnet program, 6 of 15 senior-high schools were desegregated according to a court-approved ratio of 25 to 50 percent minority in each school. Fourteen of 18 middle schools and 83 of 116 elementary schools met this enrollment criteria. The commission further noted that in fall 1978, one-third of the district's students transferred to schools outside their attendance areas pursuant to the desegregation plan. However, 53 percent of those students who volunteered to transfer were black, and only 17 percent were white. In 1978, black students comprised 42 percent and white students 51 percent of the district's total enrollment.

Comment. Not much is known about what types of magnet programs consistently attract students of different races, ethnicity, and family background. Some experts interviewed believe that magnet schools offering bilingual programs might appeal to a certain number of parents whose children speak satisfactory English but would like to learn a second language. For example, Coral Ways School in Dade County (Miami) is a desegregated, totally bilingual school. However, San Diego, as noted previously, has been less successful using this strategy.

One of the most popular types of magnets is a school for academically gifted and talented students. However, the experts were nearly unanimous in their opposition to the creation of these schools as a desegregation tool. Academic magnets for gifted and talented students are considered expensive and may reduce the quality of academic programs and the heterogeneity of comprehensive (nonmagnet) schools. This may be particularly true if unique or advanced instructional programs are centralized in the magnets. Such centralization prohibits students who are not admitted to academic magnets from gaining access to these programs. In addition, academic magnets may induce flight among parents whose children apply but are not admitted to these schools. This phenomenon may be greatest in districts that create academic magnets as components of mandatory student-assignment plans.

The relatively small size of most magnets and their specialized character may also have the effect of excluding students in need of bilingual education. If bilingual programs are centralized in magnet schools and if only small numbers of LEP students can attend these schools, other LEP students may not have access to bilingual programs. Further, when goals for racial composition in magnet schools are set, minority students from different racial and ethnic groups are sometimes treated as though they were the same. As a result, numbers of one minority group may be denied access to special programs. Racial compositions of these schools should therefore be set by considering the proportion of each different racial and ethnic group in the district's student population.

Mandatory Student Reassignment Plans

The mandatory type of desegregation plan involves reassignment of students from segregated schools to schools where their presence will increase racial balance and interracial contact. These plans are termed *mandatory* because parents have no or little choice as to their child's reassignment if they want their child to remain in that public-school system. Mandatory student-reassignment plans can be ordered by a school board (as in Berkeley and Seattle), by a court (as in San Francisco, Boston, Denver, Charlotte-Mecklenburg, and Columbus), or by the United States Department of Education (as in Baltimore, Wichita, and Amarillo).

Mandatory plans commonly employ one or a combination of reassignment techniques. The more prevalent techniques include establishing geographic attendance zones where none previously existed, redrawing preexisting attendance zones, closing old schools or constructing new ones, pairing or clustering facilities, reorganizing grade structures and establishing feeder patterns among grade levels, and reassigning and providing transportation for students where appropriate in conjunction with the implementation of any of the above techniques (see Hughes, Gordon, and Hillman 1980 for descriptions of these specific strategies).

Mandatory student-reassignment strategies are the most effective means of reducing racial isolation among schools. Although mandatory reassignment of white students produces a greater loss of whites to private or suburban schools than voluntary strategies, at least during the first year or two of implementation, it still produces greater levels of desegregation than voluntary transfer programs. Mandatory reassignment plans have proven substantially more effective than voluntary plans in increasing racial balance among schools and in reducing the numbers of or eliminating racially identifiable schools.

Evidence. In general, mandatory desegregation plans have achieved more substantial reductions in racial imbalance in all regions of the country than voluntary desegregation plans (see Taeuber and Wilson 1979). Foster (1973) found that mandatory desegregation strategies were substantially more effective in reducing levels of racial imbalance in urban school districts than voluntary strategies. Morgan and England (1981) conclude as well that mandatory strategies achieved significantly higher levels of desegregation (racial balance) than voluntary plans. Specifically, their study indicates that for elementary schools, pairing and clustering in combination with rezoning seem likely to yield the greatest success in achieving desegregation and, among other mandatory techniques, in minimizing white flight. In addition, Morgan and England found that the specific mandatory technique employed does not matter much in the desegregation of secondary schools. However, their study suggests that the use of rezoning techniques may prove somewhat more effective than other mandatory strategies for this level. Smylie (1982) found that mandatory plans achieved more than three times the racial balance of voluntary plans in large school districts. In addition, his study indicates that mandatory plans, depending on their inclusion of minority neighborhoods, eliminated virtually all schools with over 90 percent minority enrollment.

Although mandatory reassignment of whites produces more white flight than voluntary plans, Rossell (1981a) indicates that it usually produces a greater proportion white in the average minority-student's school than voluntary plans. Even where substantial white flight has occurred, interracial contact has remained significantly greater than it was before mandatory desegregation occurred (Rossell 1978a).

Some of the experts that were interviewed believe that mandatory desegregation plans are desirable because schools are more likely to make special preparation or undertake educational changes that are responsive to the needs of heterogeneous student bodies (Broh and Trent 1981; see also Hawley 1980). Minority students are more likely to be part of a critical mass of minority students when they are reassigned to white schools. A critical mass of national-origin-minority students in a school is thought to facilitate the provision of bilingual-educational programs.

Examples. In 1970 the Charlotte-Mecklenburg school district began implementation of a court-ordered mandatory student-reassignment plan.

That district's primary desegregation strategies included pairing elementary schools and redrawing attendance zones for both elementary and secondary schools. Upon implementation of that plan, Charlotte achieved 86 percent of possible districtwide racial balance and in subsequent years increased levels of racial balance as the plan was adjusted to compensate for demographic changes in the district. Prior to implementation, 22 of Charlotte's 111 schools had enrollments that were greater than 90 percent minority. Almost 60 percent of all minority students in that district attended those 22 minority schools. Upon implementation of its mandatory plan, Charlotte eliminated 19 of these minority schools and reduced the proportion of districtwide minority enrollment attending the three remaining minority schools to less than 2 percent.

Similar levels of desegregation were achieved in many districts, including Pasadena, Denver, and Hillsborough County (Tampa). In 1970 the Pasadena school district began implementation of a mandatory plan that utilized pairing, clustering, and rezoning for elementary schools. Rezoning and the construction of new facilities were used for secondary schools. Under this plan, Pasadena achieved 95 percent of possible racial balance across the district and eliminated all six of its schools that maintained over 90 percent minority enrollment prior to implementation. Before the plan was put into effect, 40 percent of Pasadena's minority-student population attended these six schools.

The principal desegregation technique used in Denver's mandatory plan was rezoning attendance areas across all grade levels. Rezoning was initially supplemented by part-time pairing of elementary schools, but this strategy was discontinued after two years. Several magnet programs were developed for secondary schools. After full implementation of this plan in 1975, Denver achieved approximately 85 percent of possible districtwide racial balance. In subsequent years, levels of racial balance increased. Prior to implementation, 11 of Denver's 119 schools had enrollments that were over 90 percent minority. Twenty-one percent of the district's minority-student population attended these schools. By 1976 Denver had eliminated all 11 schools with this minority proportion of enrollment.

In response to a federal court order, the Hillsborough County school system developed and in 1971 began implementation of a mandatory plan in which elementary and junior-high schools were rezoned and paired. Black schools became sixth-grade centers, and white schools were restructured to house students in the first through fifth grades. Attendance zones for senior-high schools were redrawn. Under this plan, Hillsborough County achieved 92 percent of possible districtwide racial balance and eliminated all 17 of its 129 schools that had over 90 percent minority enrollment. Prior to implementation, 38 percent of the district's minority-student population attended those 17 minority schools.

Magnet Schools as Part of a Mandatory Plan

In many districts, magnet schools have been used as educational options within a districtwide mandatory desegregation plan. Students are mandatorily assigned to a desegregated school, or they can opt to attend a desegregated magnet school with an educational specialization. One reason given for establishing magnet schools as part of a mandatory desegregation plan is that the inclusion of educational choices may lessen community hostility to the mandatory aspects of the plan, increase the educational attractiveness of certain schools, and as a result reduce white flight and protest. However, one unintended consequence of instituting magnet schools within mandatory plans (or as the primary desegregation technique as well) may be to stigmatize as inferior nonmagnet schools. This is particularly likely if the magnets include schools for the academically gifted, admission by selection or examination programs, or if advanced instructional programs are centralized in the magnets. Moreover, selective magnet schools may resegregate the school system by socioeconomic status and thus partly diminish the positive academic effects of socioeconomic desegregation.

Evidence. The empirical research indicates that it is the mandatory components of these desegregation plans which accomplish most reductions in racial isolation and not the magnet options. Royster, Blatzell, and Simmons conclude:

> As part of a comprehensive desegregation plan, magnet schools can assist in increasing districtwide desegregation, although indications are that most of the increase may be due to the effect of other [mandatory] techniques (1979, p. ii).

In addition, Rossell (1979) found in comparisons of magnet-only plans and mandatory plans with magnet components that in school districts with over 30 percent minority enrollment, a mandatory component is necessary in order to achieve more than a small increase in desegregation. Numerous writings from the qualitative research and most of the experts interviewed indicate that mandatory student reassignment is necessary to reduce racial isolation to any significant degree.

There is no evidence that instituting magnet schools as part of a mandatory desegregation plan lessens community hostility to the mandatory components of a plan, increases the educational attractiveness of the schools, or reduces white flight and protest. The absence of such a relationship may be explained in part by the fact that the choice to attend magnet schools within a mandatory plan is really no choice at all' with respect to participation in school desegregation. Under this type of plan, students may choose only between attending a desegregated magnet school and being assigned to a desegregated nonmagnet school.

Examples. The number and prominence of magnet schools vary substantially from community to community. Development of the specialized curricula associated with each program is left largely to local school officials in most districts (as in Boston and New Castle Consolidated). In some cases, notably in Boston and to a lesser extent Detroit, courts have ordered establishment of university, business, labor, or community-school pairings to facilitate the development and support of distinctive and responsive magnet programs. A federal district court ordered the development of several citywide magnet schools emphasizing vocational education as part of a broader, mandatory reassignment plan in Detroit. In addition to the establishment of the vocational programs, that court ordered the construction or remodeling of facilities to house them, approving a fifty-fifty cost-sharing agreement negotiated between the local and state codefendants for the construction of two new vocational centers.

Metropolitan Plans

Metropolitan desegregation plans are highly effective strategies for reducing racial and class isolation. A metropolitan plan is one that includes the central-city and surrounding suburban school districts. Desegregating a metropolitan area can be accomplished, after determination of a cross-district violation, by merging a legally separate central-city school district and the surrounding suburban school district(s) for the purpose of reducing racial isolation. Metropolitan desegregation may also be accomplished by ordering reassignment of students in districts that are already metropolitan in scope, such as countywide districts that encompass most of the residential areas in an urban region.

Metropolitan and countywide desegregation plans produce greater socioeconomic integration than mandatory plans that affect only central cities or voluntary plans, and they promote greater financial stability than central-city plans since those who live in the suburbs tend to be of higher socioeconomic status than those who live in the central city. In addition, metropolitan and countywide plans tend to produce less white flight than central-city plans and, in some cases, contribute to residential desegregation.

Evidence. James S. Coleman, Sara R. Kelly, and John A. Moore (1975); Reynolds Farley, Suzanne Bianchi, and Diane Colasanto (1979); Armor (1980); and Rossell (1978a) all find that there are higher levels of interracial contact or greater proportions of white students in the average minority-student's school under metropolitan and countywide plans than under central-city mandatory plans. This is due primarily to the fact that the white proportion of district enrollment tends to be higher to begin with in a school system that includes suburban areas. These studies, as well as the qualitative research and the findings from the authors' interviews, conclude that metropolitan and countywide plans produce less white flight than central-city plans. Less flight occurs under these plans because (1) moving out of the school district can be difficult, prohibitively expensive, or undesirable if the high-status suburbs are included in the plan and (2) in most cases, the minority proportion of district enrollment will be lower in metropolitan or countywide systems than in central-city school systems. The lower the proportion of minority students in a district, the lower the anxiety whites have about desegregation and the smaller the proportion of whites who have to be reassigned to desegregate the district's minority population. Diana M. Pearce (1980) and Gary Orfield (1981) both identify several districts in which metropolitan school desegregation has contributed to residential desegregation. This effect is discussed in chapter 4.

Examples. Most metropolitan plans are in countywide school systems that predate desegregation (such as, Nashville-Davidson County, Charlotte-Mecklenburg County, and the Florida county systems). There are only a few metropolitan school districts created for desegregation purposes. These include New Castle Consolidated (Wilmington), Jefferson County (Louisville), and Indianapolis-Marion County.

Upon implementation of its metropolitan plan in 1975, the Jefferson County school system achieved almost 90 percent of possible districtwide racial balance and reduced from 25 to 3 the number of schools across the district that had over 90 percent minority enrollments. Prior to implementation, 65 percent of all minority students in the metropolitan area attended predominantly minority schools. By 1976 the proportion of minority students attending those schools fell to less than 2 percent. Consolidation of the Wilmington and New Castle County school districts in 1978 achieved 97 percent of possible districtwide racial balance. Prior to implementation, 16 of 121 schools in the metropolitan area had enrollments that were over 90 percent minority, and 52 percent of all minority students in that area attended those schools. After implementation, the consolidated systems maintained no predominantly minority schools.

Voluntary Metropolitan-Student Transfers

Programs permitting minority students to voluntarily transfer from central-city to suburban schools have been implemented in some districts and generally have had positive impact on minority achievement. In many cases students from suburban areas are allowed to transfer to city schools, but there usually are few volunteers. In some districts such as St. Louis, voluntary interdistrict transfer programs are ordered while courts consider mandatory metropolitan remedies. These programs are normally supervised by state departments of education. Usually, transportation is provided to student volunteers who agree to participate in the program. These programs, however, have not had much impact on the degree of racial isolation in urban school districts.

Evidence. Robert Crain and Rita Mahard (1981) report that eleven evaluations have been conducted of such programs in the metropolitan residential areas of Hartford, New Haven, Bridgeport, Newark, Rochester, and Boston. Eight of these evaluations reveal achievement gains often of sizable magnitude for minority students. One study of Hartford finds that graduates of the program seemed to be more successful in pursuing careers than their cohorts who were not in the program. Some experts believe that a critical mass of students of a given race should be assured in each school participating in this type of program and suggest that critical mass be at least 15 to 20 percent.

Examples. The best known programs of voluntary metropolitan-student transfers are in Connecticut (Hartford in particular), Massachusetts (Metropolitan Council for Educational Opportunity [METCO] in Boston), and Wisconsin. State legislation in Wisconsin and Massachusetts encouraging these programs may be useful models for other areas.

Comment. It appears likely that a voluntary metropolitan program may encourage some residential desegregation of suburbs receiving students, but to date no research has addressed this question. Despite evidence of positive gains in minority achievement, it should be noted that voluntary metropolitan programs cannot be considered adequate substitutes for mandatory desegregation programs since they invariably leave central-city minority schools nearly as segregated as before such programs were put into effect.

Although these programs seem innocuous at first glance, they have in fact met with considerable political resistance both from suburbs which resist desegregation and from central cities which resist the loss of revenue resulting from declines in enrollment. Orfield (1981) suggests, however, that this type of program may be useful as a precursor to mandatory metropolitan plans since it introduces suburban districts to desegregation and helps to develop interdistrict coordination.

Considerations in Developing Pupil-Assignment Plans

The Racial and Ethnic Composition of Schools

In drawing pupil-assignment plans, almost every school district faces the question of what the optimum racial and ethnic composition of particular schools should be. *Racial balance* or the degree to which the racial compositions of individual school enrollments approximate the racial composition of the district's student population is sometimes the solution to this question. Because transportation distances needed to achieve balance may be great and because courts often have accepted the retention of some all- or predominantly minority schools in districts with large minority populations, the issue is not settled completely by a racial-balance criterion. The problem is, of course, that there are many goals that should be taken into account in drawing a pupil-assignment plan, and different goals may have different implications for the racial and ethnic compositions of schools.

The following considerations should shape decisions about racial compositions of schools. There is no precise formula that one can offer to allow these considerations to be balanced out in particular circumstances.

1. Different minority groups (for example, blacks, Hispanics, Asian and Native Americans) should be treated differently and distinctly. Hispanics have sometimes been counted as blacks and sometimes as whites, usually to minimize the assignment and transportation of white students.
2. A critical mass of between 15 to 20 percent of any particular racial or ethnic group should be maintained in each school. In multiracial or multiethnic schools, this minimum might be relaxed somewhat. The higher the socioeconomic status of the groups in question, the less emphasis needs to be placed on the group's minimum size. A

critical mass of students seems to encourage intergroup contact, discourage self-isolation, facilitate the responsiveness of teachers and administrators to the special needs of minorities—especially when remedial or bilingual programs are needed—and promote more parental involvement in the school.

3. In biracial and biethnic situations intergroup conflict may be greatest when the two groups are about equal in size. This potential for conflict may be greatest when the students involved are of lower socioeconomic status.

4. White parents and perhaps middle-class minority parents are more likely to leave or not enter the public schools if their children are assigned to schools in which they are in a racial or ethnic minority, especially in biracial or biethnic situations, or to schools in minority neighborhoods. There is some reason to believe that whites are more likely to flee when blacks rather than Hispanics comprise the majority nonwhite group. Other things being equal, the higher the socioeconomic status of whites, the more likely they are to flee from desegregation to suburban or private schools.

5. The maintenance of a critical mass of students who do relatively well academically seems to contribute not only to the achievement of these students but of students who have been lower achievers. Students seem to be influenced most by same-race peers. The size of the necessary critical mass to promote achievement seems to depend on the achievement gaps involved and the way teachers organize their classes and relate to students. These considerations are discussed in chapter 7.

Evidence. Each of these propositions represents the consensus view of the experts that the authors interviewed (see Broh and Trent 1981). Douglas Longshore (1981) found that whites were most hostile to blacks in desegregated schools that were between 40 and 60 percent white. This hostility was most clear in low socioeconomic schools, large schools, rural schools, and southern schools. Similar conclusions relating to proportion of blacks and white hostility were reached by Nancy St. John (1975) and Charles S. Bullock (1976). Charles B. Thomas (1979) and Bruce A. Campbell (1977) both found more racial hostility in situations where whites are of lower socioeconomic status.

Although the evidence is less than definitive on the question, the belief that schools should be at least 15 to 20 percent minority is widely held by experts in the field (see Koslin, Koslin, and Pargament 1972). Robert L. Crain, Rita E. Mahard, and Ruth E. Narot (1982) found poor race relations and low black-male achievement in newly desegregated southern high schools that were less than 20 percent black. That study also found generally improved achievement-test scores and race relations in schools where blacks were in the majority although there was considerable evidence of white flight as well. All other studies of school racial composition and minority achievement report a linear trend—the more white students in a school, the higher the minority achievement. However, these findings seem more related to the achievement levels of whites in these schools than to race itself.

Evidence supporting the fourth proposition related to white flight is reasonably clear and is summarized by Christine H. Rossell and Willis Hawley (1981). In addition, there is considerable evidence that black and national-origin- minority students are less prejudiced and more responsive to race-relations programs than are white students (Doherty et al. 1981; Erbe 1977; Regens and Bullock 1979).

Comment. The five propositions do not lend themselves to examples since the idea is to take them into account simultaneously. It is important to emphasize that there are many predominantly minority schools that attract and retain students of other races, have positive race relations, and demonstrate good academic performance of students. It should also be emphasized that evidence about the importance of a critical mass of students is limited to studies of cases where whites are the dominant race in the school.

One issue that continues to bedevil desegregation planners in cities with large numbers of students needing bilingual programs is how desegregation and bilingual education can be accommodated. There is a growing literature on this topic (see Fernández and Guskin 1981; Carter 1979). As already noted, the assignment of national-origin-minority children with limited-English-proficiency during desegregation must be done so as to cluster sufficient numbers of students in any given classroom or school where special assistance may be provided (bilingual instruction or English-as-a-second-language programs). The model most frequently employed to achieve this goal was first adopted in the Boston desegregation plan. In that case lawyers for the Puerto Rican Legal Defense and Education Fund recommended, and the court later approved, that LEP children be clustered in groups of twenty per grade for three consecutive grades in any selected school to which youngsters were assigned in order for a viable program to exist. Schools selected to receive these students were ones with bilingual programs.

This principle of clustering students for instructional purposes (bona fide groupings under Emergency School Aid Act guidelines) was followed in other desegregation plans such as the one developed to consolidate the Wilmington and New Castle County school districts in *Evans* v. *Buchanan*. Clustering has been incorporated by various districts (for example,

Detroit, Cleveland, Milwaukee, Kalamazoo) into compliance plans which have been approved by the United States Office for Civil Rights. In effect, national-origin-minority children who were classified as LEP were accorded assignment priority, and other children (black and white) were assigned afterwards in accordance with majority and minority ratios and variances approved by courts.

A variation of this method is found when national-origin-minority LEP students in a school with language-assistance programs are allowed to remain in that school in order to continue receiving special services. The plan submitted by the Detroit school system in response to the sixth United States Circuit Court of Appeals's 1980 order for additional desegregation between the predominantly black first district and the second district, which has significant numbers of national-origin-minority LEP students, utilizes this approach.

Socioeconomic Status of Students

One reason why desegregation improves minority-student achievement is that students from economically deprived backgrounds benefit from attending school with students of higher income families. This finding may have more to do with the achievement levels of students with higher socioeconomic status than intrinsically with socioeconomic status itself. However, teachers may behave differently when there are larger numbers of middle- and upper-class students and when the parents of these students make demands on individual schools and the system as a whole.

The influence of socioeconomic status has several implications for school desegregation. First, middle-class students should be assigned as effectively as possible in a desegregation plan. Second, a desegregation plan should be drawn to provide socioeconomically desegregated schools for low-income whites. Low-income whites can benefit educationally in the same way that low-income minorities do from desegregation. Third, in situations where it is impossible to desegregate all minority students, the benefits of desegregation should go first to those students from economically deprived backgrounds, assuming that their educational needs will be adequately addressed in the desegregated setting. As noted in the previous discussion of racial compositions of schools, racial conflict is likely to be greatest when the aggregate socioeconomic status of a school is low, especially in biracial situations where two races are of approximate proportions. Fourth, the intellectual and interpersonal resources of higher socioeconomic national-origin-minority students should be utilized, particularly of those students who have received several years of schooling in their native country.

Evidence. Coleman and his colleagues first indicated that most of the academic benefits of school desegregation to minorities result from mixing social classes (high-status whites with low-status minorities) rather than races (Coleman et al. 1966). A lack of social-class integration may reduce the academic benefits of desegregation. Charles Thomas (1979) concludes that desegregation involving low-socioeconomic whites is more likely to lead to racial tensions than desegregation involving middle-income whites. Campbell (1977) suggests further that whites of low-socioeconomic status are more prejudiced than whites of higher socioeconomic status, and when schools with socioeconomic mixes are compared, those with whites of high-socioeconomic status have less racial tension. Although it is popularly assumed that low-income minority students are often a source of discipline problems in desegregated schools, there is little evidence to support this proposition. One major study conducted in the early 1970s by Crain, Mahard, and Narot (1982) found that racial tensions in southern high schools were more serious when black students were middle income rather than poor. This may be because middle-income black students are more aggressive in their response to perceived discrimination than are students from lower income families.

As noted previously, greater white flight can be expected when the families being desegregated have the means to enroll their children in private schools or to relocate their residences in suburban school districts. Studies by Rossell (1981b) and Michael W. Giles, Douglas S. Gatlin, and Everett F. Cataldo (1976) identify this effect.

Examples. Most school systems have not explicitly utilized socioeconomic status as a criterion for desegregation although Pasadena proposed to consider socioeconomic status in its desegregation plan to achieve socioeconomic as well as racial and ethnic balance among schools. Los Angeles's 1978 desegregation plan had the effect of increasing the separation of students by socioeconomic status because schools were allowed to pair themselves in the first step of desegregation. The Los Angeles school board believed that desegregating whites with middle-class minorities would reduce white flight. In the view of the staff of the Jefferson County (Louisville) school district, the least successful schools in their desegregation plan are those which serve low-income blacks and low-income whites. Achievement-test scores are low for both white and black students who attend these schools.

Which National-Origin-Minorities Are Racially Isolated
and Should be Desegregated?

Desegregating school districts with large numbers of national-origin-minority students face the important question of whether all national-origin-minority students should be treated as minorities whose needs are taken into special account in the pupil-assignment plan. Many of the experts interviewed raised this question both because desegregation may place some national-origin-minority students in situations that are inappropriate to their educational needs and because some school systems have desegregated national-origin-minority students of certain backgrounds while leaving others isolated.

There is no empirical evidence related to the question of which students among national-origin-minority students should be desegregated, but the relevant opinion of experts and the view of the study team suggest that the principle involved is simply that persons who are not segregated should not be desegregated. This proposition, of course, raises another issue. How does one decide who is segregated? The answer to this question seems to depend on answers to several others:

1. Are the students severely deficient in English?
2. Has the group of students been and is it now the victim of discrimination by public officials?
3. Are the students involved residentially desegregated?
4. Is the income level of the students above the district's average or above the regional average?

The answers to these questions may allow districts or courts to determine who should be treated as minority for purposes of desegregation. In addition, they draw attention to the fact that the educational and social needs of many national-origin-minority students differ substantially from the needs of other students and should be treated uniquely in the desegregation plan. These considerations, in turn, draw attention to a question of the first order. What are the goals that can be achieved through the desegregation of national-origin-minority students?

National-Origin-Minority Students Should Be
Considered Distinct Groups in the Development of
Pupil-Assignment Plans

Often, nonblack minorities have been ignored, treated as black, or treated as white in the design of desegregation plans. Blacks, segregated (by the criteria given previously) Hispanics, and Asian and Native Americans not only should be defined as distinct groups, but the educational needs of these different groups also should be considered. For example, pairing or clustering schools for assignment purposes should take into account the special needs of national-origin-minority students for language and cultural-reinforcement programs.

Evidence. The experts that the team interviewed agree with this general proposition almost without exception. The research indicates that different racial and ethnic groups have different types of experiences under desegregation (see Gerard and Miller 1975; Crain and Mahard 1980; Mahard and Crain 1980; Dornbush and Fernandez 1979; Schofield 1981). An obvious point here is that the need for bilingual education among national-origin-minority students should not be assumed. It must be determined by systematic testing and teacher and parent assessment.

Drawing Subdistricts

Many school districts attempt to maintain a neighborhood element in their desegregation plans by subdividing the district into smaller racially balanced subdistricts. Students are then reassigned only within these boundaries. This approach reduces options for achieving racial balance both during the first years of the plan, particularly in the presence of implementation-year flight, and during subsequent years as the demographic characteristics of the district change.

Evidence. In an analysis of school desegregation in Boston, Christine H. Rossell and John Michael Ross (1979) suggest that it is inadvisable to draw inviolable subdistrict attendance zones even if initially they are racially balanced and particularly when there is no stable white residential area included in the attendance zone. Establishment of rigid subdistricts allows families, particularly families that comprise a racial or ethnic minority in one subdistrict, to relocate in a more desirable subdistrict within the system and precludes the school system from adjusting attendance zones to compensate for such movement and maintain racial balance among subdistricts. The advantage of a districtwide plan with no subdistricts in that school authorities are able to redraw attendance zones and reassign students from all over the district whenever necessary to stabilize schools. If a reassignment plan utilizes subdistricts for administrative purposes, the central administration should be able to redraw them when necessary.

Renovating Schools Receiving Desegregated Student
Bodies

Since minority schools tend to be located in the central city, they are often the oldest and most dilapidated schools in a system. The physical condition of central-city facilities contributes to white reluctance to attend these schools and may encourage minority students to withdraw from them when that option is present. The Massachusetts Research Center (1976) found that the newer the building to which white students are assigned, the less white flight. Daniel U. Levine and Eugene F. Eubanks (1981) conclude that magnet schools draw more white students when the facilities are attractive. The qualitative research supports this basic proportion as well. In addition, Crain (1977) identified better race relations in high schools in better physical condition, and Rossell (1977) found higher average daily attendance in schools in better physical condition. This is not to say, of course, that parents will not resist sending their children to new or renovated schools. By themselves, good facilities will not substantially reduce white flight or promote educational quality.

Example. Madison High School in Boston is a magnet school located in Roxbury, a minority neighborhood. This school, with its modern facilities, has been quite successful in attracting white students.

Placing Magnet Schools in Minority Neighborhoods
under Mandatory Reassignment Plans

One potentially effective option for minimizing white flight while maximizing racial balance within a mandatory desegregation plan is a two-stage reassignment process. The first stage is voluntary and includes the creation of magnet schools over a four- or five-month period in the preimplementation year. All magnet schools might be located in minority neighborhoods although such schools will be less attractive to whites than schools in all white or racially mixed areas. Some of these magnets might be fundamental schools in order to attract white students whose parents' image of minority schools is that they are unsafe and lacking in discipline. Magnets located in badly deteriorating facilities or the most racially isolated minority schools will be less successful than those placed in new facilities or on the border of racially isolated neighborhoods.

The first stage of the reassignment process begins with the magnet-school reassignment. After white parents are asked to volunteer for magnet-school reassignment in minority neighborhoods, additional seats in minority schools can be filled by mandatory reassignment of whites. Minorities can be reassigned by the same process. They can either volunteer for a magnet school or accept the school-district's assignment.

If one purpose of this two-stage reassignment process is to increase the prestige and resources of minority neighborhoods and schools and thus lessen white flight overall, magnet schools should not be placed in white neighborhoods. The only exception to this might be placing a magnet school in a lower income white neighborhood in which prestige and resources need to be increased as much as those in minority neighborhoods. Magnet schools may increase the status of minority schools and minority neighborhoods. However, they also may increase minority frustration if many minorities are denied the opportunity to attend a superior school in their neighborhood because it is necessary to leave seats for whites from outside the neighborhood.

Evidence. In Boston there are a significant number of whites who are willing to put their children in schools in minority neighborhoods if those schools are publicized as superior schools and if the alternative is mandatory reassignment to another desegregated school chosen by the school administration (Massachusetts Research Center 1976; Rossell and Ross 1979). In case studies of magnet programs in Milwaukee, Stamford (Connecticut), and St. Paul, Levine and Eubanks (1981) identify several characteristics that promote white enrollment at magnets in minority neighborhoods. These characteristics, shared by schools that were able to successfully attract white students, include outstanding leadership on the part of the principal, instructional programs that provide for individual attention and concentration on basic skills, attractive facilities, active recruiting of white students, and low student-adult ratios.

It is important that the first stage of volunteering be done on an individual basis rather than a school basis as was done in Los Angeles. There schools were asked to volunteer for pairings and clusters with the alternative of later mandatory pairing. The problem with this policy is that when entire schools are asked to volunteer, any given school may have enough parents who oppose and block this action. If such pairing does occur, opposing parents may withdraw their children and thus virtually eliminate any chance of achieving racial balance.

Other than this evidence that many whites, depending on the city, may be willing to volunteer for magnet schools in minority neighborhoods if the alternative is mandatory reassignment to a nonmagnet desegregated school, there is no quantitative evidence that this type of reassignment process will reduce white flight. The qualitative research is unclear on the subject.

Enriching Curricula at All Schools: An Alternative to Academic Magnets

Although academic magnet schools may reduce the perceived costs some parents who consider their children academically gifted attribute to desegregation, they also may stigmatize nonmagnet schools in a desegregated school district. In turn this may induce flight among families not admitted to the magnets. It seems desirable, therefore, to offer advanced and college-preparatory courses in all or most secondary schools in order to keep parents with high academic aspirations for their children in the public-school system, to avoid resegregation among schools, and to foster educational opportunities for all students.

Evidence. The qualitative literature supports the general proposition that curriculum enrichment will reduce white flight, but there is no quantitative evidence that addresses this consideration. The experts that were interviewed by and large endorsed the avoidance of academic magnets for academically gifted and talented students. These experts believe that academic magnets reduce advanced academic courses in regular schools and increase inequities in the school system involved. The absence of advanced courses in nonmagnet schools may mean that students who are very able in one subject but not in another will have reduced opportunities and that the motivation of students who aspire to advanced classes will be undermined. Nearly all of the national experts agreed that desegregation can facilitate the introduction and implementation of school improvements because in most cases a new agenda is set and external resources and pressures exist for change (see also Hawley 1980).

The Issue of Busing Distance

Two of the central issues in almost all desegregation suits and in all planning efforts are, first, what is the maximum amount of time a student should be on the bus? and, second, how many miles should the longest bus ride be? Of course, these two questions are related. If any argument is to be made about the effects that riding the bus has on students, it would have to center on the time involved. However, parents may be equally or more concerned about distance, perhaps because they believe that they could not respond to an emergency involving their child at a school in a part of town they do not know.

Evidence. Not surprisingly, all experts interviewed agreed that busing distances should be kept as short as possible. Of course, the shorter the bus rides in most cities, the less racial isolation can be reduced. As noted in chapter 1, it appears that riding the bus to school has no effect on student performance or attitudes toward school, but the available research does not deal with bus rides that are very long (for example, an hour or more each way). Neither research nor the experts can tell us if there is a maximum time or distance a child should ride a bus to school before there are harmful effects. There is some but very limited research suggesting that whites are more likely to leave the public schools if their children are bused long distances as part of a desegregation plan. However, this appears to be only a short-term effect.

Chapter 1 cited studies that have addressed this concern generally indicate that busing itself has no adverse effect on learning. After examining data from a large number of desegregated southern school districts, J. Davis concludes that "there is no evidence that busing *per se* . . . [or] attending one's own neighborhood school has any effects, positive or negative, on school achievement or social climate" (1973, p. 119). Barbara Zoloth (1976b) examined the effects of the amount of time spent riding the bus and concluded that it has no relationship to student achievement. Two other studies, both of Jefferson County, support these findings. Gerald L. Natkin (1980) found that busing had no impact on the achievement-test scores of either black or white second-grade students. Edward J. Hayes (1981) reached a similar conclusion in his analysis of grade-point averages of black high-school students in that district.

There is some research on the relationship between busing distance and white flight. All studies of central-city school districts have been of the implementation year, and they find a relationship between busing distance and white flight (Rossell 1981b). The studies of countywide and metropolitan school systems, by contrast, find no relationship although most were of postimplementation years. Rossell's (1981b) analysis of Los Angeles determined that there was a relationship between busing distance and white flight only in the implementation year. Parents who do not withdraw their children at that time do not withdraw them later because of a long bus ride (see also Massachusetts Research Center 1976).

One-Way or Two-Way Busing

Desegregation plans which assign and transport minority students into predominantly white schools but do not assign and transport white students, or at least not many white students, to minority neighborhoods are called *one-way busing plans*. Two-way plans require minorities and whites to share the burdens of attending a school outside one's neighborhood.

When minority students are mandatorily reassigned and transported to white schools but whites are not reassigned to minority schools (as in Riverside, California and Ann Arbor, Michigan), there is a greater reduction in racial isolation than if the plan is completely voluntary. There is generally less white flight from one-way than from two-way reassign-ment and transportation. However, under such one-way reassignment plans, desegregation may be viewed as a minority problem, and minorities are considered the outsiders. In addition, mandatory reassignment of minorities but not of whites contributes to the idea that whites have control over their own fate but minorities do not.

Evidence. No empirical evidence exists that one-way busing plans are harmful to minority students. Rossell (1978a) finds that two-way busing plans, especially when they involve young children, lead to substantially more white flight from desegregation than one-way plans. Mandatory black reassignments, by contrast, whether as a part of one-way or two-way plans, seem not to have provoked black flight and protest even when blacks disproportionately bear the burden of busing. Blacks in most cities have been willing to accept the disproportionate burden of one-way plans such as those in Riverside, Hillsborough County (Tampa), and Milwaukee. Although black protest against disproportionate busing ap-pears to be increasing in other cities such as those in Nashville-Davidson County and in Fort Wayne and Portland (see Alexander 1979), blacks by a two-to-one margin say that they are willing to bus their children to schools outside their neighborhoods in order to achieve desegregation (Harris 1981).

Regardless of their effect on students, protest, and flight, one-way busing plans raise equity questions with which each community must deal. The experts that were interviewed, generally advocate two-way plans because of equity and the long-term support desegregation may have from minority communities. Two-way plans provide planners and implementors with more options to reduce racial isolation. In addition, they substantially reduce the likelihood that schools in minority com-munities will be closed and that new schools will have to be built. Two-way plans may facilitate housing desegregation, especially where options for white flight are not great.

Implementing Pupil-Assignment Plans

Desegregation That Begins at the Earliest Possible Grade Is Most Beneficial

The benefits to children will be greater if school desegregation begins with the first grade or kindergarten. However, because of parental op-position, most desegregation plans omit kindergarten and some also exclude the early primary grades. Beginning desegregation in the middle elementary grades or in junior-high school may be harmful to student achievement and complicates efforts to promote positive race relations. Changing both schools and classmates in the middle elementary grades disrupts instructional processes, limits students' access to programs if those programs are not offered in their new schools, and requires that students adjust to different peers and social environments. Moreover, racial and ethnic attitudes develop early, and adjusting to multiracial or multiethnic environments and avoiding racial and ethnic stereotypes are much more difficult for older than for younger students. The exclusion of students with limited-English-proficiency may facilitate provision of bilingual education in some instances but hinders linguistic and ethnic contact.

Evidence. Crain and Mahard (1981) have reviewed ninety-three empirical studies examining relationships between desegregation and student achievement. Both that survey and its predecessor present substantial evidence that desegregation begun in kindergarten or the first grade enhances minority achievement-test scores much more than desegregation begun in later grades (Crain and Mahard 1981). However, although Paul Wortman (1981) found significant relationships between desegregation and achievement, he did not identify as strong a relationship between early desegregation and improvements in minority test scores.

Little direct evidence from studies of desegregated schools exists that allows one to state with great confidence that early desegregation has a more positive effect on race relations than later desegregation. There are, however, a number of empirical and theoretical reasons for expecting this relationship. Empirical research on the development of racial awareness and racial attitudes indicates that young children tend not to be as conscious of racial differences or to have developed the elaborate stereotypes that older children have acquired (Katz 1976). Coleman and his colleagues found that desegregation at the earliest possible grades was associated with better race relations in later years of schooling (Coleman et al. 1966). In addition, Holt in her expert testimony before the court in the original *Brown* v. *Board of Education* (see Kluger 1977) and a number of experts that were interviewed believe that desegregating young children fosters better race relations.

One unintended consequence of a desegregation plan that includes early grades may be greater white flight at least when students are initially reassigned. Rossell (1978a), Rossell and Ross (1979), and the Massachusetts Research Center (1976) found more withdrawal of white elementary students than white secondary students upon implementation of mandatory desegregation plans.

Despite evidence that it is not in the best interests of children to delay desegregation, the Dallas and Los Angeles school systems, both under court order, have excluded students in kindergarten through third grade from mandatory reassignment in response to parental opposition. In Nashville-Davidson County, a federal district-court judge excluded students in kindergarten through fourth grades from reassignment under a modified mandatory plan that was to go into effect in fall 1981.

Phasing in Pupil-Assignment Plans

Many school districts implement their desegregation plans in stages in the hope that the process will not be disruptive or unmanageable. Thus, in the first year of desegregation the first through eighth grades may be desegregated, and in the second year the ninth through twelfth grades are added to the plan, as in Racine, Wisconsin. Plans can also be phased in by geographic area as in Boston. In this second method of phasing in plans, one area of the school district is desegregated in the first year, and the remaining areas are desegregated in the second or third year. While this process may facilitate management, phasing in desegregation plans leads to greater white flight than implementing them at one time.

Rossell (1978a), Armor (1980), and Morgan and England (1981) found that phasing in a desegregation plan leads to greater white flight than one would expect from the total amount of reassignments because there is greater flight during the first year in anticipation of future reassignments. In short, this finding suggests that the more warning people are given about desegregation and the more time they have to act, the more white flight occurs. The national experts interviewed were nearly unanimous in disapproving phased in plans.

Maximizing the Efficiency of Student Assignment and Transportation

Busing is a symbol on which desegregating and desegregated communities focus. If the pupil assignment and transportation processes are conducted efficiently and smoothly, parents may tend to have more confidence in the ability of the school administration to deal with other aspects of the desegregation process. For example, where appropriate, bilingual or bicultural personnel should be assigned to school buses and sites to reduce confusion and clarify instructions. The efforts school administrators make to facilitate the efficiency of student assignment and transportation may foster more positive community attitudes about desegregation and as a result may serve to reduce flight from desegregation.

Evidence. There is no quantitative evidence to support this consideration of efficiency although it makes intuitive sense. Some of the experts interviewed and several qualitative commentaries support this strategy (see Broh and Trent 1981).

Example. There are numerous ways that school systems can ease the anxiety and confusion that accompany initial pupil reassignment. For example, the associate superintendent of the Stockton school district reported in an interview that he traveled with the director of research to every desegregated school district in California to learn which strategies improve implementation efficiency. They found that one school district tried to get first graders who could not read on the right bus in the morning and afternoon by putting different colors on the front of each bus and then tagging students with the appropriate color. Unfortunately, this same district found that 6 percent of their students were color blind. The Stockton administrators found another school district which had anticipated that problem and put animals on the front of the bus, only to discover that first graders cannot always tell one animal's silhouette from another. The Stockton administrators decided to cover all bases by putting colored animals on the front of each bus and then tagging each student with his or her colored animal. This strategy minimized the number of lost youngsters and led these administrators to believe that it greatly enhanced public confidence in the plan and, as a result, reduced flight.

Stability in Pupil-Assignment Plans

Among the considerations desegregation planners should take into account is the desirability of stability in the relationships students have in their schools with their peers and teachers. Thus, once racial isolation has been substantially reduced, changes in pupil assignments should be minimized. Such stability may be particularly important in promoting parent and community support for schools and desegregation and in meeting the needs of national-origin-minority and other students who require bilingual and other special instructions programs.

There appears to be no empirical research on the importance of stability in the context of school desegregation. However, the local and national experts that the team interviewed and the members of the study team agree that stability is very important to the successful implementation of desegregation plans over time.

Promoting stability in desegregation plans appears to have several possible advantages. These advantages include:

1. Minimizing changes in the composition of a student cohort is likely to minimize conflict over which group will control what territory and to facilitate the development of good interpersonal relationships, especially among junior-high and high-school students.
2. Minimizing changes for individual students will probably reduce the personal anxiety many young people feel in new settings and will increase continuity in the curricula students experience. When movement is necessary, sending and receiving schools should coordinate their curricula.
3. Stability in teacher-student relationships should facilitate understanding of students' learning needs (assuming stereotypes are avoided and high expectations are held). The maintenance of social order and discipline in the school should be facilitated because few students will be unknown to those in authority (Gottfredson and Daiger 1979).
4. Minimal changes in pupil-assignment plans and in the number of different schools students attend should help parents feel more confident about being involved in the education of their children. Uncertainty about the schools that their children will attend probably causes some parents to flee public schools.

This emphasis on stability is not meant to diminish the importance of dealing with resegregation among and within schools. The stability argument can be and has been used as an excuse not to reduce racial isolation. What is suggested is that when plans are drawn and the problem of resegregation among schools is considered, the stability issues raised here should be taken into account. School systems that phase in plans by grades or geographic areas will invariably induce instability. Likewise, efforts to minimize desegregation initially keeps the issue in the courts so that pupil reassignment remains a lingering prospect.

In initial assignment plans, and when additional transfers are necessary, attempts might be made to (1) keep families together, which some experts that were interviewed observed is particularly important in national-origin-minority settings; (2) limit the number of schools to which students in a sending school should be reassigned so that there will be a critical mass of students reassigned who know each other; and (3) transfer teachers and students together so that students reassigned will still know and be known by several teachers.

Summary

The primary objective of a pupil-assignment plan is to reduce or eliminate instances of unconstitutional segregation among schools. Research clearly indicates that plans which rely primarily on voluntary choice are not effective means to reduce districtwide racial isolation, particularly in large school systems and in those with over 30 to 35 percent minority enrollment. Under certain conditions magnet programs can effectively reduce racial isolation, but in most districts a mandatory component is necessary to achieve any substantial districtwide desegregation.

The research and experiences of school districts around the country indicate that mandatory student-reassignment strategies are the most effective means of reducing racial isolation among schools. Although mandatory plans produce greater white flight than voluntary plans, at least during the first year or two of implementation, they still result in greater desegregation and interracial contact than no plan or plans in most districts that rely on voluntary choice. Metropolitan and countywide plans that include central-city and suburban school districts produce greater socioeconomic integration and greater financial stability than central-city mandatory or voluntary plans. In addition, metropolitan and countywide plans tend to produce less white flight than central-city plans and, in some cases, create conditions that contribute to residential desegregation.

A critical mass of 15 to 20 percent of any particular racial or ethnic group should be maintained in each school if possible. Desegregation plans should also take into account the socioeconomic and academic status of students who are reassigned to produce socioeconomic and academic desegregation. The research indicates that different racial and ethnic groups have different experiences under desegregation. Different minorities, therefore, should be treated as distinct groups with different needs that should be addressed by desegregation plans.

The creation of magnet programs under mandatory plans may reduce some resistance to the forced aspects of desegregation and may contribute to districtwide desegregation if the programs are housed in predominantly minority schools. However, establishment of academic magnets may promote racial, socioeconomic, and academic resegregation; stigmatize non-magnet schools as inferior; lead to the flight of white families whose children are not admitted to these programs; and result in minority protest among those families whose children cannot attend these special schools in their own neighborhoods. It seems desirable, therefore, to enrich curricula in all schools and to offer advanced and college preparatory courses in all secondary schools.

Although most experts agree that busing time and distance should be kept as short as possible, the available evidence indicates that riding the bus, at least as it is required under most desegregation plans, has no impact on learning or on the social climates of schools. There is some evidence that during the first year of implementation there is a relationship between busing distance and white flight in central-city school systems, but there appears to be no relationship after that first year. In other words, parents who do not withdraw their children before or during the first year of a mandatory desegregation plan generally do not withdraw them later because of a long bus ride.

The experts assert that plans that involve busing should be two-way plans that involve both white and minority students. In many districts the time and distance of busing cannot be shared equally among minorities and whites because of the racial composition of student populations. Although these plans lead to greater white flight than those that reassign only minority students, two-way plans are recommended by experts because of equity and the long-term support desegregation may gain from minority communities. One-way busing of minorities, however, does not appear to adversely affect the benefits that they receive from schools.

Research on academic achievement and racial attitudes suggests that desegregation should encompass at least twelve grades and would be even more effective if it also included kindergarten. Phasing in plans leads to greater aggregate white flight due to anticipation of future reassignments. School systems should maximize the efficiency of student reassignments and transportation and promote stability in assignments after initial implementation. However, districts should not use efficiency and stability as arguments to minimize the amount of desegregation through the system or to avoid dealing with significant resegregation if the demographics of districts change over time.

Pupil-assignment strategies have important educational and social as well as political and economic implications. However, research indicates that the many educational and social outcomes that are attributed to desegregation are not so much a factor of pupil-assignment strategies as they are of the strategies that districts and individual schools develop and implement to address the educational needs of students and create positive learning and social climates. These strategies are identified and discussed in the chapters that follow.

Notes

1. Unless otherwise noted, figures of changes in racial balance and in numbers of predominantly minority schools presented as illustrative examples of progress under different types of desegregation plans are based on biannual pupil-enrollment surveys administered and released by the United States Office for Civil Rights and are contained in Smylie (1982).

2. Armor's (1980) method consistently yields the most negative long-term impact. John Michael Ross, B. Gratton, and R.C. Clarke (1981)

find a nonnegative impact only in suburban school districts. While countywide school districts in their sample have almost the same loss rate as the control group in the fourth year, it is not enough to make up the implementation-year loss. Morgan and England (1981) conclude that the effect of school desegregation on white-student loss is not long-term. Their data from fifty-two large school districts indicate that regardless of school level (elementary or secondary), postimplementation white-enrollment declines are only slightly larger in magnitude than preimplementation declines. Similarities between pre- and postimplementation rates of decline are identified as early as the first or second year after initial implementation.

3. This increase is seen in a cohort analysis comparing magnet school enrollment in kindergarten through eighth grade in 1980 to enrollment in first through ninth grades in 1981.

4

Using School Desegregation to Effect Housing Desegregation

It has long been known that housing segregation creates segregated schools. More recently, it has been contended that the reverse is also true—segregated schools can create or reinforce housing segregation (Pearce 1980). Meyer M. Weinberg (1980) and Gary Orfield (1981) identify a reciprocal relationship between school and housing segregation. In Diana M. Pearce's words:

> School and housing segregation are so closely linked that they are often thought of as two facets of a single problem, that of urban segregation. In terms of cause and effect, however, school segregation is increasingly seen as a result of housing segregation. Urban dynamics, however, are seldom as simple or uni-directional as such a formulation suggests. That school segregation has contributed to housing segregation has been increasingly recognized by both social scientists and the courts in such cases as Denver, Columbus, and [Charlotte-Mecklenburg County] (1980, pp. 1–2).

The United States Supreme Court acknowledged this linkage in its 1971 opinion in *Swann* v. *Charlotte-Mecklenburg Board of Education:*

> The locations of schools may . . . influence the patterns of residential development of a metropolitan area and have important impact on the composition of inner-city neighborhoods. . . . [S]chool board decisions may well promote segregated residential patterns, which, when combined with ''neighborhood zoning,'' further lock the school system into the mold of separation of the races (cited in Pearce 1980, p. 2).

In finding Cleveland and that city's public-housing authority guilty of unconstitutionally segregating public housing, United States District Court Judge Frank Battisti wrote in *Robertson* v. *Perk* (1972):

> Since this city is faced with such a massive segregation problem, a dispersal of urban housing patterns seems to be the most reasonable alternative to a massive busing program to eliminate the resulting segregation in the public schools (cited in Weinberg 1980, p. 2).

Desegregated housing would greatly reduce or eliminate the need for school desegregation, particularly mandatory student reassignment. However, as both Orfield (1981) and Pearce (1980) note, few efforts have been made by local or federal officials to promote residential desegregation in order to reduce prospects for mandatory student reassignments or to treat housing desegregation as a goal in itself. Although there appear to have been few initiatives to move from housing desegregation to school desegregation, some evidence now exists that school desegregation can under certain circumstances promote housing desegregation and thus reduce the need for mandatory student reassignments.

Reductions in housing segregation through school desegregation can occur for at least four reasons. First, when a school district is completely desegregated (that is, there are no neighborhoods that are excluded from the plan), there is lessened pressure for whites with young children to move out of racially mixed neighborhoods to white neighborhoods since the district has guaranteed racial balance among all its schools. Second, white or minority parents can move anywhere in the school district knowing that their children will not be the only ones of their race in their new school. Third, school desegregation makes racial steering by real-estate agents more difficult since they can no longer use the racial composition of a neighborhood school as a guide to the neighborhood's prestige (see Pearce 1981). Nor can real-estate agents intimidate whites by arguing that certain neighborhoods have schools of inferior quality based on racial composition. Fourth, when the desegregation plan ensures attendance at one's neighborhood school where the neighborhood attendance zone is residentially integrated, white and black families who want their children in neighborhood schools have an incentive to live in integrated neighborhoods.

The only comparative study of the relationship between school desegregation and housing desegregation is Pearce's (1980) exploratory analysis of changes in residential racial composition in seven matched segregated-desegregated pairs of school districts. This analysis assumes that the critical factor in this relationship is the presence or absence of white enclaves in school-desegregation plans. Pearce's data indicate that school districts with districtwide desegregation usually experience substantially greater reductions in residential segregation of blacks and whites than urban areas with only partial school desegregation. This effect is not limited to the first few years of school desegregation. Pearce found that reductions in residential segregation continued at least into the second decade of desegregation. Thus, although this study needs to be extended to other urban areas, it appears that extensive districtwide school desegregation stimulates residential desegregation.

This analysis does not, however, suggest that districtwide school desegregation always results in housing desegregation. Rather it indicates that districtwide desegregation creates conditions that remove certain benefits for families to relocate in segregated neighborhoods. In particular, districtwide student reassignment involving all neighborhoods promotes the dissolution of white enclaves that may draw white families who seek to avoid school desegregation. Under this type of plan, families know that wherever they live in the school district, they will be involved in the school desegregation process.

In order to promote housing desegregation, school-desegregation plans should incorporate a number of strategies that create both incentives for living in or moving into racially mixed neighborhoods and disincentives for moving out of these neighborhoods. Several communities with desegregating or desegregated school districts have recognized the relationship between housing and school desegregation and have developed and implemented strategies to promote both goals simultaneously. Various aspects of these communities' experiences are reported by Pearce (1980), Orfield (1981), Weinberg (1980), George K. Cunningham and William L. Husk (1979a), and the Kentucky Commission on Human Rights (1977, 1980). The strategies proposed here and the discussions that follow are based on these assessments and on interviews with local and national experts (see Broh and Trent 1981).

Preserving Desegregated and Stabilizing Racially Changing Neighborhoods

In communities with neighborhood schools, a small migration of minority residents into an all-white neighborhood or a noticeable change in the minority enrollment may result in white flight from the schools. If the flight is not arrested, the result will be a segregated school and a segregated neighborhood. The right kind of school-desegregation plan can slow the process of racial change and encourage residential desegregation. The ideal desegregation plan for this purpose would contain the following components:

1. The desegregation plan should be based on accurate projections of racial compositions for several years in advance rather than on existing figures which may be out of date before the plan is implemented. In particular, projected increases in Asian and Hispanic populations, especially in urban areas, should be taken into consideration by relocation planners.
2. Mixed and changing neighborhood schools should be designated as schools where students will not be reassigned and bused out. In many cities, whites in these neighborhoods are bused in one direction in order to desegregate a ghetto school while minorities are bused in

the opposite direction to further desegregation in a white neighbor-hood (as is done in Columbus). This often occurs when a computer program is used to minimize the total amount of transportation. Instead, students who attend these schools should be exempted from reassignment and busing. This exemption is important because it counteracts negative market tendencies and encourages individual inclinations to remain in the integrated neighborhood (Pearce 1980).

3. These mixed neighborhood schools should also be given guarantees of racial stability through a provision to expand facilities with port-ables, through annual adjustment of attendance boundaries where helpful, and through the promise of busing in rather than busing out white and minority students as needed to supplement the racial com-position of enrollment. Since this means one-way busing for the whites or minorities brought into the neighborhood, these new stu-dents should be drawn from nearby areas so that busing time will be short and there will be a tendency for sending and receiving neighborhoods to recognize that they have a common interest in residential stability.

4. Schools in segregated neighborhoods should not be exempted if they are desegregated by the voluntary transfer in of white or minority students (as was done in Los Angeles). Voluntary transfers provide no incentive for neighborhood desegregation and increase the busing distance for other students (see discussion of Milwaukee's magnet school plan in Orfield 1981).

5. Adjoining segregated neighborhoods of opposite-race composition can be placed in the same school-attendance zone to create a no-bus desegregated neighborhood as long as there is some reasonable chance that whites will be willing to move into the minority area and minorities into the white area sometime in the future to create a truly desegregated residential area. However, this strategy has the same risks as does the creation of inviolable subdistricts discussed in chapter 3. Paired segregated neighborhoods can become imbal-anced as a result of white flight to more desirable areas of the district, thus reducing chances for both school and residential desegregation. Chances that such relocation may occur are reduced when guarantees of racial balance are made or metropolitan reassignments are made by the school district.

Examples. In Stockton, neighborhood attendance zones were examined and redrawn where necessary to create schools which would be exempt from busing by virtue of desegregated residential areas or adjoining seg-regated neighborhoods. As a result, Stockton experienced white move-ment in two directions—out of the school district and into the central city where desegregated attendance zones had been created. The highly segregated Philadelphia school system has done some interesting things to maintain racially mixed neighborhoods, including the creation of magnet schools to serve racially mixed neighborhoods. Baltimore, another highly segregated district, has established middle schools to maintain racially mixed neighborhoods. In Louisville-Jefferson County desegregated neighborhoods are exempt from busing, and the local fair-housing organization has vigorously promoted residential desegregation as an alternative to busing. As a result of residential desegregation in this district, several new schools were exempted from busing when the system redrew its attendance zones in 1980.

Incentives for Segregated Neighborhoods to Desegregate

Rarely is any neighborhood, particularly a white neighborhood, able to establish a collective will to encourage opposite-race families to move in. However, in Shaker Heights (Ohio) white neighborhoods have worked to attract blacks in order to decrease the pressure of black in-migration on adjoining neighborhoods in danger of becoming segregated (Weinberg 1980). A school-desegregation plan can encourage racial desegregation of housing by providing incentives to neighborhoods which receive opposite-race migrants.

One important incentive would be to exempt residents of a neighborhood that attracts opposite-race families from busing as soon as school enrollment in that neighborhood reaches a certain level of racial desegregation even if this racial mix is lower than that which characterizes the district as a whole. An effective school-desegregation plan ideally would include coordination between the school system and other city agencies to provide information about the benefits, at least in terms of exemption from reassignment and busing, of recruiting and accepting opposite-race families. Information about different neighborhoods should also be provided for opposite-race families considering relocation. In addition, neighborhoods should be helped to organize politically so that they can work to attract opposite-race families or, alternatively, to accept scattered site public housing or use federal Section 8 rent subsidies to promote residential relocation.

Example. In Louisville-Jefferson County, the Kentucky Commission on Human Rights provided counseling for blacks and publicized those white neighborhoods into which they could move and be exempted from busing. As a result, blacks have moved into suburban

Jefferson County, and many white neighborhoods have begun to actively recruit black families to exempt themselves from busing (Cunningham and Husk 1979a; Orfield 1981; Kentucky Commission on Human Rights 1980).

Incentives to Encourage Individuals to Move into Opposite-Race Communities

A segregated neighborhood school-assignment policy provides no encouragement to minority or white families who are considering the possibility of moving into an area occupied predominantly by opposite-race families. A districtwide school-desegregation plan may ensure at least a minimum presence of racial groups in each school but provides no positive incentives for residential relocation.

One incentive to induce individuals to move into opposite-race neighborhoods is to guarantee that the children of these families will not be reassigned and bused out even if they do not constitute a large enough group to create a desegregated school. This exemption is difficult to provide if a grade-reorganization plan is implemented such that all elementary-school students attend, for example, fifth grade in minority areas and first through fourth grades in white areas. In this situation, there is a disincentive for whites to move into predominantly minority neighborhoods since they will find their children bused for more years than if they had remained in their white neighborhoods.

Another way to ensure that individuals who live in desegregated neighborhoods are not bused and still maintain racial balance in the school system is to establish magnet schools in minority neighborhoods. Seats in these schools should be guaranteed for children of white families who have moved into these communities. In most districts, locating magnet schools in white neighborhoods is not as useful to desegregation as placing them in minority neighborhoods. This is partly because magnet schools in white neighborhoods might serve as enclaves for whites who resist being reassigned to schools in minority neighborhoods. In addition, magnets located in white neighborhoods provide no incentives for whites to remain in racially changing or opposite-race neighborhoods if their children may be eligible for these programs no matter where they live in the district (see Orfield 1981).

A supplemental strategy for ensuring no busing for those who move into opposite-race neighborhoods is to design a plan which reassigns only a proportion of students in each grade, leaving a full range of grades for both minority and white students in neighborhood schools. A family moving into an opposite-race neighborhood would be given the option of staying in their desegregated neighborhood school for all grades or being reassigned and bused out to other desegregated schools. These strategies could ultimately reduce the amount of reassignment and transportation of students.

Examples. In Wichita, black students are reassigned and transported according to their street addresses. However, if they move into a predominantly white area, they are exempt from busing (Pearce 1980). In Louisville-Jefferson County any students moving into an area where they constitute a racial minority are immediately exempt from reassignment and busing. Between 1978 and 1980, 722 black families relocated in formerly white neighborhoods of Jefferson County. Orfield (1981) and Cunningham and Husk (1979a) attribute this movement, at least in part, to the exemption incentive.

Creating a School District Office for Housing Desegregation

Since reducing housing segregation reduces the need for student reassignment and busing for school desegregation, it seems advantageous for a school district to be concerned with housing patterns and housing policy. However, school-district administrators are educational experts rather than housing experts. There appear to be few school districts which have the expertise to systematically deal with housing issues.

To foster desegregated housing, school districts should establish an office explicitly concerned with the problem of housing segregation and the relationship between housing and school desegregation. This office would have six major functions:

1. Prepare policy analysis and policy recommendations for the school board and publicize the school board's positions on this issue.
2. Develop an overall plan for housing patterns with its own staff or assist local housing agencies to do so. Such a plan would attempt to project the pattern of residential movement of minorities and whites into the future and thereby identify areas which are likely to be good targets for the school district's efforts either to prevent residential and school resegregation or to introduce desegregation.
3. Coordinate the school district's efforts with other agencies and lobby for effective policies which would help the district desegregate its schools. Coordination activities might include making decisions jointly with housing agencies about the location of magnet schools to develop desegregated residential areas. The school district might

also be able to encourage local public-housing agencies to locate public housing so as to reduce the need for reassignment and busing. In addition, the school district might review all proposed private-subdivision developments in order to minimize their adverse effects on school desegregation.

4. Advise the school district on the best use of its real estate. Many school districts own land originally purchased for school construction and which is no longer needed for these facilities. This land could be disposed of in such a manner as to further housing desegregation.

5. Through its own staff or the staff from another city agency ensure that counseling services are provided to families. This is especially important for families eligible for federal rent subsidies under Section 8 of the Housing Authorization Act of 1976 who would benefit from making a desegregating move but who might be quite unfamiliar with opportunities available to them. The counseling office could also provide useful services to white families from the suburbs returning to the city. Of particular interest would be counseling services provided for teachers who are often assigned to schools in opposite-race neighborhoods as a result of desegregation and who might wish to live closer to their place of work.

6. Provide liaison services with neighborhood improvement groups. These groups may be able to organize a drive to exempt their neighborhoods from busing by recruiting opposite-race families or persuading them to accept subsidized housing. Such housing could be either new construction or subsidies applied to existing buildings. An organizer and technical-assistance official might be very helpful to these neighborhoods. (For examples of the work of neighborhood improvement groups to foster housing desegregation, see Weinberg 1980.)

The housing office should be staffed by individuals with proven expertise and experience in housing and real estate and a commitment to school desegregation. It should be served by an advisory board of individuals who bring expertise, influence, and channels of communication to other government agencies and private organizations.

Examples. The Riverside Unified School District has performed many of these functions for the last ten years, and as a result all but four schools are desegregated by neighborhood-attendance zones. The Louisville-Jefferson County housing authority's figures indicate that over one-half of the 1,413 black families who signed Section 8 leases since 1978 moved into white suburban Jefferson County (part of the metropolitan school district). This relocation was facilitated by the merger of the separate city and county agencies into one office which counseled families and co-ordinated their relocation. Although not part of the school system in Jefferson County, the activities of this agency are those that school districts could promote.

Scattered-Site Public Housing

One way to desegregate residential areas is to locate subsidized housing units to serve minority families in white neighborhoods. Each site should be relatively small and should be scattered throughout the school district. School desegregation plans, in turn, can take these housing patterns into account when developing or modifying student reassignments. For example, a white neighborhood that accepts minority subsidized housing might be exempt from reassignment and busing if a certain minority proportion of neighborhood-school enrollment is achieved.

Examples. In Charlotte-Mecklenburg County, school officials, the community relations commission, real estate brokers, and housing and county planning officials developed a system for consultation and identification of sites for construction of new subsidized housing. This consortium also worked to encourage predominantly white neighborhoods to accept scattered site housing. The community was generally receptive to this initiative because receiving neighborhoods would then become exempt from busing. Local experts interviewed in Denver, Minneapolis, and Seattle report scattered-site housing was employed to further school desegregation. In 1980 a federal district court ordered that any white St. Louis neighborhood that accepted subsidized housing which brought its school enrollment to at least 20 percent black, would retain a neighborhood school.

Including Local, State, and Federal Housing Authorities in School-Desegregation Remedies

Court cases involving a number of school districts have indicated that federal, state, and local housing policies can further segregation of neighborhoods and hence the segregation of schools. Although housing authorities may not be legally liable for segregation among schools, it follows logically from the relationship between housing and school segregation that a school-desegregation remedy should involve local, state, and federal authorities that affect housing as well as school districts. The requirement that subsidized housing be located so as to further residential desegregation is one obvious way in which housing authorities can share in creating a desegregated school district and reduce levels of student reassignment and busing.

Examples. Two of the most significant school-desegregation cases that involve housing authorities are in St. Louis and Yonkers (New York). In St. Louis a federal district court ordered the school board, city and state officials, the United States Department of Housing and Urban Development, and the United States Department of Justice to devise a plan to administer federal housing programs in the St. Louis metropolitan area in a manner that would support school desegregation (Orfield 1981). Although Judge Battisti suggested dispersal of urban-housing patterns in Cleveland as an alternative to mandatory student reassignments and busing, such dispersal did not occur, and housing authorities were never entered as litigants in the case. In 1976, four years after this alternative was proposed, Judge Battisti found the Cleveland school district unconstitutionally segregated and ordered a districtwide mandatory student-reassignment plan to remedy racial isolation (Weinberg 1980).

Summary

The literature, as well as a number of court cases, identifies a close relationship between housing and school segregation. Although housing desegregation would greatly reduce the need for school desegregation, particularly mandatory student reassignments and busing, few initiatives have been taken to promote residential desegregation to reduce racial isolation in neighborhood schools. The primary empirical research on housing and school desegregation suggests that the broader the scope of school desegregation, the fewer opportunities remain for families to move from racially integrated to racially segregated neighborhoods in order to enroll their children in segregated schools. Indeed, in several districts with metropolitan or districtwide school desegregation, residential desegregation has increased at a greater rate than in comparable districts with only partial desegregation.

There are a number of strategies that may be incorporated in school-desegregation plans to provide direct incentives for residential desegregation. Students who live in desegregated neighborhoods and students who move into opposite-race neighborhoods should be exempted from mandatory reassignment and busing out of those neighborhoods. Schools that become desegregated through residential integration should be given guarantees of racial stability.

School systems should establish an office concerned with housing patterns and housing policy to coordinate school-district desegregation efforts with local, state, and federal housing authorities and private real-estate agencies. This office may also perform a public-information function and counsel families about housing opportunities to promote neighborhood-school desegregation. School systems should consult with housing authorities about the location of subsidized public housing. In addition, whenever possible, government housing authorities should be involved in the development of school-desegregation plans.

5

Preparing and Involving Parents and the Community

Between the time a court orders desegregation and the time the plan is actually implemented, school districts have an opportunity to prepare parents and the community to ensure that desegregation will be implemented smoothly and work well. However, most school districts do not take full advantage of this opportunity. The fears that many parents have of violence in the schools, of the unknown, and of losing control of their children's lives have important effects on their behavior and, ultimately, on the outcome of desegregation. The school district and the political, business, and grass-roots leadership of a community need to deal with these anxieties if desegregation is to be successful. Typically, the school district does not adequately address parents' concerns nor does it involve community groups, particularly in the preimplementation planning stages. The mass media often exacerbates fears by focusing on disruption, white flight, and protest. The business and political leadership usually remains silent.

A number of studies stress the importance of community involvement in planning school desegregation. Robin Williams and Margaret Ryan (1954) and Morton Inger and Robert T. Stout (1968) argue that access of community groups to the decision-making process is vital to early public acceptance of school-desegregation plans. Everette Rogers (1962) also asserts that citizen participation in planning desegregation results in greater community commitment to social change. In describing the relationship between community involvement in and later support of school desegregation, Charles V. Willie and Susan Greenblatt note:

> In order to make effective use of citizen participation, citizens must be allowed to participate in the planning from the outset. Although much citizen participation in planning is more symbolic than real, it may have a positive effect in avoiding conflict if participation takes place *before* specific decisions are made about how to desegregate. If citizens feel that they have a mechanism that channels their opinions to school administrators, they are more likely to accept the final plan that emerges (1981, p. 340).

In a survey of 131 community organizations located in forty desegregated school districts, Lorraine M. McDonnell and Gail L. Zellman (1978) found that groups ranging from elite business and civic groups to civil-rights organizations and small neighborhood groups can help build broad-based public support for school desegregation, especially during the planning stages. They can disseminate information to make certain that the community understands the logistics of the desegregation plan. In addition, these groups can serve as a countervailing source of political power against officials who are reluctant to implement the plan. Furthermore, McDonnell and Zellman found that community involvement through these groups can provide legitimacy to the public and credibility for unpopular policy. They can also promote parental involvement in the schools.

Community and parental involvement in the schools after implementation may ultimately be as important as preimplementation involvement, especially if it gives parents the feeling that they have some control over their children's education and their future. David J. Armor and his colleagues (1976) and John E. Coulson and his associates (1976) found that parental involvement in schools and classroom activities related to increases in student achievement. Jean B. Wellisch and her associates (1976) identify a similar positive effect. In addition, the extensive human-relations study by the System Development Corporation found evidence that parent involvement in school activities can improve interracial attitudes among minority students (Doherty et al. 1981). However, many administrators and teachers view education as a professional matter in which laymen should not intervene except perhaps in ways defined by educators. When the context is as highly politically charged as school desegregation, that kind of attitude may only create additional problems for the school district.

There are a variety of approaches and specific activities that may be effective in preparing parents and the community for desegregation and promoting their support for an involvement in desegregated schools. This chapter focuses on how acceptance for school desegregation is gained. Chapter 7 turns to other strategies for increasing the involvement of parents in the continuing educational activities of their children's schools.

Communitywide Multiethnic Citizen-Parent-Teacher-Student Committees

Many school districts have formed broad-based citizens' committees to work with school-district personnel in designing desegregation plans. These committees typically represent all major racial and ethnic groups as well as parents and education, business, and political leaders. Members are usually drawn from across the community. Their authority and function can vary from having formal veto power on desegregation strategies (which is highly unusual) to serving as an informal advisory group. The major purpose of these committees is to maximize the acceptability of the plan to the community, given the constraints imposed by courts or other governmental agencies. The range of issues with which such committees deal also varies. Usually groups formed during the preimplementation period examine the details of a plan and assist in designing implementation procedures and activities.

These committees should equally represent all elements of the community and all racial and ethnic groups even if that means representation on these committees is disproportionate to group representation in the community. Equal committee representation provides equal opportunities for groups who are in the minority in the community to influence the work of these committees. In districts where more than one national-origin-minority group reside, separate meetings and committees should be established by language group to ensure maximum parent participation and accurate dissemination of information.

A committee that serves to facilitate initial desegregation may not be appropriate to the implementation of the plan, depending on how the committee is formed, its preimplementation functions, and the tasks given its members. One difference might be the relative role of parents. It seems desirable to find some way to select parents that will ensure that they represent the views of other parents and to increase their role and influence on these committees after implementation. School-level parent involvement is also of great importance and should be promoted both before and after implementation.

Evidence. Although there is no quantitative evidence supporting the efficacy of these communitywide committees in increasing community acceptance or reducing white flight and protest, the experts that the authors interviewed agree that this type of group is important to effective desegregation. The consensus literature stresses that these committees can provide greater issue clarity in planning and reasonable treatment of sensitive issues in the final plan (Murphy 1980; Smith, Downs, and Lachman 1973; United States Commission on Civil Rights 1976). This literature asserts further that these committees may help establish a basis for broad support of the final desegregation plan.

The qualitative literature identifies a positive relationship between active multiethnic parent-teacher-student committees and public support for school desegregation. Monroe Billington (1966) suggests that these committees played an important role in fostering public acceptance of desegregation in many Missouri school districts. M. Hayes Mizell (1966–1967) identified similar relationships in his study of South Carolina school districts.

In addition, the qualitative literature supports strategies that call for parent and citizen involvement in planning and monitoring school desegregation to promote positive race relations and to avoid resegregation after implementation. Boyd Bosma (1977) argues that lack of community participation in planning for desegregation is linked to the isolation of minority teachers and the deterioration of race relations among schools after implementation. In a study of Boston, Kelly M. Alexander (1975) found that communitywide groups are often helpful in improving race relations among students and members of school staffs. Joyce D. Miller (1975), Nancy L. Arnez (1978), Sylvia Demarest and John F. Jordan (1975), Lawrence Wright (1973), and Leon Hall (1979) each call for more community involvement to prevent resegregation resulting from disproportionate minority suspensions of pushout practices. In a study of school officials from throughout the Southwest, Hardy R. Murphy (1980) found communitywide multiethnic citizen-parent-educator committees effective in reducing levels of resegregation.

The experts interviewed agree that nonparent citizens can play important roles on these committees prior to the implementation of desegregation plans. However, once implementation has begun, steps should be taken to increase the role and influence of parents in these groups.

Examples. School officials interviewed in Riverside believe that the existence of communitywide committees was critical in minimizing protest prior to desegregation and ensuring peaceful implementation. They thought that the small amounts of protest and the generally peaceful implementation of desegregation plans tended to reduce white flight in their district. The United States Commission on Civil Rights (1976) reports that immediately following the 1971 court order school administrators in Hillsborough County (Tampa) organized a 156-member citizens' committee to review plans and options developed by the school district. Committee members included black and white community leaders as well as advocates and opponents of school desegregation. All meetings of the committee were open to the public and were advertised to promote citizen attendance. The press was present at each meeting and reported on all the proceedings. The commission reported that school administrators and private citizens cited community and media involvement as a major factor in public acceptance of desegregation in that district.

It is important that these communitywide committees work closely with the school administration and have school officials' cooperation. In Los Angeles, the citizens' committee was appointed by the court and had an adversarial relationship with the school administration which rejected each of its proposed plans. This experience suggests that in the planning stages these committees should probably be appointed by or with the approval of the school district.

One example of the type of problems that can be avoided by the effective involvement of minority parents is suggested by Milwaukee's experience. In that city, notices to parents specifying options among schools and programs were sent out in English with no translation provided to limited-English-speaking families until after the deadline for the submission of choices. As a result, many Hispanic parents exercised no choice for their schoolchildren. Some redress eventually occurred, but the active involvement of Hispanic parents in planning educational options and preparing these notices could have prevented this situation.

Providing Information about Desegregation to Parents and the Community

School systems cannot depend solely on the media to inform parents about every aspect of school desegregation, student reassignments, or the programs offered by schools to which their children are reassigned. Nor can communitywide committees serve as a vehicle to best communicate with parents. Thus, school districts should develop ways of informing parents about desegregation that might include dissemination of understandable and even upbeat written materials that describe the details of the desegregation plan, its rationale, student assignments, and the nature of the educational services available to students. The best approach to communicating with parents may be to emphasize the quality of the schools students will be attending at the same time that the logistics of the pupil-assignment plan are spelled out. In systems with limited-English-speaking populations, information should be provided in the native language of those groups.

Walk-in parent meetings might be held in both residential neighborhoods and in neighborhoods of receiving schools. Teachers can be the best source of information about schools and instructional programs and might be encouraged to visit parents at their homes. In addition, school-level committees, perhaps in conjunction with parent-teacher associations (PTAs), can serve important communication functions for parents.

In providing information to parents and to the community, school districts should be aware of the influence of the print and electronic media on public opinion. It is critically important that school systems develop positive relationships with the mass media and adopt strategies to foster comprehensive coverage of both public education in general and school desegregation in particular. Strategies to promote these relationships and comprehensive media coverage will be discussed later in this chapter.

School districts should also develop and implement strategies to correct misinformation that shapes community perceptions and opinions about school desegregation. Promoting comprehensive coverage of desegregation in the mass media may serve to correct much of this misinformation. School systems might also establish public-information offices and rumor-control centers that can provide information directly to parents and to members of the community and can serve as information-resource centers for newspaper and television reporters. (See chapter 6 for discussion of how to establish a district-level public-information office.) These centers may be staffed by teachers, parents, and nonparent citizens.

In some districts, community organizations have joined to form non-partisan groups to disseminate information about school desegregation to both parents of public-school children and to other members of the community. Although these community-based information centers may perform valuable functions, school systems themselves should take primary responsibility for disseminating information to parents and to the public for two reasons. First, school officials are privy to first-hand information about the schools and students. Second, by taking responsibility for disseminating information to the public, the school system displays its commitment to clarify misinformation, promote public knowledge and support of the public schools and desegregation, and facilitate parent and citizen participation in the schools. School systems might work in conjunction with community groups to assess public perceptions and public opinion and to disseminate information.

Many school systems assume, often incorrectly, that minority populations, especially blacks, support the desegregation effort. The experts placed particular emphasis on the need to communicate to minorities what the purposes of the plan are and what services will be available to their children.

Evidence. Allen and Sears (1978) found that confusion about the details of desegregation plans seems to increase parent and community opposition to school desegregation. Almost all the experts the authors interviewed agree with this finding and suggest that one way to reduce such opposition is to provide parents and the community with complete information about the desegregation plan and its implementation.

The United States Commission on Civil Rights (1976) reports that information and rumor-control centers have been effective tools for keeping the community informed about school desegregation. The commission asserts that through these centers parents have been provided with a

readily accessible line of communication to learn about educational programs, student assignments, and bus routes and to clarify rumors.

Example. In St. Louis, twenty community organizations, agencies, and
local colleges and universities joined to form the Coalition for Information
on School Desegregation. The coalition's expressed purpose is to assist
the public to understand the issues of interdistrict school desegregation
in the St. Louis metropolitan area. This group, the membership of which
includes local chapters of the League of Women Voters and the National
Conference of Christians and Jews, the St. Louis Archdiocesan Schools,
and St. Louis University, publicizes information about the city's desegregation litigation and its implications to school systems and citizens in
the metropolitan area. In addition, it operates a speakers bureau that
invites researchers, desegregation planners, and community leaders to
address desegregation issues and to provide a broad research and comparative context to local questions. The coalition coordinates its activities
with the metropolitan school systems and the area's mass media.

Emphasizing Educational Programs That Will Result from Desegregation

One of the peculiarities of school-desegregation litigation is that it is one
of the rare cases in which a defendant is found guilty of a violation of
the law and is ordered to take an action which does not impose a traditional
punishment or cost. Litigation is ordinarily a zero-sum game—what one
party gains, the other loses. In civil cases the guilty defendant is required
to pay damages; in criminal cases the guilty defendant pays a fine or is
imprisoned. Thus, it is only natural for the white community to assume
that if it has been found guilty of segregation, desegregation is the punishment. Proponents of desegregation and defendant school systems do
not like to debate whether desegregation is beneficial and will often
defend desegregation by simply pointing out the constitutional mandate
for the elimination of illegal segregation. However, by doing so, proponents and school systems may increase the anxieties of the white community by stressing the fact that they have been found guilty and implying
that they should be or are being punished. For this reason, it is important
to emphasize that desegregation is not a punishment, that it does not harm
white children, and that it is an opportunity for all students to benefit
from educational innovation.

Perhaps because demands for desegregation usually come from minority groups, school officials often fail to provide minority parents and
minority communities with information about the potential benefits of

desegregation. For example, Hispanic parents need to be assured that bilingual and other special programs can and should be part of desegregation plans. These parents need to be assured that the programs which they are provided in segregated schools will not be lost to desegregation.

Evidence. There is no empirical research on this issue in the context of school desegregation. However, studies of political attitudes and conflict resolution illuminate the way in which zero-sum thinking dominates public attitudes about policymaking. Several experts stressed the importance of conveying positive changes resulting from desegregation rather than justifying desegregation in terms of the past wrongs or inequities experienced by minorities. Under some conditions, desegregation can create opportunities for introducing new programs and instructional innovations in schools. In his study of five large school systems undergoing desegregation, David L. Colton (1979) found that a desegregation order serves as a catalyst for quite extensive redistribution of school resources and usually increases the amount and sources of school-district revenues in the form of desegregation assistance.

Increased revenues from desegregation assistance, even discounted by the costs of pupil reassignment, and the redistribution of district resources can lead to new and better instructional programs, greater capacity for change, and better trained staff. For example, Abdin Noboa (1980) indicates that desegregated school systems are more likely to offer bilingual education programs than are those that are predominantly of one race or ethnic group. In addition, Anne H. MacQueen and John E. Coulson (1978) found in longitudinal evaluations of the effects of federal assistance to desegregating districts (through the Emergency School Assistance Act) that over time these new resources were associated with improved academic achievement.

Comprehensive Media Coverage

Since the greatest white flight in most school districts occurs in anticipation of and during the first year of implementation, those who flee are generally people who have never experienced desegregation. Typically, these individuals do not know anyone who has experienced desegregated schools, yet they believe their children's education will suffer when their schools are desegregated. The question is, From what source do these people get their information? In most cases, the answer is the mass media.

This is also true after a desegregation plan is first implemented. Few parents have contact with any more than a small number of other parents and so rely on the media to tell them how school desegregation is faring, what kind of education their children are receiving, and particularly what kinds of disturbances and racial tensions exist in the schools and in the community. Thus, the mass media can have a substantial impact on the climate of opinion in a community and on the outcomes of desegregation.

Because the mass media serve as the primary sources of information on the costs, benefits, and risks of school desegregation, it is important that some agency provides the newspapers, radio, and television with a wide range of information on school desegregation, including evidence on school performance both before and after implementation. Press releases might be provided about new and innovative school programs. This is a full-time responsibility which requires someone skilled in public information and marketing. While a school district might be willing to undertake such a task after school desegregation is first implemented, it is unlikely it will do so before implementation. During the preimplementation period, some other agency, perhaps in the state government, should accept this responsibility.

In districts with national-origin-minority populations, care should be taken to provide information in the language and through the media of these groups. Where appropriate, this information should emphasize the interrelationships among civil-rights initiatives resulting in race desegregation and leading to bilingual education and other special instructional programs.

State agencies can play an important role in facilitating comprehensive coverage by collecting information about desegregation and providing it to the media. These agencies may compile comparative information about desegregation in different cities within the state and about desegregation in other states to provide a context within which local media may develop single-district coverage.

Evidence. Although the media have a liberal reputation among many opposed to busing and mandatory desegregation, Christine H. Rossell (1978b), Reginald Stuart (1973), Weinberg and Martin (1976), and Levinsohn (1976) argue that local and national media coverage tends to emphasize antibusing protest, white flight, and interracial conflict as products of desegregation. William R. Grant (1976), formerly a columnist for the *Detroit Free Press*, identifies the inability and unwillingness of the press to report certain aspects of school desegregation issues. He asserts that reporters often do not understand the legal, political, and educational intricacies of desegregation plans.

The quantitative research identifies a relationship between the perspectives of press coverage and public reaction to school desegregation. Rossell (1978b) found a correlation between negative media coverage of school desegregation and white flight. In addition, Allen and Sears (1978) identify a relationship between negative coverage and negative parental attitudes toward desegregation.

Examples. One very important activity school districts can initiate during the preimplementation period which will not make them appear to be pro-desegregation but which almost always results in positive media coverage is organized bus trips for white parents to visit minority schools. The *Los Angeles Times* extensively quoted white parents who went on these trips as to how much better the schools were than they expected, how learning actually occurred, and how the distance did not seem that long when someone else was doing the driving.

The superintendent of the Charlotte-Mecklenburg school district reported in an interview that he could not have accomplished what has been done with respect to desegregation without the cooperation of a supportive print and electronic media. In that city there was live television coverage of discussions of the desegregation plan. Well-planned efforts to cultivate positive relationships with the media have been undertaken in the New Castle Consolidated and Louisville-Jefferson County school districts. In New Castle private industry helped the school district foster this relationship, and in Louisville self-censorship agreements were worked out with local newspapers in order to facilitate coverage of both positive and negative aspects of desegregation.

A citizen's group worked closely with the schools and the media in Columbus to provide reporters with information and news sources. A similar initiative was undertaken by the Coalition for Information on School Desegregation in St. Louis. In Massachusetts the state education agency contracted with the University of Massachusetts to collect information about desegregation in the state and elsewhere and to provide that information to the agency for dissemination to the media.

Supportive Community Leadership

Encouraging community leadership to play a more positive role in desegregation controversies and in public education in general can be an effective strategy for promoting positive public reaction to desegregation. Leaders of the same race and ethnicity as the persons they hope to influence will be most effective. While it is important to gain the support of communitywide and elected leaders, it is equally if not more important to gain the support of neighborhood or grass-roots leadership that has the capability to guide persons on a neighborhood or individual basis.

Evidence. There is no quantitative evidence that communitywide elected leadership has any substantial direct influence on public acceptance of school desegregation, white flight, and protest. Rossell (1978b) argues that such influence exists but is more indirect by contributing to the perspective of newspaper and media coverage of schools and desegregation. This may be because desegregation is an issue for which there is often no leadership from city officials and business leaders. The United States Commission on Civil Rights (1976) points out that with the exception of school-board members in some communities, local elected officials have no direct authority over the public-school system. However, the commission finds that the public response of elected leaders to desegregation can have an impact where controversy exists:

> Where public officials actively support the desegregation process, the community generally directs its attention toward making the process work. Even where political leaders have actually opposed the specifics of a court order, . . . if they take a position of ''obedience to the law,'' the result is a positive contribution to the desegregation process (1976, p. 95).

The commission found that the support of elected leaders furthered public acceptance of school desegregation in a number of districts, including Springfield (Massachusetts), Newport News, and Minneapolis.

J.G. Hayes (1977) and Garth Taylor and Arthur Stinchcombe (1977) suggest that if leadership activity is to be successful in minimizing negative reactions to desegregation, that activity should originate from and be exercised at the neighborhood or grass-roots level or from religious and social groups that can reach members on an individual basis. Thus, although it is clearly desirable to have communitywide leaders endorsing the public schools and desegregation, announcements from afar about the need to obey the law may not be sufficient if antibusing leaders are actively influencing opinion and behavior at the grass-roots level.

Behind-the-scenes political activity in which various groups are influenced to acquiesce to or even support desegregation may be influential in shaping behavior. On the basis of experience in districts such as Boston and Louisville-Jefferson County, political leaders who built their careers on opposition to desegregation may not last long after the desegregation plan is implemented. The case evidence suggests that opposition to busing is usually a source of only short-term glory (Rossell 1981a).

Example. In October 1972 chamber of commerce officials in Memphis established IMPACT (Involved Memphis Parents Assisting Children and Teachers), an organization to promote community acceptance of school desegregation. Beginning in November of that year, three months before implementation of the plan, IMPACT began a campaign which included newspaper and television advertisements, fact sheets, a telephone rumor-control center, neighborhood meetings, a speaker's bureau, and church and neighborhood organization support. John Egerton (1973) asserts that IMPACT and the community leadership operating through that organization had a substantial positive impact on public acceptance of desegregation in Memphis.

The Catholic hierarchy in a community can exert influential leadership by announcing that their schools will not serve as a haven for those fleeing public-school desegregation. In Cleveland and Milwaukee, the Catholic church has taken this position with the support of most nuns and priests.

Parent Visitations to Receiving Schools before Implementation

Parents whose children are reassigned in a desegregation plan normally know little or nothing about the schools to which their children are being transferred. Without such knowledge, unfounded fears based in part on media-influenced stereotypes may take hold. In addition to providing complete information about the desegregation plan, school officials might consider a series of parent-exchange visits between schools. Parent fact-finding groups can be formed to collect information about new schools, but all parents should be involved in visits to schools to which their children are reassigned.

One successful type of visit takes the form of an open house. Staff and parents of the receiving school play host to staff and parents of sending schools in a celebratory atmosphere of cakes and cookies accompanied by visits to the classroom. Any visitation program should not be limited to the period before schools open. They should be scheduled to continue throughout the year not only to keep parents informed about the school and their children's progress but to promote parent involvement in other school activities. As noted previously, these visits also provide the material for positive media coverage of desegregation.

Evidence. There is considerable agreement among the experts the authors interviewed and in the qualitative literature that these visitation programs are useful in gaining acceptance of desegregation. The United States Commission on Civil Rights (1976) reports, for example, that a number of school districts have been able to allay the fears and anxieties of parents and promote their support for desegregation by instituting orientation and visitation programs.

Examples. Parent visits were very successful in Los Angeles in the schools where they were held. The former chairman of the Human Relations Advisory Council in the New Castle Consolidated district reported in an interview how several Sunday open-house activities in the schools helped allay the fears of white parents regarding schools in black neighborhoods while reducing black parents' fears of racism. In Denver a series of picnics and home visits were held and reportedly involved more than one hundred thousand people. In Louisville-Jefferson County and Cleveland some parents rode buses to the schools that their children were to attend in distant neighborhoods and reported back to other parents in their neighborhoods. Both Columbus and Dayton school systems conducted summer orientation programs for parents.

Multiethnic In-School Parent-Teacher Committees

Following desegregation, some school systems have formed in-school committees that provide information, advice, and guidance to parents, teachers, and students, and serve as mediating bodies to resolve grievances. These committees, made up of parents and teachers of individual schools, contribute to effective desegregation if they are committed to its goals, know what to do to make it effective, and remain multiethnic in membership. These organizations can reduce resegregation by providing an interpretation of experiences and behaviors encountered by parents, teachers, and students in order to prevent responses that result in student withdrawals from classes or activities by choice or decree. The success of in-school committees is heavily dependent on the commitment and responsiveness to them by school administrators.

Although these committees have met with some success, it must be emphasized that obtaining and sustaining the participation of low-income and minority parents is often difficult since many must travel greater distance and may have employment obligations that make participation difficult. Unless special arrangements are made to overcome such obstacles, in-school parent-teacher committees can and often do become all-middle-income or all-white over time. Chapter 7 explores this matter further.

Evidence. No empirical research explicitly examines this strategy of in-school committees. Qualitative assessment of these committees are alluded to by authors calling for greater parent (especially minority-parent) involvement in the schools (see, for example, Forehand and Ragosta, 1976). Their reasoning is that such involvement increases community and parent ownership, support, and concern for the school which may no longer be a neighborhood school and that parents provide examples for their children.

In an assessment of desegregation in Missouri school systems, Daniel J. Monti (1979) concluded that multiethnic in-school parent-teacher grievance panels were effective tools to handle discriminatory disciplinary procedures and to solve problems such as racially motivated pushouts and suspensions. The consensus literature also supports the formation of these in-school committees. The United States Commission on Civil Rights (1976); Al D. Smith, Anthony Downs, and M. Leanne Lachman (1973); and Garlie A. Forehand and Marjorie Ragosta (1976) each suggest that committees which provide school-desegregation information and counseling services for and handle grievances of parents, teachers, and students help improve race relations in schools, avoid resegregation, and improve public response to desegregation.

Local and national expert opinion reinforced the need for these committees. Several local experts that were interviewed specifically noted the positive consequences of community involvement in grievance-dispute resolution at the school level. Almost all of the local respondents indicated that the success of in-school committees depends upon principals encouraging and supporting the active involvement of parents in schools. Local experts agreed that these committees should function in an advisory capacity, as did the national experts.

Efforts to Bring Families Back to the School District

In many communities, most of the families who leave the public schools to avoid desegregation do not move out of the school district (Lord 1975; McConahay and Hawley 1978; Cunningham, Husk, and Johnson 1978). School systems should maintain contact with these parents, identify their concerns, and provide programs for their children and information that might attract them back to the public schools. Parent-teacher-student associations can play a major role in such recruitment efforts as can community organizations, but school-district officials should take primary responsibility for this activity.

School districts might also attempt to attract parents back to the school system and keep those already there by creating all-day schools which will serve a child-care function before and after school until the parent comes home from work. Such schools could be much more attractive to working parents than a private school from which their children have to be transported in the middle of the workday to often costly after-school day-care centers.

Evidence. There is no quantitative evidence that this strategy would be successful although many school systems have initiated efforts to improve public relations in their communities in order to reduce flight, enhance public support for schools, and attract students from private schools. Empirical research indicates that many school districts experience less than normal white-enrollment declines in the fourth and fifth years of implementation (Coleman, Kelly and Moore 1975; Rossell 1978a; Ross, Gratton, and Clarke 1981). This trend suggests that there are parents willing to remain in or return to the public-school system. Interviews with personnel in countywide school systems further indicate that there are indeed white parents returning to the public-school system.

Examples. Little Rock runs day-care centers in its school system. Parents of public-school students in that district and in Nashville-Davidson County and Charlotte-Mecklenburg County have compiled materials, invited private-school parents and parents of preschool children to the schools, and instituted recruitment activities. The local teachers' organization in Nashville-Davidson County launched a public-relations campaign that included advertisements for the public schools on city buses. These activities are usually initiated by parents. Generally, school systems have not seen themselves in the business of marketing their products.

In 1980 an organization of approximately one thousand white parents called Parents for Public Schools was formed in Little Rock. The group initiated an advocacy campaign to dispel rumors of poor quality, tension, and disruption in the public schools. It ran ads in newspapers and over television and distributed bumper stickers and T-shirts. According to the school superintendent, the district does not experience a significant white flight problem but rather a problem of persuading whites to enter the system or return from private schools. However, due to the efforts of the district to improve instructional quality and provide special programs and perhaps to the activities of Parents for Public Schools, Little Rock has been able to draw some whites back from private schools. Gregory Jaynes (1981) reported that in the 1980–1981 and 1981–1982 school years, eighty-two white students left private schools to return to Little Rock's Central High School. Several Nashville-Davidson County high schools have experienced a return of white students to public schools in recent years.

Summary

The effectiveness of school desegregation depends in large part on preparing members of the community for desegregation and involving them in developing and implementing the plan. Community and parent involvement in the schools after implementation may ultimately be as important as preimplementation involvement. In order to prepare the community for desegregation and promote postimplementation involvement in schools, districts should establish communitywide multiethnic citizen-parent-teacher-student committees to assist in planning and implementing desegregation. The work of this type of committee may continue after implementation although its function should be altered to address postimplementation concerns. Parents should generally play a greater role after implementation of the desegregation plan.

Parents and other members of the community should be provided with full, clear, and accurate information about the desegregation plan and its implementation. The central administration of a school system should take primary responsibility for this public-information function, perhaps by establishing a public-information office. This office might work with citizen-information groups to collect and disseminate information to the public and to the media to promote comprehensive coverage of the process and progress of school desegregation.

School systems should further take initiatives to gain the support of the elected, business, and grass-roots leadership of a community to promote desegregation. School administrators and community leaders may best encourage public support by emphasizing the educational opportunities that are associated with desegregation rather than emphasizing only compliance with the law.

The information about schools and school desegregation made available by the school district and the media importantly influence public and parent perceptions. However, these sources cannot provide parents and other members of the community all the information they need and perhaps want to know. Desegregating districts should try to bring parents and other citizens to schools both before and after implementation of desegregation and involve them in educational and extracurricular activities. Multiethnic in-school parent-teacher committees may be formed to address concerns of students, parents, and educators at the school level. In addition, school systems should maintain contact with parents who have withdrawn their children from desegregating schools to attract them back to the system.

This chapter has focused on gaining acceptance for school desegregation. Chapter 7 deals with other strategies for facilitating school desegregation that involve parents in the continuing educational activities of their children's schools.

6

Organizing at the District Level for Continuing Implementation

Most of the literature and debate about school desegregation is focused on the pupil-assignment plan and community preparation on the one hand, and school-level policies and activities on the other. How a district organizes so as to best promote desegregation receives little discussion despite some recognition by experts that this can make or break implementation of the plan. Many of the strategies discussed throughout this book have implications for what a school district should do, that is, what things it should encourage and support, but too little attention is given by most policymakers to how the governance and administrative systems of a district should be structured.

Central administrations of school systems are often confronted with a variety of demands and challenges that relate to achieving effective desegregation. These include compliance with the desegregation order, coordination of personnel and resources, educational accountability, strengthening the public-information function, promoting community involvement in schools, and promoting school-level support for and implementation of desegregation-related policies and activities. This chapter briefly presents several ideas and strategies to facilitate district-level organization and activities to address these demands and challenges. For the most part, the ideas presented here are gleaned from interviews with local and national experts and from the observations of the study group. Although there is no real evidence, aside from a relatively lengthy discussion of monitoring commissions, that these proposals are effective, it seems highly likely that improving the capabilities of district-level organizational structures will affect the success of desegregation plans.

Organization of Essential Administrative Functions

As it does for school-level functions, desegregation places new demands on district-level administration. If no effort is made to establish a discrete administrative capability responsible for fostering effective desegregation, it is unlikely that the opportunities created by desegregation will be realized or that the problems it introduces will be dealt with adequately. However, establishing a separate office for desegregation may reinforce propensities to view desegregation as something apart from the central functions and activities of the district. In turn, this may result in failures to adapt to desegregation and to coordinate the full resources of the district in ways that break down the false dichotomy between educational equity and educational quality.

The answer to this dilemma seems to be to establish a small, professionally staffed unit in the superintendent's office and to give that unit the responsibility of increasing the motivation and capability of offices that administer the central functions of the district. If there is resistance to desegregation within the administration, it will not be overcome for long, if at all, by going over the heads of key administrators. Of course, some districts may be so recalcitrant that judges or state agencies will find it necessary to displace all or some of a superintendent's authority by appointing a desegregation czar and establishing an operational office. In Cleveland, for example, the court appointed a desegregation administrator who was responsible only to the court and established Cleveland's Office of Desegregation Implementation. However, the very concept of a *czar* raises questions about the validity of this technique, and it should be seen as a last resort.

One function an administrative desegregation unit might perform is to work with the administrator(s) responsible for curricula to make human-relations objectives a significant and well-integrated element of all learning activities. In addition to fostering the attainment of human-relations objectives through regular curricula, there appear to be some special desegregation-related needs of the system that this unit can address through technical assistance or the identification of external expertise and resources. These needs include:

1. Facilitating linkages among various special-education programs the coordination of which is always difficult and is often exacerbated by desegregation.
2. Coordinating and enriching in-service training activities. This should not lead to centrally developed in-service training but could result in the better use of external resources, such as those available through state agencies, and in the identification of individuals and programs within the district that can be helpful to others.
3. Encouraging expertise in financial management and full deployment of external resources (see Colton and Berg 1981).
4. Facilitating community and staff review of instructional materials and patterns of participation in extracurricular and elective offerings in order to eliminate biased presentations and to ensure inclusions of relevant minority contributions.
5. Conducting formative program evaluations. It is important to the

capacity of the school system that principals and teachers as well as parents be provided with information about the progress of desegregation in general and about the effectiveness of particular programs. Schools can learn from each other's experiences but only if the district coordinates evaluations and dissemination of information. Evaluations should treat the different racial and ethnic groups in the district as distinct populations.

This office might be the unit with which the district's housing expert is affiliated (see chapter 4). In addition, this administrative unit should coordinate its activities with the district's public-information functions.

Involving Teachers and Principals in the Development of Desegregation-Related Policies

One of the most important determinants of effective school desegregation is the commitment of teachers and principals to the plan and the capability of school-level personnel to implement it and to go beyond the minimal activities it prescribes. A basic management principle concerning motivation and skill development is that those who must implement a program should be involved in developing the relevant policies and practices (Berman and McLaughlin 1977). However, few districts directly involve principals, much less teachers, in drawing the plan or in program development. In particular, teachers' unions, when they decide to do so, can make important contributions to effective desegregation. An example of such a contribution is the interpersonal-relations training program developed by the United Federation of Teachers in Detroit.

Strengthening the Public-Information Function

When desegregation occurs, the public generally wants to know more about schools. Too often, the information they seek is not available, and rumors and anecdotes, usually negative in character, dominate the flow of information. Thus, establishing a professionally staffed public information office should be a high priority for desegregating districts. This office should work in conjunction with other information and rumor-control activities of community organizations and should coordinate dissemination of information to the media (see chapter 5).

Strengthening Evaluation Capabilities

Desegregation creates needs for information, and new programs require assessment. School systems undergoing desegregation will also experience increased demands for accountability. The inability or unwillingness of some districts to respond to such demands feeds suspicions of poor quality and is counterproductive. Moreover, a capacity for sophisticated evaluation of activities and programs can provide important management information that usually helps to improve programs and allocate resources. For example, simplistic reporting of test scores on a school-by-school basis invariably understates the effectiveness of school-system efforts to improve educational quality.

Although there is no evidence on the consequences of such a program, some members of the study team believe that school districts should be required to provide detailed information about achievement and student attitudes for each major ethnic group in each school, including those omitted from the plan. The purpose of providing this information is twofold. First, it may be used to identify unsuccessful schools so that they may receive special attention. Second, it can identify the strengths and weaknesses of the overall desegregation plan so as to allay needless fears and concentrate the public's and the school district's attention on the real problems.

The evaluation capabilities of a school system can be improved by employing an independent specialist to analyze school-level achievement data for each major ethnic group and by requiring each school to administer questionnaires to students, principals, and teachers. Questionnaires are commonly used in evaluations of special programs; however, they are not used routinely by school districts for more general self-evaluation.

Robert L. Crain, Rita E. Mahard, and Ruth E. Narot (1982) argue that courts or civil-rights agencies can do little directly to improve school quality or ensure building-level compliance with the spirit of a desegregation order. However, courts can do a great deal to establish a climate of intelligent discussion about school problems. Parents have very few means to determine if the schools their children attend are doing an adequate job. Published test scores are little help since they normally pool minority and majority students who may come from very different neighborhoods and economic backgrounds. Test scores will normally show wide differences between poor and wealthy neighborhoods, and only a trained analyst with access to past as well as current scores can identify schools in which students' performance is above or below what can be considered average. Armed with this information, the school system and the public would be able to focus attention on problem schools and use exemplary schools as models.

Mechanisms for Monitoring Compliance and Effective Implementation

If there were no serious problems of commitment to desegregation within the school system, there would be no need for court and state-agency actions that usually result in comprehensive desegregation plans. In addition, there is no guarantee that court or state-agency action will reverse resistance and engender district commitment to desegregation. Thus, the desegregation process will be expedited in most districts by some type of monitoring group. It seems important, however, that school systems recognize the incongruity of the watchdog functions of a monitoring group and the facilitative, supportive functions of the administrative desegregation unit proposed previously. Placing these two different types of functions in the same organizational unit will probably result in neither being performed very well.

Many desegregation orders mandate that a citizen's committee monitor the operation of the plan and verify that it is being implemented properly. While the primary function of monitoring groups is to provide information to the court or agency ordering the plan, in practice monitoring groups provide valuable information about the progress of school desegregation to the public in general and to the school system itself. These groups can also identify a wide range of educational problems that arise in desegregating school districts and in many cases prompt school systems to act to resolve them. Monitoring committees, which school districts themselves might establish, can assist desegregation by helping create a climate of public opinion which is concerned with school quality rather than with debates about the merits of busing.

Examples. Jennifer L. Hochschild and Valerie Hadrick (1981) examined a number of monitoring groups in school systems across the country. In addition to the more obvious factors such as leadership, commitment, organization, and funding which determine these groups' effectiveness, Hochschild and Hadrick indicate that differences in mandate, strategy, and purpose have a great impact on the viability and success of these groups. For example, Denver's Community Education Council (CEC) has been one of the most successful and influential monitoring commissions. Initially, the function of the CEC was unclear, but eventually the council was given authority to review all district proposals which would have an impact on the system's desegregation efforts, and it received quasi-party status in the courts. This degree of autonomy appears to have been a crucial factor in the CEC's effectiveness. In contrast, the difficulties of the Los Angeles Monitoring Committee stem in large part from the ambiguity of the court's mandate for the committee. In that district, community members recruited for participation on subcommittees eventually lost interest because there was no clear understanding of the function or role of the group (King 1980; Hochschild and Hadrick 1981).

There are two distinct approaches to the monitoring process: first, systemwide research and analysis, and, second, specific problem solving or complaint resolution. The Denver CEC is organized around complaint resolution and has succeeded in affecting several programmatic changes such as persuading the court to order activity buses for children who want to participate in extracurricular activities. The council's quasi-party status allows it to participate in long-range planning as well, and it has petitioned the court for hearings on affirmative action, in-service training, and pupil assignment. The Tri-Ethnic Committee in Dallas is also structured around individual complaint resolution and has succeeded in instituting a uniform disciplinary system which provides a three-part hearing for students charged with serious infractions of discipline codes.

Monitoring groups in Portland and Boston are examples of the systematic approach to overseeing desegregation implementation. Basing many of its recommendations to the court on public forums, questionnaires, and the results of national research, the Community Coalition for School Integration in Portland helped develop the Comprehensive Desegregation Plan which was submitted to the school board in April 1980.

The Office of School Monitoring and Community Relations (OSMCR) in Cleveland provides a good example of how monitoring groups can build community support for school desegregation. The primary function of OSMCR is data collection rather than complaint solicitation, and the organization apparently has succeeded in providing extensive information to the community that has helped to reduce stiff opposition and resistance to desegregation. Some monitoring groups have been able to work with the media to ensure accurate and fair coverage of desegregation issues. This relationship was cultivated in Cleveland due to the efforts of OSMCR's full-time press secretary who had previously been a journalist.

Summary

The manner in which districts organize so as to best promote desegregation and respond to its demands is crucial to the successful implementation of desegregation plans. One strategy to promote effective continuing implementation is the creation of a small, professionally staffed unit for desegregation in the superintendent's office to enhance and coordinate the capabilities of offices that administer the central functions of the district and to address desegregation-related needs of the district. Desegregating school districts should also organize to promote the active involvement of both teachers and principals in the development of desegregation-related policies.

When desegregation occurs, the public generally wants to learn more about the schools. In order to provide complete and accurate information about the process and progress of desegregation and the educational quality of schools, districts should establish a professionally staffed public-information office. In addition, school systems undergoing desegregation experience increased demands for accountability. Districts should develop a capacity for sophisticated evaluation of activities and programs to provide management information for improving programs and resource allocation as well as information to direct the district's and the public's attention to addressing educational problems of the system.

In many school districts, monitoring groups have been created to verify that desegregation plans are implemented properly. These groups serve the courts or agencies that order plans but may also serve to provide valuable information about the progress of desegregation to parents and the community. In conjunction with districts' evaluation activities, monitoring groups can identify a range of educational problems that result from desegregation and may prompt school systems to resolve them. The effectiveness of the organizational units described previously depends on leadership capabilities, commitment, funding, support from district-level administration, and clarification of roles and functions.

7 Changes within Desegregated Schools

In the Detroit desegregation case, *Milliken* v. *Bradley* (1977), a federal judge ordered the adoption of various educational components as appropriate remedies to past segregation. The United States Supreme Court confirmed that these aspects of the desegregation plan were justified by the Constitution, arguing that ''pupil assignment alone does not automatically remedy the impact of previous, unlawful racial isolation'' (*Milliken* 1977, pp. 287–288). Thus, school systems that expect to achieve effective desegregation need to be concerned not only about pupil-assignment plans but also about how they can effectively respond to the educational and social needs of their students.

Because desegregation is often preceded by years of litigation and controversy about the creation of racially or ethnically mixed schools, it is all too easy to think of desegregation in its narrowest sense as an event that begins and ends with initial implementation of a pupil-assignment plan. However, it is at this point that the process of interracial schooling begins for students. This chapter identifies a number of policies, practices, and strategies which there is reason to believe will help create school and classroom environments that foster academic achievement and improve relations among majority and minority students. By contributing to the creation of positive learning and social environments and to the promotion of positive intergroup relations, these strategies may also serve to discourage voluntary resegregation among students, as commonly observed in cafeterias and playgrounds. They may also reduce the likelihood that students will be suspended for discriminatory reasons or segregated within schools because they are erroneously assigned to racially identifiable special classes or programs.

The strategies identified and discussed in this chapter are based on the recognition that desegregated schools are often more academically and socially heterogeneous than segregated schools. This academic heterogeneity makes strategies to reduce rigid tracking and ability grouping essential to effective desegregation. Similarly, academic heterogeneity suggests the use of cooperative team-learning models and other instructional strategies that have been designed for academically heterogeneous classrooms. The social, racial, and ethnic diversity of desegregated schools requires the development and implementation of conscious strategies to ensure a reasonable balance of power and recognition among groups to foster interracial interaction, encourage previously excluded groups to participate in the life of the school no matter which group the school previously served, and foster equitable treatment of all students while being responsive to the different needs of students from different backgrounds.

Many observers are discouraged by the apparent absence of many close friendships among students of different races and ethnic backgrounds in most desegregated schools. The experts that were interviewed tend to agree that such self-segregation, in itself, is not evidence that relations among groups are unfriendly. These experts emphasize that students group together for many reasons, including neighborhood ties and nonacademic interests, and that these reasons are often unrelated to racial or ethnic differences or prejudices. The tendency for intraracial associations means, of course, that the interracial and interethnic interactions which are essential to achieving good race relations are not an automatic outcome of school desegregation and must be promoted through specific programs and activities in the school.

Most of the strategies identified here have a much greater chance of success if administrators, teachers, and staff members are knowledgeable of and committed to desegregation, organizational change, and educational innovation. Indeed, school desegregation presents most educators with new experiences and opportunities which challenge their professional capabilities and their personal values and dispositions. It is important, therefore, that school systems provide in-service training to prepare educators for changes in schools that result from desegregation and to assist them in effectively implementing special activities of desegregation plans. Strategies for in-service training for desegregated schooling are discussed in chapter 8.

Organizational and Personnel Changes

Maintaining Smaller Schools

Smaller schools may be more effective in achieving desegregation and fostering integration once student bodies are racially and ethnically mixed. Greater proportions of students are likely to participate in some extracurricular activities in smaller schools. Also, there is less chance for student anonymity and, therefore, less chance for marginal students to isolate themselves or drop out because they have no investment in the school. Interactions among students, and between students and adults, are easier to facilitate in an environment where many of the people know each other. This might make improving race relations an easier objective to accomplish. Moreover, parents whose children comprise a minority proportion of a student body may feel more comfortable in smaller settings.

Whites often overestimate the proportion of minorities in a given environment, and, probably, the more nonwhites in the environment and the larger the school, the more they overestimate. Thus, white flight might be reduced in smaller schools simply because the proportion minority will seem smaller and less threatening than in larger schools.

Small schools may also have disadvantages. Very small schools are costly to operate and may make it difficult to offer certain types of programs, especially when their student bodies are heterogeneous. For example, bilingual-education programs could be difficult to implement or maintain in small schools. On the other hand, one can imagine a small school organized around bilingual instruction.

Evidence. Roger G. Barker and Paul V. Gump (1964) and James S. Coleman and his colleagues (1966) studied variables correlated with school size and found that student participation in school activities is higher and students express a greater sense of belonging in smaller schools. The interviews with local experts suggest that students are more likely to have interaction with greater numbers of their schoolmates in a smaller environment. In addition, Gary D. Gottfredson and Denise C. Daiger (1979) studied disruption in 600 schools and found that lack of order and discipline, which parents perennially view as the biggest problem in the public schools, is demonstrably easier to remedy in environments which are characterized by interpersonal familiarity. (See Plisko and Noell 1978 for data on parents' views of disruption in public schools.) Ultimately, establishing and maintaining order and discipline should reduce white flight and improve instruction. For example, Rossell (1981a) found that lower levels of implementation-year white flight in Los Angeles were associated with smaller minority schools. Although not dealing specifically with desegregation, Jame W. Guthrie's (1980) review of the research and literature on the relationship between school size and instructional outcomes concludes that small schools have the advantage.

Examples. Few desegregating school systems appear to have tried to maintain smaller schools for the educational reasons cited previously. On the other hand, many magnet schools have been established by desegregating systems, and most of these facilities are quite small. Discussions about these schools often stress the sense of community they are able to develop. For example, Mary H. Metz (1980) describes a magnet school in Milwaukee the small size of which contributed to successful implementation of instructional programs and to a sense of shared commitment among parents, teachers, and students to the school and to the educational process. The literature on alternative schools provides several examples of well-integrated successful small schools (see Fantini 1976).

Maintaining Smaller Classrooms

Almost all teachers and parents share the belief that small class size makes for better schooling. Smaller classrooms tend to reduce student-teacher ratios and provide greater opportunities for teachers to give attention to individual student's needs. In addition, they provide greater opportunities for students to know and learn about one another, which may foster positive race relations in desegregated classrooms and throughout desegregated schools.

Since enrollment in most school systems is declining rapidly and many teachers consequently face unemployment, and since most school systems are experiencing financial stress, maintaining small classrooms may be a costly strategy to implement. A federal or state program aimed at retaining teachers in desegregating and desegregated school systems may help reduce class size which, in turn, could have positive educational consequences for students. Such positive consequences might also help reduce white and middle-class flight from desegregating school systems.

Smaller classes also eliminate one justification for within-class ability grouping. Teachers frequently argue that they need to break a large class into smaller, more homogeneous groups for instruction. A smaller class makes that less necessary.

Evidence. Research on class size and achievement demonstrates that classrooms with less than twenty students show increases in achievement with reduction in size (Glass and Smith 1978; Glass et al. 1982). This research also finds that reductions in student-teacher ratios which result from small class size promote more positive pupil attitudes toward peers, teachers, and school.

There is no evidence of a relationship between smaller classes and levels of white flight. However, one could reasonably argue on theoretical grounds that the achievement gains and the positive pupil attitudes that are associated with small class size could remove several of the perceived educational costs associated with school desegregation.

Reorganizing Large Schools to Create Smaller, More Supportive Environments

If smaller schools or classes are not practical, large elementary and secondary schools can create smaller, more effective, and supportive learning and social environments by dividing students into units, houses, or clusters within which they can establish closer contacts and relationships. Creation of these smaller environments may promote many of the positive achievement, attitudinal, and social outcomes associated with small schools and classrooms. In particular this strategy may facilitate student participation in learning and social activities, provide greater opportunities to build peer relationships, and increase levels of student-teacher contact which may lead to higher academic performance. Furthermore, creation of smaller environments should help schools maintain order and discipline.

Evidence. The qualitative evidence indicates that this strategy is a particularly effective way of reducing student anonymity and marginality. Susan C. Kaeser (1979a, 1979b), Joan First and M. Hayes Mizell (1980), the United States Commission on Civil Rights (1976), and the National School Public Relations Association (1976) suggest that creating smaller learning and social environments tends to keep misbehaving and low-achieving students supported and involved in activities and, thus, reduces the likelihood of disorder. This strategy is supported further by Gottfredson and Daiger's (1979) findings that teachers with fewer different students with whom they must regularly interact are less likely to be victimized and that the schools in which they teach are less likely to have high rates of student disorder.

Desegregating Faculties and School Staffs

Desegregated school systems should have desegregated staffs and faculties. A desegregated school with an all-white teaching staff will have more difficulty obtaining good student performance and preparing students for a range of adult roles. Minority students in a school with an all-white teaching staff are more likely to be faced with discriminatory behavior, lower expectations for their performance, and discrimination in assignment to ability groups and in grades received, and they are more likely to be alienated from the school. Moreover, it seems important that minority students be provided role models and that they see minority staff in positions of authority. The benefits to national-origin-minority students of same-background teachers seem to be enhanced when national-origin-minority teachers have bilingual and bicultural capabilities.

Evidence. The available research generally supports this strategy, but it also makes clear that many teachers are as effective or more effective with students of another race than other teachers are with students of their own race. Given this, the evidence generally supports the idea that staffs, especially teaching and administrative staffs, should be desegregated.

Bridge, Judd, and Moock (1979) conclude from their review of the very limited research on this subject that minority elementary-school students have higher achievement when they have minority teachers, other things being equal. In a study of Emergency School Aid Act human-relations programs, William J. Doherty and his colleagues (1981) indicate that minority teachers tend to afford minority students more attention in nonacademic situations and to be more equitable in their instructional groupings. Joyce Epstein (1980) reports that black teachers are less likely than white teachers to place black students in lower instructional tracks.

Charles H. Beady and Stephen Hansell (1981) found no differences in the expectations black and white fifth- and sixth-grade teachers held for the performance of black and white students in elementary and secondary schools. Black teachers, however, did have substantially greater expectations for black students' college attendance and completion. Crain and Mahard (1978a) indicate that black students of equal achievement-test performance in schools of the same student-racial composition have higher grades if there are more black teachers on the staff, and will be more likely to attend college. This study was unable to determine whether these outcomes were a result of negative bias on the part of white teaching staffs or positive bias on the part of racially mixed staffs. The net effect seems to be, however, that minority students were better off in schools with more minority staff members. Arnez (1978) links disproportionate minority suspensions to a lack of minority teachers and principals.

Local and national experts that were interviewed strongly support desegregating faculty and staff. Sixty-five percent of those interviewed on the local level gave a racially balanced staff high priority. The national experts stressed the importance of a racially mixed staff in order to correct the perspectives of students about the relative status of minority and majority group members and to provide role models for minority students. In addition, Murphy (1980) reports from a survey of 132 southwestern school districts that educators believe that racially mixed faculties are important to effective desegregation.

Although minority teachers are often underrepresented in desegregated schools, bilingual-education programs often have more than their share of Hispanic teachers, leading to overrepresentation in staff. In Riverside this situation was criticized by the United States Office for Civil Rights (Carter 1979).

Employment of Minority Counselors in Desegregated High Schools

Minority students in desegregated schools tend to benefit from having counselors of their same race or ethnicity. Minority counselors are usually more effective in establishing a rapport with these students. A desegregated high school which has, at a minimum, one minority counselor will tend to be more effective in keeping minority students in school. Minority counselors are likely to be sensitive to the needs and concerns of minority students and will be of more assistance than white counselors in placing minority students in traditionally black colleges. However, if the full benefits of minority counselors are to be secured, these individuals should have training in the nature of opportunities at predominantly white colleges so that a desegregated college experience is made available to students who can do well in desegregated settings. Counselors in schools with students of limited-English-proficiency should speak the language(s) of those students.

Evidence. Jomills H. Braddock and James M. McPartland (1979) have shown that desegregation is self-perpetuating—that minority students in desegregated high schools are more likely to attend desegregated colleges than minority students in segregated high schools. Although this is what one would expect desegregation to do, this outcome may not always be beneficial for all minority students. For example, Gail E. Thomas (1980) indicates that blacks in traditionally black colleges are more likely to obtain degrees than those who attend predominantly white institutions. It seems, therefore, that some black students in desegregated high schools would benefit from knowledge about opportunities in traditionally black institutions of postsecondary education. Crain and Mahard (1978a) found that black students in predominantly white southern high schools which have black counselors are more likely to attend traditionally black colleges, presumably because black counselors are aware of such opportunities. In addition, this study indicates that students in high schools with black counselors are more likely to obtain scholarship aid at both black and white colleges.

Employment of an Instructional-Resource Coordinator in Each School

Desegregated classrooms often have very heterogeneous student bodies, and the traditional book-lecture-workbook approach is inadequate to address the different instructional needs of students. Teachers in these classrooms should be able to identify and acquire a wide variety of learning materials. Unfortunately, teachers do not often have the time or knowledge to locate and select the materials they require to teach in heterogeneous classrooms.

An instructional-resource coordinator is a certified teacher who has no classroom responsibilities and whose primary function is to assist classroom teachers in selecting and obtaining all sorts of relevant instructional materials (for example, books, workbooks, films, computer programs, and so forth). The presence in each school of such a staff member would release classroom teachers from their responsibility to independently obtain resources and free them to devote more time and attention to instruction and the proper use of these materials. Thus, the presence of a resource coordinator could have a positive impact on the achievement of both minority and majority students in desegregated schools. In addition, a resource coordinator can introduce high-technology equipment such as television and computers in classrooms and help ensure their proper use. A coordinator can help plan complex school activities and major field trips, facilitate the use of parents and other volunteers in classrooms, and serve as a helpful, nonthreatening colleague to assist staff members with specific instructional problems.

Evidence. The *Southern Schools* report (1973) attempted to measure the impact of a large number of school resources on student achievement. The resource in high schools which was most clearly related to achievement was the presence of a person whose title was *audio-visual coordinator*. Less than 10 percent of southern high schools employed such a staff member in the early 1970s, but the schools that did had markedly higher black and white achievement. In a later analysis, Crain, Mahard, and Narot (1982) found that schools with resource coordinators had unusually good race relations and speculated that this was because students were more involved in more varied and interesting school activities and because teachers, freed from the need to lecture continuously, had more interaction with students.

The Educational Testing Service is studying an experimental use of computers for basic-skills instruction in the Los Angeles public schools (Ragosta, Holland, and Jamison 1980). The school system placed a full-time coordinator in each school, and the Educational Testing Service has concluded that even in a nonexperimental setting, such a coordinator is necessary to ensure proper and effective use of this technology.

Examples. The Louisville-Jefferson County district staffed its new middle schools with full-time instructional-resource coordinators. These individuals provided materials to classroom teachers and also served as peers with whom teachers could talk about problems. A related strategy was also implemented in this district. An Emergency School Aid Act (ESAA) funded materials workshop for teachers representing a number of schools met once a month for a year. This workshop was judged to be the most successful of all that district's ESAA projects. The group served as a source of materials and ideas and provided social support for teachers, many of whom were in buildings with weak administrators.

Additional examples of the use of resource coordinators may be found in Kim Marshall's (1975) description of her duties in this role at Martin Luther King School in Boston. The Citizen's Council for Ohio Schools' publication *Orderly Schools that Serve All Children* also describes the work of coordinators in several exemplary schools (Kaeser 1979a).

Curricular and Instructional Changes

College-Preparation Programs in All Secondary Schools

Although magnet schools for the academically advanced student may reduce the perceived costs of desegregation, particularly to the persons whose children attend them, they also may stigmatize nonmagnet schools in desegregated school districts as academically inferior. College-preparatory courses offered in each secondary school (except in specialized schools) provide instructional diversity to all students, prevent stigmatizing nonmagnet schools, and may help retain middle- and upper-middle-class students in the public-school system. Provision of these preparatory programs may be of particular importance in reducing the flight of students who may not be admitted to academic magnet schools or of students who may fear the loss of instructional quality as a result of school desegregation. (See discussion of curricula enrichment as an alternative to academic magnet schools in chapter 3.)

Evidence. There is no quantitative evidence that supports the proposition that college-preparatory programs in all secondary schools or overall curricula enrichment will reduce white flight. However, the qualitative literature indicates that these programs, as part of upgrading curricula throughout a school system, will improve students' performance. Smith, Downs, and Lachman (1973), and the United States Commission on Civil Rights (1976) find that enriching curricula on a districtwide basis enhances academic achievement. In addition, there is some indirect evidence that college-preparatory programs have particular relevance to Asian American students. In reanalyses of the 1966 Coleman data, George W. Mayeske and Albert F. Beaton (1975) and Anthony E. Boardman and Anne S. Lloyd (1978) confirm the importance of college-preparatory programs to the aspirations as well as the achievement of these students. Several local and national experts that were interviewed also emphasized the importance of college-preparatory programs for both minority and majority students.

Multiethnic Curricula

During the past fifteen years, a considerable amount of effort has been expended on developing various curricular models and materials which reflect the diversity of the U.S. population and culture. This effort is evidence of a widespread consensus that such curricula have a positive effect on interracial and interethnic understanding. Two trends in this development have been most notable. First, textbooks have been revised. Second, many schools have developed minority-oriented courses. These two trends are similar in that they both seek to provide students with more information about minority groups than do more traditional textbooks and curricula. They are different, however, in that one incorporates materials of special relevance to minority groups within the regular curriculum, whereas the other tends to isolate it in special units or courses.

A great many school systems now say that they use some type of multiethnic curricula. It is assumed that doing so will enhance ethnic pride and reduce negative ethnic stereotypes. Ideally, the presence of such curricula should further the extent to which students receive an education which accurately reflects the contributions of various racial and ethnic groups to U.S. society. Ethnic-studies courses are said by their advocates to serve some of the same purposes as multiethnic curricula. However, some experts argue against the use of minority-studies programs in secondary schools because they often do more damage than the good they accomplish by resegregating students. Other experts argue that ethnic-studies courses should not be seen as a substitute for a multiethnic curriculum but rather as an integral component of a comprehensive multiethnic curriculum which builds understanding of other cultures as well as knowledge about and pride in one's own. Multiethnic curricula can also be linked to the development of English-language skills in bilingual classrooms.

How can a good multiethnic curriculum be distinguished from an unsatisfactory one? It is not uncommon for publishers to tout as multiethnic texts those which are basically similar to traditional texts but have pictures of a few blacks or Hispanics scattered throughout their pages. Furthermore, the mere utilization of multiethnic texts hardly constitutes a multiethnic curriculum. Many experts believe that a comprehensive multiethnic curriculum would be reflected in many other aspects of the school as well, including its wall displays, its library, its use of the community, and its assembly programs. The effectiveness of multiethnic curricula that address the needs of national-origin-minority students will be enhanced if a critical mass of these students is present in particular schools.

Evidence. Almost all the experts interviewed and a good number of those persons who write about the effectiveness of school desegregation stress the importance of multiethnic curricula to effective school desegregation. Several qualitative and quantitative studies suggest a weak but positive relationship between the use of multiethnic curricula or minority-oriented courses and positive student race relations (see Forehand and Ragosta 1976; Genova and Walberg 1980; Litcher and Johnson 1969; Doherty et al. 1981). A few studies show no effect, but there do not appear to be any which identify a negative relationship. Even if multiethnic curricula have no consistently strong impact on race relations, the experts and the qualitative literature stress the obvious advantage of presenting a balanced and hence potentially more accurate picture of U.S. society to students.

Robert E. Slavin and Nancy Madden (1979) show that multiethnic curricula is less effective than interracial interaction in achieving better race relations among students. This study suggests that dissemination of information, by itself, is not enough to promote good race relations. Rather, multiethnic curricula seem most effective in classrooms and schools which also provide opportunities and activities for positive interracial interactions. It seems likely then that interracial interaction and multiethnic curricula reinforce each other and have an additive effect.

The necessity of examining closely material which purports to be multicultural or multiethnic is made clear by Gaston Blom, Richard Waite, and Sara Zimet (1967). This study found that a text designed as part of an urban-multiethnic series (1) had more of its stories set in suburban than urban settings, (2) had a higher proportion of failure themes than comparable traditional texts, (3) devoted the stories about blacks exclusively to those about black families living in stable white neighborhoods, and (4) restricted blacks in its stories to family roles rather than having them appear in both family and work settings. James A. Banks (1979) provides some useful checklists which schools and educators can employ in order to assess the extent to which they do provide a complete multiethnic curriculum.

The Montgomery County (Maryland) school district instituted a program whereby its teachers developed multicultural units for use in the system's schools. A carefully selected group of teachers were paid during one summer to construct these units, which were to be introduced to other teachers during in-service training sessions.

In Minneapolis, the curriculum has been changed to reflect the background, heritage, and history of all minorities so that minority and majority students might learn about the contributions to the United States made by these groups. A school-board member who was interviewed stated that not only did minority students learn about themselves but they also learned that many of their beliefs about students of other races or ethnic backgrounds were inaccurate.

Comprehensive Student Human-Relations Programs

Each school should develop a two-part human-relations program for its students: first, curricula and activities for individual classrooms and, second, special programs for the entire school. The classroom aspects of the program would include multiethnic textbooks, role-playing projects, and discussions of race relations as they occur in the classroom, the school, the community, and U.S. society generally. The most important classroom aspect of this program would be to assign students to interracial groups to work together on class projects or otherwise create opportunities for black, national-origin-minority, and white students to interact. Obviously, these curricular changes should be thought out in advance; they will not be as effective if introduced after interracial conflict arises.

Programs that appear most effective are those that are integral to the day-to-day learning experience and social interactions of students. In other words, the more integrated with other activities and the less obvious human-relations activities are, the more integration among students they are likely to achieve. One reason for this appears to be that although teachers and administrators may think that good human relations are desirable objectives, they often do not place this goal above other, more traditional goals of schools, such as teaching reading, math, language arts, or history.

The special-programs aspect of a human-relations program would include activities such as multiracial schoolwide student committees, special movies, assembly speakers, and schoolwide recognition of the birthdays of minority political and social leaders and of other important events in U.S. race relations. One idea the study team found attractive is to teach students about the desegregation controversy in their own community, especially the reasons why the judge, the state or federal agency, or the school board required desegregation.

These special schoolwide programs should not be regarded as substitutes for the curricular aspects of the school human-relations program. Furthermore, the specifics of individual special programs may not be as important as the fact that their presence symbolizes to students that administrators, teachers, and staff have a high regard for positive human relations. The more teachers and principals talk about the importance of good human relations and behave accordingly, the more impact specific programs are likely to have on students. It is very important that human-relations programs begin in kindergarten (or before where appropriate) because attitudes toward other races and cultures may be significantly shaped by the time students are ten to twelve years old. Human-relations programs should seek to foster understanding of and interaction among different minorities as well as among whites and racial and ethnic minorities.

Evidence. Experts on school desegregation are in considerable agreement about the importance of human-relations programs although they differ on how much change can be achieved through them. Most agree that interracial and interethnic contact is essential to making substantial gains in race relations and that textbooks are not substitutes for more experiential learning. All experts agree that human-relations programs should begin at the earliest grade, as does the available research on the formation of race-related attitudes (see Katz 1976).

Slavin and Madden (1979) found that assigning students to interracial teams in classrooms was the most effective of the eight practices they studied for improving race relations among students. This practice was strongly correlated with positive racial attitudes and behavior for both whites and minorities. John B. McConahay (1981) reviewed the experimental studies of interracial cooperative teams and found that across the variety of settings and a number of techniques for setting up the teams, the practice produced more positive attitudes and behavior and improved academic achievement in some instances. (For a further discussion of cooperative learning techniques see the next section.)

The effects of special programs or curricular materials on race relations were not as strong as those for interracial teams, but Slavin and Madden (1979) report some association with positive attitudes among whites. Crain, Mahard, and Narot (1982) found that schools purchasing human-relations materials had better race relations, and Doherty and his colleagues' (1981) human-relations study found that special programs directed toward students produced improved attitudes and behavior and improved self-concept among minority students. This latter study, the most extensive to date focusing on human-relations programs, found that strategies were most effective when they (1) were coordinated with the regular instructional program, (2) increased intergroup contact, and (3) were supported by school and district officials.

Examples. Experts agree that the best types of human-relations programs are those that are so well integrated with the curriculum, instructional practices, and extracurricular activities that it is not possible to identify them as being distinct programs. An example of an instructional strategy that subtly involves human-relations objectives is the various approaches to cooperative learning. However, more visible student human-relations programs and limited programs can also have positive effects. Meg Gwalt-ney (1979) describes student human-relations programs that are conducted by a school district located in a large eastern industrial and commercial center where minorities comprise 53 percent of the student population. Student communication workshops, involving between twenty and twenty-five students per workshop, some parents, and one or two teachers, are held during the school day at various locations including some outside the schools. Students participate in human-relations exercises that are designed to increase trust and reduce threat among themselves and particularly among students of different racial and economic backgrounds. Teachers who attend are encouraged to continue the workshop exercises in the classroom.

In Cleveland, the court ordered implementation of a program in which students explore the history of segregation and the desegregation suit in that city. No evidence on that program's effectiveness is yet available. In Shaker Heights, the school system instituted a number of human-relations activities for elementary-school students. These activities included development of a resource room to which white and minority students may go for recreation after lessons are completed. The room is designed to encourage interracial interaction during play. Another activity is a hands-on program sponsored by a local museum. Students of different races are encouraged to interact in a learning environment outside the classroom.

Minneapolis secondary-school students participate in the formulation of human-relations guidelines and are involved in planning and conducting schoolwide lectures and seminars on human-relations topics. Over the school year, a variety of ethnic observance days are set aside, and schools participate in programs designed to foster understanding of a number of ethnic cultures, not merely black and Hispanic. The Green Circle program, which involves activities designed to increase student awareness of racism and sexism, has been implemented with apparent succcess in many school systems, including Nashville-Davidson County and New Castle Consolidated.

Cooperative-Learning Strategies for Heterogeneous
Classrooms

One set of techniques widely utilized to improve student relations, promote the academic performance of low-achieving students, and minimize the problems of teaching academically heterogeneous classrooms is *co-operative learning*. These techniques usually involve the creation of teams of students. Each team of roughly four to six students represents the full range of ethnic, ability, and gender groups in the classroom. Academic work is structured so that the students on each team are dependent on each other but also so that disparity in achievement levels does not automatically lead to disparity in contributions to goal attainment. So, for example, one team-learning technique (Jigsaw) is structured so that each child is given information which all group members need to complete their work. Another team-learning technique (Student Teams-Achievement Division—STAD) provides rewards for improvement in academic performance so that students with weak academic backgrounds have the potential to contribute as much to the success of the team as do the best students.

The work of Susan J. Rosenholtz (1977, 1982) and Elizabeth G. Cohen (1980) on multiple-abilities curriculum models suggests promising results in fostering equal participation and influence in cooperative-learning groups. Rosenholtz (1977) found that children considered high in reading ability and status in group reading tasks also have high status in groups with tasks that do not require reading. Multiple-abilities instructional approaches are designed to counter the effects of such status generalization in academically heterogeneous and racially integrated classrooms.

One of the advantages of these cooperative-learning techniques is that they are relatively easy to implement. They can be used by a single teacher without requiring the cooperation of other teachers and administrators. Also, they can be used for only a portion of the school day or for only a short period of time over the semester. Finally, they do not require a major investment in learning new techniques or in setting up administrative procedures. Books and manuals which explain implementation procedures are available as are some instructional materials already organized for student team learning. There are many varieties of cooperative and team learning. For example, national-origin-minority students might serve as tutors in foreign-language courses.

Evidence. Considerable evidence suggests that various types of cooperative learning techniques (1) lead to higher than usual academic achievement gains for low-achieving students who are involved, and (2) almost always improve relations between majority- and minority-group children. However, considerable care needs to be taken in designing cooperative-learning experiences so that they do not put low-achieving students at a disadvantage. Teachers who understand the basic theory of cooperative learning are more likely to be effective in adapting particular programs to their classroom situations.

The research revealing positive effects of various structured cooperative-learning team strategies is strong although the impacts of some of these techniques, such as Teams-Games-Tournament (TGT) and STAD, have been more frequently studied than those of others. Both Robert E. Slavin (1980) and Shlomo Sharan (1980) in independent reviews of the research on cooperative-learning techniques identify both achievement gains and improved relations among students. Some studies examined in these reviews have been conducted in classrooms with Hispanic as well as Anglo and black students. The conclusions drawn from this research are generally similar to those found in the more numerous studies of biracial classrooms. Perhaps because the evidence on cooperative- and team-learning strategies is so strong, the national experts that were interviewed chose cooperative learning with great frequency as a specific means for minimizing resegregation within schools.

Later research suggests that cooperative-learning techniques may not have the same degree of positive effects on white and minority students. Robert E. Slavin and Eileen Oickle (1981), in an analysis of the STAD technique, confirmed earlier findings that cooperative-learning groups made significantly greater gains in academic achievement than nonteam classes. However, this positive effect was disproportionately due to outstanding gains by black students. White students seemed to benefit academically from team learning as well but not as much as black students. This study also found a small but significant increase in cross-racial friendships among students in cooperative-learning groups, and this effect was due primarily to whites gaining black friends. Sandra B. Damico, Afesa Bell-Nathaniel, and Charles Green (1981) also found that white students in cooperative-learning groups developed more friendships with blacks.

The evidence relating to the impact of encouraging academic cooperation between majority and minority students without employing specific well-tested team techniques is less clear, but it does support the idea that positive impacts will result. The United States Commission on Civil Rights (1976) found support among school administrators for academic cooperation as a means of reducing resegregation. Slavin and Madden (1979) found that assigning black and white students to work together on academic tasks consistently related to positive outcomes on six different indicators of student interracial attitudes and behavior. Similar findings about positive benefits of team-organized schools are reported by Damico, Green, and Bell-Nathaniel (1981). David W. Johnson and Roger T. Johnson (1981) found that cooperative-learning experiences promoted more interracial interaction in instructional and recreational activities than individual-learning experiences. In addition, recent studies indicate that cooperative intergroup contact in the classroom may improve at least some students' self-concepts and attitudes toward school, especially for blacks (see Doherty et al. 1981).

Studies by Julie T. Stulac (1975), Cohen (1979), and Rosenholtz (1982) provide evidence that multiple-abilities intervention helps to equalize status and participation in small heterogeneous groups of both single-race and multiracial composition. In addition, Cohen (1980) and Janis Ahmadjian-Baer (1981) both found that low-achieving minority students exhibited more active learning behavior in classrooms that use this approach. There is no evidence on the relationship of the behavioral changes to achievement outcomes in the multiple-abilities environment.

Although these studies identify the positive impact of a variety of classroom procedures which encourage cooperative intergroup contact, there is research which suggests that several factors may influence just how effective such contact is in improving race relations. Specifically, Fletcher Blanchard and his colleagues show that the positive impact of cooperation is greatest when the group succeeds academically (Blanchard, Weigel, and Cook 1975). The research suggests further that whites are more attracted to blacks who perform competently in a group situation. This evidence, combined with research by Cohen, Rosenholtz, and others indicates that careful attention should be paid to structuring cooperative learning so that situations are not created in which participation and status of different groups are very unequal.

Examples. The models for cooperative learning that are most widely discussed in the literature include TGT, STAD, Jigsaw, small-group teaching, and multiple-abilities classrooms. Descriptions of these models follow.

Teams-Games-Tournament. TGT is built around two major components: (1) four- to five-member student teams and (2) instructional tournaments. Teams are the cooperative element of TGT. Students are assigned to teams according to a procedure that maximizes heterogeneity of ability levels, sex, and race. The primary function of the team is to prepare its members to do well in the tournament. Following an initial class presentation by the teacher, the teams are given worksheets covering academic material similar to that to be included in the tournament. Teammates study together and quiz each other to be sure that all team members are prepared.

After the team practice session, team members must demonstrate their learning in the tournament, which is usually held once a week. For the tournament, students are assigned to three person tournament tables. The assignment is done so that competition at each table will be fair— the highest three students in past performances are assigned to table one, the next three to table two, and so on. At the tables, the students compete on simple academic games covering content that has been presented in class by the teacher and on the worksheets. Students at the tournament tables are competing as representatives of their teams, and the score each student earns at the tournament table is added into an overall team score. Because students are assigned to ability-homogeneous tournament tables, each student has an equal chance of contributing a maximum score to his or her team since the first place scorer at every table brings the same number of points to the team. Following the tournament, the teacher prepares a newsletter which recognizes successful teams and first-place scorers. Although team assignments always remain the same, tournament-table assignments are changed for every tournament according to a system that maintains equality of past performance at each table. (For a complete description of TGT see Slavin 1978.)

Student Teams-Achievement Divisions. STAD uses the same four- to five-member heterogeneous teams used in TGT but replaces the games and tournaments with simple, fifteen-minute quizzes, which students take after studying in their teams. The quiz scores are translated into team scores using a system called *achievement divisions*. The quiz scores of the highest six students in past performance are compared, and the top scorer in this group (the achievement division) earns eight points for his or her team, the second scorer earns six points, and so forth. Then the quiz scores of the next highest six students in past performance are compared, and the process continues. In this way, student scores are compared only with those of an ability-homogeneous reference group instead of the entire class. A bumping procedure changes division assignments from week to week to maintain equality. Students know only their own division assignments; they do not interact in any way with the other members of their division. The achievement-division feature maintains the equality of opportunity for contributions to the team score as in TGT. A complete description of STAD appears in Slavin (1978).

Jigsaw. In Jigsaw, students are assigned to small heterogeneous teams, as in TGT and STAD. Academic material is broken into as many sections as there are team members. For example, a biography might be broken into early years, schooling, first accomplishments, and so forth. The students study their sections with members of other teams who have the same sections. Then they return to their teams and teach their sections to the other team members. Finally, all team members are quizzed on the entire unit. The quiz scores contribute to individual grades, not to a team score as in TGT and STAD. In this sense, the Jigsaw technique may be seen as high in task interdependence but low in reward interdependence as individual performances do not contribute directly to a group goal. In the Jigsaw technique, individual performances contribute to other's individual goals only. Since the group is not rewarded as a group, there is no formal group goal. However, because the positive behavior of each team member (learning the sections) helps the other group members to be rewarded (because they need each others' information), the essential dynamics of the cooperative-reward structure are present.

Slavin (1978) constructed a modification of Jigsaw called *Jigsaw II*. In Jigsaw II students all read the same material but focus on separate topics. The students from different teams who have the same topics meet to discuss their topics and then return to teach them to their teammates. The team members then take a quiz, and the quiz scores are used to form team scores as in STAD. Thus Jigsaw II involves less task interdependence and more reward interdependence than Jigsaw.

Small-Group Teaching. Small-group teaching is a general organizational plan for the classroom rather than a specific technique. It places considerable emphasis on group decision making, including assignment of group members to tasks, and on individual contributions that make up a group product rather than a less well-defined group task. Cooperative rewards are not well specified; students are simply asked to cooperate to achieve group goals (Slavin 1980).

Multiple-Ability Classroom. Mixed-ability groups are assigned cooperative-learning tasks which require a number of abilities and do not exclusively rely on reading, writing, and computation skills. In addition, students are prepared for the task by discussing the range of abilities it requires and are instructed that although no group member will possess all of the necessary skills, every member will be able to contribute at least one. The multiple-ability assignments may be preceded by expectation training in which low-status students are prepared for special tasks which they then teach to other students (Cohen 1980).

These various cooperative-learning techniques have been implemented in hundreds of school systems throughout the country. The STAD procedure has been endorsed by the United States Department of Education as an idea that works. Detailed information about this program and assistance in adopting it, is available from the National Diffusion Network, United States Department of Education, 400 Maryland Avenue, S.W., Washington, D.C. 20203.

Peer Tutoring

The most common peer-tutoring model is cross-age tutoring in which older children teach younger children and both tutor and tutee are usually low-achieving students. Peer tutoring can be used within age groups and for students of all levels of academic ability. The rationale for peer tutoring can apply to integrated, multiage, or nongraded classrooms to accommodate diverse achievement levels and to foster improved race relations among students (Gartner, Kohler, and Riessman 1971).

Evidence. In a review of the research on peer tutoring, Linda Devin-Sheehan, Robert S. Feldman, and Vernon L. Allen (1976) identify considerable evidence that this strategy promotes cognitive and affective gains for older, low-achieving tutors. However, the literature they survey on comparable effects for tutees is more equivocal. Some studies show positive academic and attitudinal changes for both tutor and tutee, but others have found that the benefits for the former do not also accrue in same measure to the latter. Positive results have been found for both black and white same-race pairs; however, very few studies reviewed in this survey examined mixed-race pairs. One that did found that cross-race tutoring produced greater interracial interaction and acceptance for both tutor and tutee although there were no significant gains in achievement.

In a recent analysis of sixty-five evaluations of peer-tutoring programs, Peter A. Cohen, James A. Kulik, and Chen-Lin C. Kulik (1982) found that these programs have positive effects on the academic achievement and the attitudes of those students receiving tutoring. These students outperformed students who did not receive tutoring on examinations and developed more positive attitudes toward the subject matter covered in the programs. This analysis found similar positive outcomes for students who served as tutors. The studies analyzed suggest that achievement outcomes for tutees are stronger when programs are structured and are of short duration. They also appear to be stronger when lower level skills are taught and when programs emphasize math rather than reading skills.

Maximizing Parent Involvement in Education Activities

A strong consensus exists that involving parents in the school is an important strategy for successful desegregation. At both the elementary and the secondary levels, the use of parents as either paid or volunteer aides can be important. This is especially true if the aides are parents of the bused-in group of students since involvement of these parents increases the school's channels of communication with the sending school community. At the elementary-school level, parental-involvement strategies are often intended to improve achievement by helping parents supervise homework and tutor both students in the school and their own children at home.

Many desegregating school systems lack the staff and materials to provide the enriched multiethnic curricular and extracurricular experiences necessary to promote various goals of desegregation. The utilization of parents, especially minority parents, as resource persons and as role models can be an effective means of overcoming such deficits. These programs tend to fade away over time, however, and teachers and principals must learn how to use parents in significant ways to achieve desired outcomes in order to keep parents interested in maintaining their involvement. Although desegregation can increase the distance between home and school for some families, schools can take steps to involve parents that they usually do not take, such as conducting parent-teacher conferences in the students' neighborhood when the schools they attend are not close to home. (See chapter 8 for discussion of in-service strategies to increase parental involvement in schools.)

Evidence. No empirical study has examined the impact of parents working in educational capacities in desegregated schools. The qualitative literature does offer support for this strategy. The United States Commission on Civil Rights (1976) and Murphy (1980) both support this as a meaningful and effective method for reducing within-school racial isolation. Murphy (1980) found particularly strong support for using Hispanic parents as school-resource persons to enhance multiethnic curricular content and orientation.

There is little systematic evidence from research on the process of desegregation that relates to parental involvement; other research attests to the usefulness of this strategy. The benefits of involving parents depend on whether parents are directly engaged in the education of their children. As Herbert Walberg points out, ''Programs for parental cooperative teaching and specific reinforcement of school lessons at home, often in inner city neighborhoods, have proven beneficial in 16 of 17 studies'' (1982, p. 5). PTA meetings and parent-teacher conferences are good but inadequate ways to involve parents.

Virginia Shipman and her colleagues found that mothers who said they felt welcomed and supported by their children's schools participated more in their children's education (Shipman et al. 1976). Armor and his associates (1976) found for black, not Hispanic, students that schools' efforts to involve parents and the community in school decision making related to increases in reading achievement. John E. Coulson and his colleagues (1976) found achievement in desegregated schools to be related to levels of parent involvement in classroom activities. Jean B. Wellisch and her colleagues (1976) assert that parent aides were more effective than paid outsiders in promoting achievement and positive relationships among students in desegregated schools.

Examples. The United States Commission on Civil Rights (1976) reports that in Charlotte-Mecklenburg County the PTA obtained federal funds to hire a staff member to solicit and coordinate parent volunteers to tutor students (see also United States Commission on Civil Rights 1973). In an interview, the superintendent of Charlotte said that since the volunteer program has been in effect, over ten thousand parents have participated in various school activities. In addition, the commission (1976) notes that parent volunteers in some school districts have become a part of regular school operations. In Denver, for example, a parent organization sponsors monthly programs at individual schools that include cultural-exchange activities. In Hillsborough County, parents have volunteered in increasing numbers to participate in class parties and field trips.

A useful inventory of ways to involve parents in schools is contained in *Working with Your Schools,* a publication of the United States Commission on Civil Rights' State Advisory Committees in Arkansas, Louisiana, Texas, and New Mexico. In addition, the Pittsburgh public-school district has published guidelines and a checklist for parents to promote learning outside of the classroom ("Helping Children Learn" 1982). These guidelines suggest strategies parents may use to tutor their children at home.

The extent to which schools can go to engage parents in their children's education is suggested by New Haven's involvement of parents in the district's reading program. The New Haven plan has eighteen components ranging from recipes for increasing reading skills, to parent workshops and courses, to various forms of parent information (Criscuolo 1982).

Grouping, Tracking, and Academic Resegregation

Eliminate the Grouping of Students in Separate Classes by Ability in Elementary School

Students are separated by ability level for at least some or all of their instruction in most U.S. schools. In elementary schools, students are often assigned to separate classrooms according to their ability when they reach a particular grade level. Ability is usually measured by standardized tests, grades, and teacher reports. This practice should be eliminated in elementary schools that seek to desegregate effectively.

Another form of academic resegregation is the division of children within a class into recognizable ability groups. If the groups are more or less permanent and are continued across subjects, this practice can be as dysfunctional as ability grouping among classrooms. Indeed, within-class groupings may be more damaging because they reinforce stereotypes and may result in student self-devaluation. However, groupings for instruction in particular subjects for portions of the school day should not necessarily be eliminated.

Evidence. The evidence is clear that these assignment practices tend to segregate students by race. Warren G. Findley and Miriam M. Bryan (1971) and Roger Mills and Bryan (1976) argue that ability measures, such as standardized tests, sort students by socioeconomic status and race and that teacher reports and grades are also biased by assumptions related to race and socioeconomic status. Studies by Findley and Bryan (1971) and Epstein (1980) also indicate that this assignment practice does not improve achievement for low-ability or high-ability groups. This generalization seems to apply even to very low-achieving students, assuming that students experience good teaching. One major analysis, conducted by the National Institute of Education (1978a), found that in three out of four schools studied students in need of compensatory education who were mainstreamed did better than those in special classes. In the fourth school there was no difference between the groups. In a review of the research on compensatory education, Carl H. Haywood (1982) concludes that pull-out programs in which students are grouped by ability are ineffective and that students in heterogeneous classrooms do score higher on tests of performance. Further, the achievement and self-esteem of low-ability students generally seem to be harmed by grouping, and race relations cannot be improved when students are separated in segregated classrooms or groups for instruction.

Findley and Bryan (1971) provide evidence that teachers prefer classes with a limited range of ability if they are assigned to groups of students with high or average ability but not if they are assigned to classes with low ability. It is the popularity of ability grouping with teachers and not its obvious instructional value that has guaranteed the continuation of this practice. Empirical research reviewed by Epstein (1980) indicates that eliminating tracking in the elementary schools will have little effect on achievement scores but that flexible grouping (allowing for status change) and other organizational structures (active-learning and equal-status programs) can have positive effects on student and particularly black-student achievement.

Examine Carefully Within-Class Ability Groups That Do Not Change

More than three-quarters of elementary-school teachers group children for reading and mathematics. Often children grouped on the basis of one skill (usually reading) are kept in these groups for other subjects and classroom activities, and this may be quite inappropriate. Schools should examine grouping practices carefully to determine whether they are flexible and clearly reflect students' abilities. Is it possible for children to move up? Do students, in fact, improve and move to higher ability-level groups?

Evidence. Within-class groupings for reading and math based upon standardized measures of ability or upon experiences a child first brings to kindergarten or first grade usually segregate students by race within groups in the classroom. Within-class groupings by ability for reading and math are not clearly superior to other methods of organizing a classroom, though this depends on the extent of heterogeneity. Epstein (1980) found that black students did better in less resegregative programs; they benefited from participation in equal-status learning programs and from flexible grouping.

Teachers prefer ability grouping because it limits the range of student experience and knowledge (which they call ability) with which they must contend at any one time. The need to continually reexamine the rigidity of grouping procedures is underscored by the findings of Epstein (1980) and Harold B. Gerard and Norman Miller (1975) that teachers who express low support for integration are more likely to use homogeneous grouping strategies than those who support it.

Evidence on the impact of within-class grouping on race relations is inconclusive. Schofield (1981) suggests that this is due to the variety of ways in which in-class groups may be used. In general, however, McConahay (1981) concludes that race relations are improved by interracial contact and seldom improve in the absence of such contact.

A danger of stable within-class grouping is that decisions made about children's abilities that are made very early in their school careers (kindergarten or first grade) will be simply honored by each succeeding teacher providing little chance for change. If those early decisions are left unexamined by teachers, principals, parents, or children, they become self-fulfilling prophecies. This possibility is strengthened by evidence that students who have been classified as less able may receive less instructional time, attention, and material than more able students (Rist 1970; Oakes 1980; Green and Griffore 1978).

Eliminate Rigid and Inflexible Tracking and Grouping
in Secondary Schools

Two types of grouping occur at the high-school level. One is a form of ability grouping, sometimes called *leveling,* in which courses such as English and mathematics are taught with different levels of difficulty. The other arrangement, usually called *tracking,* refers to differentiated curricula. Three tracks are generally utilized on the secondary level: college preparatory, vocational, and general. Leveling should be limited, flexible, and determined for each subject separately. Students and parents should be allowed to choose among levels of courses upon recommendations from school personnel. Tracking should also be flexible, and students should be allowed to choose from both college preparatory and vocational courses. Students should not have to declare or commit themselves to the college preparatory or vocational track so that they have separate criteria to meet for graduation depending upon track membership, therefore, excluding themselves from post-high-school options.

Evidence. The evidence is clear that leveling and tracking tend to segregate by race. Annegret Harnischfeger and David E. Wiley (1980) found black, Hispanic, and foreign-born students overrepresented in lower levels and in vocational and general tracks. In addition, A. Guy Larkins and Sally E. Oldham (1976) indicate that leveling and tracking not only resegregate students while they are in their leveled or tracked classes but that they affect students' schedules for all other classes. This leads to resegregation in classes not consciously tracked. The experts that were interviewed suggest that schools eliminate grouping by ability and allow students to choose freely among vocational or college-preparatory courses without having to declare themselves in a particular track.

The empirical evidence of the impact of tracking and leveling on race relations is quite mixed, but generally it suggests a negative impact. Crain, Mahard and Narot (1982) conclude that selective ability grouping in newly desegregated southern junior- and senior-high schools (sorting English and other basic classes by ability while leaving electives, gym, and other courses heterogeneously grouped) tends to have harmful effects on achievement but beneficial effects on race relations. However, this study finds that ability grouping in elementary school has harmful effects on both achievement and race relations. Robin D. Froman (1981) identifies negative impacts on low-ability groups (which have high concentrations of minority children in desegregated districts) and no consistently positive impact on high-ability groups.

Student outcomes identified by other studies are also mixed and seem much more likely to be related to teacher behavior, student-teacher interaction, and the structure of the instructional process within groups rather than the grouping itself. There is a limit to the diversity that classroom teachers can handle. Carolyn M. Evertson and her colleagues argue that without expertise in classroom management and knowledge of instructional strategies most appropriate for heterogeneous classes, extreme student diversity will defeat most teachers and the learning needs of students will not be met (Evertson, Sanford, and Emmer 1981). A recent analysis of leveling by Jeannie Oakes (1980) indicates that students assigned to lower levels spend less time on instruction, and their teachers have lower expectations for their work. Also, Oakes finds teacher clarity and teacher enthusiasm greater in high-level than in low-level classes. Although it is widely believed that leveling and tracking keep middle-class whites in desegregated schools, there is no evidence to support this contention. In fact, almost all school systems use the practice, including those with high levels of white flight.

National experts were nearly unanimous in rejecting or urging extremely restricted use of ability grouping at all levels of instruction. Similarly, the consensus literature generally attributes detrimental effects to ability grouping and tracking. Smith, Downs, and Lachman (1973) conclude that these practices have negative impacts on academic achievement and lead to within school and within class resegregation. These impacts are also identified by Forehand and Ragosta (1976) and the United States Commission on Civil Rights (1976).

*Nondiscriminatory Identification and Placement of
Students*

The development of policies and procedures for identifying and placing students in special curricula in nondiscriminatory ways calls for school administrators, staff members, and teachers to be trained in assessment procedures that will reduce the disproportionate assignment of minority students to special curricula (EMR [educable mentally retarded] for example). Moreover, school systems should develop explicit policies governing such placements. For example, LEP students should not be tested in English. Schools should seek linguistically and culturally relevant information and advice in order to reach informed decisions regarding special-education placement of national-origin-minority students.

Evidence. Systematic research on the effects of alternative assessment procedures on the classification of minority students is virtually non-existent. An application of Jane R. Mercer's (1973) technique did produce a reduction in the identification of Hispanic children in California as retarded. The use of learning-potential assessment led Milton Budoff (1969) to conclude that a large number of I.Q.-defined retardates do have learning ability and are not mentally retarded but educationally retarded. Erwin C. Hargrove and his colleagues (1981) found in a case study of the implementation of Public Law (P.L.) 94–142 that schools in which the referral process was more consultative referred fewer students for testing. Their analysis found no relationship between race and referral rates. Richard L. Weatherly (1979) found evidence of strong bureaucratic constraints on the deliberations of interdisciplinary teams used to determine student referrals that frequently reach professional consensus before parents are involved and consider only a narrow range of service options.

Clear evidence exists that when bilingual children are tested in their primary language their performance is stronger. For example, when the plaintiffs (nine limited-English-speaking children classified as EMR) in *Diana* v. *State Board of Education* (1970) were retested in Spanish, only two of them scored below the I.Q. cutoff for EMR, and the lowest score was only three points below the cutoff.

Bernard Mackler (1974) calls for an assessment team approach (interdisciplinary model) to prevent the resegregation of minority students. Both local and national experts emphasize the importance of this strategy as does the United States Commission on Civil Rights (1976).

A variety of alternative assessment procedures have been developed that are intended to reduce reliance on standardized intelligence tests. These include but are not limited to the following techniques.

1. Criterion-referenced assessment describes a child's test performance in terms of level of mastery of specific skills rather than in comparison with statistically determined norms. It is a method of test interpretation rather than a type of test; no normative or peer-referenced implications are drawn. Examples of criterion-referenced assessment include mastery testing and domain-referenced testing (see Mayo 1970; Nitko and Hsu 1974).

2. Learning-potential assessment uses a test-teach-retest paradigm in order to assess the child's actual learning ability and strategy. The Learning Potential Assessment Device (LPAD) is accompanied by *instrumental enrichment*, educational techniques designed to facilitate development in the area of cognitive deficiency identified by the LPAD (see Feuerstein 1979; Haywood 1977).

3. Interdisciplinary assessment combines the perspectives of a variety

of professionals who have worked with the child, including the child's classroom teacher. Under P.L. 94–142 the parents are included in the procedure, as well as the child when appropriate. The rationale for this type of assessment is that multiple sources of information about the child's behavior in a variety of settings will reduce reliance on test scores in making placement decisions and thereby reduce minority disproportion (see Mackler 1974).

4.   The consultation model prescribed by Richard A. Johnson (1976) is not a method of psychological assessment but rather a process by which the necessity of testing is determined. In this model, the school psychologist consults with the referring teacher and other school personnel to devise ways of working with the child in the regular classroom. Testing follows only if these strategies are not effective. The rationale is that in many cases a teacher's referral may be a request for help and should not automatically be interpreted as a step toward special-education placement.

5.   The System of Multicultural Pluralistic Assessment (SOMPA) integrates several approaches to nondiscriminatory assessment in an attempt to control for different sources of bias. The SOMPA, developed by Jane R. Mercer and June F. Lewis (1978), adopts pluralistic norms for standardization, includes an ecological assessment of adaptive behavior, and uses the interdisciplinary process with emphasis on parent involvement. Although its psychometric basis remains controversial, the SOMPA represents the best organized model of nondiscriminatory assessment available at this time (see Cook 1979).

Student Discipline Techniques and Resegregation

Establish Clear and Consistent Expectations for
Student Behavior in Each School

During the initial year of desegregation, some students in new schools experience anxiety and different expectations and standards for behavior. When behavioral expectations are ambiguous and when they are applied inconsistently, students become confused and sometimes hostile. Increases in minority suspensions following implementation of desegregation plans may occur in part because minority students are more often reassigned to previously white schools than white students are reassigned to previously minority schools and because greater proportions of minority students than whites are required to adapt to or assimilate different sets of rules and different cultural and behavioral expectations. (See Metz

1978 for assessment of tensions students experience when they must adapt to different rules and behavioral expectations.)

Special attention to cooperative and open development of a set of behavioral expectations at each school during the initial period of desegregation may help reduce disproportionate minority suspensions. This does not mean that developing a new code of conduct in which rules are uniform in all schools is sufficient. The key point here is that minority and majority parents and students must come together with teachers and the principal to arrive at some common agreement about and understanding of the way everyone is expected to behave in school. Agreement about expectations must be communicated to all persons in the school, including teachers and staff members. If the approach taken is one of understanding differences in acceptable behavior rather than one of total adjustment of minority children to the majority expectations, then minority suspensions are likely to be reduced.

Evidence. The qualitative literature supports this approach to reducing misbehavior for all students during desegregation. For example, Galen N. Drewry (1955) contends that allowing the greatest possible participation of teachers and students in drawing up codes and rules is crucial to fair discipline. In this way, he argues, the cultural norms of all groups will be reflected in the administration of discipline. The national experts interviewed support this approach and stress the early notification of and communication with parents when infractions occur.

Gottfredson and Daiger's (1979) analysis of data from 600 schools also provides strong support for this approach. Specifically, this study finds that order will increase if the following measures are adopted.

1. Develop schools or educational environments of smaller size where teachers have extensive responsibility for and contact with a limited number of students (for example, schools within schools, curriculum integration, and so forth) and where steps are taken to ensure adequate resources for instruction.
2. Administer schools in ways that are clear, explicit, and firm.
3. Promote cooperation between teachers and administrators especially with respect to school policies and sanctions for disruptive behavior.
4. Develop school rules that are fair, clear, and well publicized and apply the rules in ways that are firm, consistent, persistent, and evenhanded.

Also, Edmund T. Emmer's (1979) research emphasizes the importance of establishing and enforcing classroom and school norms early in the school year.

Analyze Carefully the Reasons for Disproportionate
Minority Suspensions

Students are suspended from school for a wide variety of reasons, and minority students are often suspended in disproportionate numbers in relation to their percentage in the school or district. Minority suspensions frequently increase immediately after implementation of a desegregation order, particularly in previously all-white schools. In some cases, the use of suspensions may be an attempt to limit the impact of desegregation.

Although some infractions—such as truancy, possession of drugs or weapons, and the like—are objectively measurable, many others—such as disrespectful behavior, insubordination, and dress code violations—require personal judgments by school officials. Most of the questions raised about unfair disciplinary actions relate to sanctions for these ill-defined offenses.

Schools should keep records of suspensions that note the reason for the punishment, the teacher or staff member involved, and the race and sex of the student disciplined. Collection and assessment of this information allows the school principal, parents, and others to analyze the reasons for suspensions, by race and sex, and to determine if particular teachers or staff members are experiencing problems that require attention. Until the leadership in a school understands the causes of disproportionate minority suspensions in that school, solutions are impossible.

Evidence. The relationship between local support for desegregation and perceptions of increased discipline problems identified by Peter O. Peretti (1976), and reports by school officials interviewed that communication problems contribute to increased discipline problems, underscore the importance of monitoring suspensions subsequent to desegregation. Gordon Foster (1977) and the Study Group on Racial Isolation in the Public Schools (1978) found that in some cases, where detailed records have been kept, minority students were suspended more often for subjective and less serious offenses than their majority peers. At the order of a federal district court, the Columbus school system has undertaken careful analysis of suspension and other data. Second-year data revealed slightly more suspensions, but the racial disproportionality was reduced from the first year (Columbus Public Schools 1980). Cleveland analyzed suspensions by reason and race but did not use these data in revising their discipline code (Kaeser 1979b).

Limit the Number of Offenses for Which Suspensions
and Expulsion Can Be Used

Suspensions are used extensively in U.S. schools, generally for behavior that is not considered dangerous to persons or property. As many as one-half of all suspensions are for violations of attendance policy. The widely varying suspension rates among schools, sometimes schools with similar student bodies in the same city, suggest that considerable discretion is exercised in the use of this technique for dealing with student infractions.

Student advocate groups, such as the Children's Defense Fund and the South Eastern Public Education Project, and professional associations, such as the National Education Association, the National Association of Secondary School Principals, and the American Association of School Administrators, all agree that the overall numbers of suspensions ought to be reduced. All of these organizations have recommended ways that this might be accomplished.

One place to begin reducing suspensions is to prune suspendable offenses from a district's discipline code. Most districts have a laundry list of fifteen to twenty-five offenses. Eliminating suspension for truancy, tardiness, and other absence-related offenses is a first step. A second category of offenses for which suspension should be limited are those that are vague and require subjective determination, such as failure to comply with authority.

Examples. Sample disciplinary codes are available from the following organizations.

Children's Defense Fund
1520 Hampshire Avenue, N.W.
Washington, D.C. 20036

Harvard Center for Law and
  Education
6 Appian Way, 3rd Floor
Cambridge, MA 02138

Southeastern Public Education
  Program
1338 Main Street, Suite 501
Columbia, SC 29201

American Association of School
  Administrators
1801 North Moore Street
Arlington, VA 22209

Citizens' Council for Ohio
  Schools
451 The Arcade
Cleveland, OH 44114

National Education Association
1201 16th Street, N.W.
Washington, D.C. 20036

National Association of
  Secondary School Principals
1904 Association Drive
Reston, VA 22091

Create Alternative In-School Programs in Lieu of Suspensions

Both disruption and disproportionate minority suspensions defeat the purposes of desegregation and reduce public and parent support for the school system. When suspensions are disproportionately minority, they can have the effect of resegregating students. This is particularly a problem in schools where minorities comprise relatively small proportions of student bodies. In part because of this resegregative effect and perhaps because of the severity of suspension as a punishment, teachers and administrators may be reluctant to suspend disruptive students in the absence of alternative disciplinary techniques.

Many school systems have developed in-school programs as alternatives to student suspensions. These alternative programs include student referral centers, time-out rooms, in-school suspension, pupil-problem teams, counseling and guidance programs, and Saturday and evening schools. Uncritically instituting one of these programs will not guarantee a reduction in disproportionate minority suspensions. Indeed, if in-school alternative programs remove substantial members of minority students from regular classes for long periods of time, these alternatives may themselves contribute to within-school resegregation. The causes of disproportionate minority suspensions in a particular school must first be understood, and programs should be developed to address those causes.

Effective alternative in-school programs to suspensions in desegregated schools have five important characteristics.

1. They identify the individual problem that led to the misbehavior.
2. They provide assistance, support, encouragement, or active intervention for solving the problem. This includes help for teachers and students. Sometimes teachers have problems dealing with particular kinds of student behavior.
3. They actively work at helping the student keep up with academic work or catch up if the student is behind.
4. They reduce dramatically or eliminate totally the number of out-of-school suspensions.
5. They do not over time resegregate students within the school.

Programs based on all of these characteristics can help schools reduce resegregation and the educational costs that result from suspension and avoid out-of-school suspensions whenever possible.

Evidence. The use of alternatives to suspensions is increasing, but evaluation data tend to be incomplete or fail to address fully the impact on the resegregation of students. Many alternative programs point to reduced use of out-of-school suspensions (see National Institute of Education 1979; Moody, Williams, and Vergon 1978). There is also evidence of low recidivism in some programs. For example, the National Institute of Education (1979) describes a counseling program in which fewer than 12 percent of participants have been subsequently suspended, and an in-school suspension center in which 93 percent have neither been suspended nor returned to that center. Even without a reduction in racial disparity, a reduction in numbers of students suspended should reduce resegregation.

After the creation of in-school suspension programs under a court order, the Dallas school district reported a black suspension rate of close to 40 percent, the proportion of black enrollment. In Jefferson Parish (Louisiana), four out of five middle schools in which an intervention room was established reduced their minority suspensions by 28 percent while in the unserved schools, minority suspensions increased by 29 percent (National Institute of Education 1979). The Positive Alternative to Suspensions (PASS) program in Pinellas County (Florida) reduced suspensions or held them constant while an increase was observed in control group schools (Bailey 1978). That program includes regular classroom instruction in human relations, basic encounter groups for students and staff, time-out rooms, parent training, and school and home survival courses for students with behavior problems. After the PASS program was introduced in all Pinellas County high schools, the number of suspensions was cut by more than one-half.

Administrators of in-school suspension programs and observers continue to express concern about the degree of racial isolation and disproportionality of minority representation in alternative programs themselves. Arnez (1978) cites Louisville-Jefferson County as an example of a district in which referrals to a separate-school program were overwhelmingly black while those to an in-school program were mostly white. Robert F. Arnove and Toby Strout (1980) observed similar situations in other large cities. Participants in the National Institute of Education conference on disciplinary programs observed that in-school suspension centers could become just as disproportionately minority in composition as were out-of-school suspensions. These programs can become identified as minority programs, especially when they involve a voluntary transfer to an alternative school (National Institute of Education 1979).

Other effective programs are described in *Creative Discipline,* a periodical published by the South Eastern Public Education Project, and in studies edited by First and Mizell (1980), and by Charles D. Moody, Junious Williams, and Charles B. Vergon (1978). Reference should also be made to Foster's (1977) study of the Hillsborough County schools and to Willis J. Furtwengler and William Konnert's (1982) research on the effectiveness of discipline strategies.

Student Organizations and Extracurricular Activities

Desegregated Student Governments

It is important that the formal student leaders of a desegregated school be representative of the racial and ethnic groups of that school. Student governments can play an important rule in establishing a favorable racial climate in schools. However, in newly desegregated schools, elections may become racial referenda with bloc voting that prevents members of the school's smaller racial or ethnic group from obtaining seats in the government. The principal should act in this situation to make it clear to the student body that a one-race student government is unacceptable.

Principals have used a variety of techniques to ensure that student governments are desegregated. Some have replaced conventional student councils with multiethnic student committees which have a fixed number of seats for each group. Others have required elections to be among slates of candidates, with each slate representative of the school's racial mix. Some principals have simply announced that they will not approve any elections which do not result in a multiethnic group of officers. Each of these techniques have their limitations, but all will work. The authors do not recommend proportional-representation systems of voting because they generally result in confusion and encourage students to vote for their own group.

Election of multiracial student governments is a necessary first step to improve racial climates, but by itself is not a panacea. In particular, the election of a minority class president in a majority-white school is not evidence that any of the school's racial problems are solved.

Evidence. Crain, Mahard, and Narot (1982) present evidence that integration of the student elite is a valuable desegregation technique. In addition, there are some case studies that support this idea (Rist 1979).

Example. In Charlotte-Mecklenburg County, school administrators established a six-to-three representation of white and black students for student-government councils. The school board rejected the administration's plan, but the students independently adopted this guideline for student government representation. Student race relations in that system are considered good.

Student Human-Relations Committee

Many southern communities created biracial citizen committees to deal with local racial issues. Although they were advisory bodies with no formal power, they nevertheless often were able to intervene in racial issues and resolve problems before they got out of control. Many high schools in the South have formed similar biracial or multiracial human-relations committees with students. These groups receive information and complaints from other students and convey to the administration information about problems and recommendations for their solution. They also organize human-relations activities, develop special projects, and provide rumor control. In many cases, these committees are given credit for preventing racial confrontations. When a problem does occur, there is a ready-made source of trained student leadership to help solve it.

Biracial or multiracial committees and human-relations committees are sometimes elected, sometimes appointed by the student government, and sometimes appointed by the principal. In some committees, the officers and the other committee members are volunteers.

Evidence. Forehand and Ragosta (1976) conclude that student human-relations committees contribute to the effectiveness of desegregated high schools by promoting positive interracial climates. Crain, Mahard, and Narot (1982) present additional evidence in support of this proposition.

Integrated Extracurricular Activities

A great deal of evidence has been presented in this chapter that good race relations can best be brought about by personal contact between white and minority students in an atmosphere of cooperation toward a common goal. This means that for desegregated junior-high and high schools, extracurricular-activities programs may be a central mechanism for creating real integration. Not only will a strong extracurricular-activities program strengthen school race relations, but the improved student morale could enhance achievement as well.

Schools must generally do two things: first, they must offer enough different kinds of extracurricular activities to involve virtually every student, and second, they must work to ensure that all these activities are integrated. To do this, schools must assign staff time to extracurricular activities and must plan their programs carefully to minimize organizations that will appeal to only one group or organizations that elect their own membership on diffuse grounds (such as overall popularity) that will often be racially biased. The principal should monitor extracurricular activities carefully. In a desegregated school there must be adequate transportation to allow students to remain after school. This may be expensive, but the potential benefits seem substantial. Alternately, some schools have scheduled a time period during the school day for extracurricular activities. Since few teachers have special training in the management of extracurricular programs, in-service training is important.

The capacity for some types of extracurricular activities needs to be established early by the school system. For example, schools without instrumental music programs in early grades are not likely to have desegregated bands or orchestras in later grades. Extracurricular programs that most need strengthening include:

1. Female athletics programs. There is reason to believe that minority girls have a particularly difficult time being integrated within desegregated schools.
2. Programs for junior-high-school students.
3. Intramural athletics in larger schools.
4. Interest clubs (electronics, automotive, foreign language, clothing, computers, bowling).
5. Service organizations (volunteer groups for in-school or out-of-school programs). These must be controlled to prevent them from becoming prestige clubs.
6. Human-relations groups.

These programs can be made more effective if a socially and ethnically representative group of the school's participants are involved in planning, developing, and supporting extracurricular activities. Such group planning may reduce the occurrence of one-race activities.

Strong extracurricular-activities programs will also work to build community support for desegregated schools. They involve parents in the school through assistance in activities and attendance at games and concerts, are a good source of media attention, and provide opportunities for students to make contact with adults (through, for example, fund-raising activities). However, extracurricular activities often become resegregated unless efforts are made to prevent this from happening.

Evidence. There is also some empirical evidence that minorities are underrepresented in extracurricular activities. Theory and research suggest that participation in extracurricular activities, especially in those activities requiring cooperation (such as athletic teams or music groups), can have a strong positive impact on intergroup relations. The theoretical work is derived from researchers such as Gordon W. Allport (1954) and Muzafer Sherif (1958). Slavin and Madden's (1979) analysis shows that participation on interracial athletic teams is associated with positive intergroup relations. Crain, Mahard, and Narot (1982) identify a number of positive benefits associated with high levels of extracurricular participation and find that achievement is higher in schools with strong extracurricular programs. In a more recent analysis of southern desegregated high schools, Crain (1981) found that high levels of black and white student participation in extracurricular activities promote increased incidences of interracial contact, improved self-esteem, and led to more positive attitudes toward school, more personal contacts with teachers, and more parental involvement in schools. Marian Rogers, Norman Miller, and Karen Hennigan (1981) found that cooperative recreational activities sharply increased interracial interactions among girls.

The qualitative literature supports this strategy. Reports by the Southern Regional Council (1973, 1979) assert that extracurricular activities are effective ways to foster desegregation and reduce levels of resegregation. The consensus literature is nearly unanimous in its support for this strategy (Smith, Downs, and Lachman 1973; Forehand and Ragosta 1976; Murphy 1980). In addition, the experts that were interviewed provide considerable support for integrated extracurricular programs but do not link it directly or solely to the reduction of resegregation.

On the issue of how to develop effective extracurricular programs, 86 percent of the interviewees recommend some form of postimplementation community involvement ranging from in-school committees to districtwide committees. The local experts reported that these committee efforts were effective in producing student acceptance of desegregation in their districts.

Examples. The Shaker Heights (Ohio) school system will not fund or otherwise support extracurricular activities that are not racially integrated. Some schools in that district have converted the homeroom period into a social-group activity. One school grouped entering ninth graders together with a teacher into a homeroom period and left the group and teacher together for the four years of high school. Each homeroom was ethnically balanced and conducted various social activities over the four years. There was considerable resistance to this program from some teachers who felt unskilled in groupwork. Some school systems have emphasized the importance of extracurricular activities by taking them as an indication of the success of their overall efforts. In Stockton, for example, student participation is used as a measure of evaluation of integrative results of desegregation (Carter 1979).

Summary

School systems that expect to achieve effective desegregation need to be concerned not only about pupil assignment and the racial, ethnic, and socioeconomic compositions of schools but also about how schools respond to the educational and social needs of their students. In other words, districts should be equally concerned with desegregated schooling as they are with desegregating schools.

Desegregated schools are often more academically and socially heterogeneous than segregated schools. This academic heterogeneity makes issues concerning class and school size, tracking, and ability grouping important to effective desegregation. In addition, academic heterogeneity suggests a need for cooperative-learning techniques and other instrumental strategies that have been designed for academically heterogeneous classrooms. The social heterogeneity of desegregated schools requires the development and implementation of conscious strategies to ensure a reasonable balance of power and recognition among groups to foster interracial interaction, encourage previously excluded groups to participate in the life of the school, and foster equitable treatment of all students while being responsive to the different needs of students from different backgrounds.

The interracial and interethnic interactions that are essential to achieving good race relations are not an automatic outcome of school desegregation and must be promoted through specific programs and activities. These programs and activities include integrating a multicultural and multiethnic perspective into curricula and the noninstructional activities of schools. They should also be structured to promote friendly, equal-status contacts among students of different races and ethnic backgrounds and opportunities for them to work together toward common goals.

The maintenance of order in desegregated schools is essential and should be an early and high priority. Schools should also examine their disciplinary procedures and techniques to avoid tendencies in newly desegregated schools toward resegregation. Students and all staff members should be called upon to develop codes of discipline that are substantively fair and that can be administered in an equitable manner.

The effectiveness of school desegregation can be enhanced by strategies to actively involve students of different races and ethnic backgrounds in all school activities, including student organizations and extracurricular activities. Effective desegregation can further be enhanced by increasing the involvement of parents in the classroom and in other activities of schools.

The strategies presented in this chapter are those that the research indicates are effective in increasing student achievement, promoting positive interracial interactions, and avoiding resegregation after initial implementation of desegregation plans. Certainly, most of these strategies will not be effective without modification to the particular characteristics of individual schools and classrooms. However, the availability of a great number of instructional strategies and techniques for organizing and managing schools and classrooms that have been found to be effective in the research leads one to a very important point—in desegregating and desegregated schools there need not be a tradeoff between educational equity and educational quality.

Most of the strategies contained in this chapter have a much greater chance of success if administrators, teachers, and other staff members are knowledgeable about and committed to desegregation, organizational change, and educational innovation. Desegregation presents most educators with new experiences and opportunities which challenge their professional capabilities and personal values and dispositions. It is important, therefore, that school systems provide in-service training to prepare teachers for change and to help them develop and implement the instructional and management strategies that meet the needs of their students and that promote changes in schools to achieve effective desegregation.

8

In-Service Training for School Desegregation

School desegregation presents most educators with new experiences which challenge their professional capabilities, personal values, and dispositions. It follows that in-service-training programs should provide teachers with knowledge, insights, and skills to cope with change. Such programs are thought to combat rigidity in teachers' attitudes and instructional practices by facilitating the development of flexibility in dealing with new instructional demands and challenges in relations with students and colleagues.

The intuitive sensibility of the need for in-service training in desegregating schools is reflected in the provisions of many desegregation plans for public elementary and secondary schools. Most desegregation experts agree that in-service training is necessary to prepare educators for changes in schools that result from desegregation (see Broh and Trent 1981; James A. Banks 1976; Felkner, Goering, and Linden 1971; Genova and Walberg 1980). For example, William H. Banks, Jr. (1977) observes that many of the problems experienced during the desegregation of the Louisville-Jefferson County schools might have been avoided if the district provided teachers and administrators with more extensive and better planned training to deal with anticipated and unanticipated change.

Despite agreement among researchers and academicians and the requirements of desegregation plans, educators frequently express skepticism about the usefulness of in-service training for desegregation. Indeed, such doubt regarding the effectiveness of often uncritically planned and implemented in-service programs may be well founded. Although most desegregation experts emphasize the importance of in-service programs, remarkably little research has undergirded the case for the effectiveness of particular desegregation-training strategies. The greatest portion of the literature on desegregation-specific training is qualitative and descriptive. Few empirical studies examine this type of training.

The evidence on desegregation-specific training is problematical for a number of reasons. First, studies measure a variety of outcomes to identify effective or successful in-service-training activities. Most deter-

Portions of an earlier version of this chapter appeared in Mark A. Smylie and Willis D. Hawley, *Increasing the Effectiveness of Inservice Training for Desegregation: A Synthesis of Current Research* (Washington, D.C.: National Education Association, 1982).

mine program effectiveness in terms of change in participants' attitudes, behavior, or proficiency; few measure effectiveness in terms of changes in student attitudes, behavior, or academic achievement. Many studies stress effects of training on the attitudes and behavior of educators, usually measured by perceptions of participants themselves, their supervisors, or other observers rather than by more systematic and objective modes of assessment.

A second problem of the research on desegregation-specific in-service training is that the impact of programs on participants or students is seldom measured over time. Most evaluations are administered immediately after programs conclude but before teachers attempt to apply training in the classroom. As Meyer Weinberg notes:

> The most basic problem of existing research on inservice training is the failure to study the practical classroom application of findings. Typically, a summer workshop is held; participants are pretested and posttested; a positive change in attitudes may be recorded. This outcome is hailed as evidence of a successful experience. But no effort is usually made to discover whether the classroom teacher acts any differently when he or she returns to the classroom (1977, p. 240).

Another problem of the existing research on in-service training for desegregation is the validity of generalizing findings of specific studies to broader contexts. Most research examines training in a single school or district. Programs studied are usually developed and implemented to meet specific needs and concerns of educational settings that differ in terms of student and staff characteristics, school organization, and styles of administrative leadership. It is risky, therefore, to apply strategies found to be effective in these limited contexts to other educational settings. Findings of research on specific programs may serve to guide the planning and conduct of other programs, but they cannot be used to justify wholesale adoption of program models because they have been determined to produce positive outcomes in other schools and districts.

In the research, as in practice, distinction is often made between training for desegregation and general in-service training. In many respects, however, these types of training are very similar. The problems teachers and administrators confront in desegregated settings are usually variations of the problems and opportunities they encounter prior to desegregation. At the bottom line, the goals of desegregation-specific and general in-service training are the same—promoting student achievement, improving classroom management and discipline, promoting positive relations among students, and stimulating curricular innovation. If problems of desegregated settings are variations of problems encountered by educators in nondesegregated contexts, useful information about the effectiveness of different approaches to conducting desegregation-specific training can be gained from research on general training programs. Many of these studies shed light on relationships between training and both educator and student outcomes alluded to but not demonstrated by studies of desegregation-specific training.

The chapter is concerned primarily with strategies that promote useful and effective in-service programs in desegregated schools. As is the case with general in-service training, the effectiveness of in-service training for desegregation depends on at least four factors: (1) the manner in which training is conducted, (2) the content of training, (3) which groups participate, and (4) who conducts the training programs. Each of these factors is discussed in this chapter. In addition, this chapter presents the findings of research that assesses the impact of in-service training on educators and students.

Strategies for Planning and Conducting In-Service Training for Desegregation

The design of an in-service program involves two basic types of decisions: first, what topics should be addressed? and, second, how should training be conducted? Most discussions focus on the first of these questions. Yet, unless in-service training is developed in ways that promote learning and behavioral change, efforts spent designing the content of programs will have little consequence. Often, strategies used in providing educators with in-service training lack the sophistication of instructional strategies that educators themselves employ to facilitate learning in the classroom.

Few studies empirically examine the effectiveness of particular approaches to desegregation-specific training on teacher and administrator attitudes and behavior or consider how such training affects student achievement and race relations. Despite the lack of such direct evidence, some agreement exists that certain general strategies of in-service education will enhance the knowledge and capabilities of educators. Each strategy should be considered in planning and implementing in-service programs.

General Strategies

General strategies for planning and implementing in-service training for desegregation are similar to those for in-service training in nondesegregated settings. (Useful research on effective inservice education includes the work of Mohlman [1982], Burrello and Orbaugh [1982], and Howey,

Bents, and Corrigan [1981].) These strategies follow a general sequential and cyclical pattern.

1. The planning and development of in-service-training programs should be preceded by a needs assessment by members of a school's staff.
2. Planning of the content and procedure of in-service training should be based on the needs assessment. Specific goals for training and strategies for their achievement should be well established in this process.
3. Means should be developed at the start to evaluate consequences of training. Evaluation criteria should coincide with training goals.
4. Actual training should reflect the goals established in the planning process and should address the specific problems and needs identified in the initial assessment.
5. Training sessions should be evaluated to determine whether program goals were addressed and training procedures were followed. Anticipated and unanticipated outcomes of training should also be assessed. Evaluation should be made continuously to determine the impact of training over time.
6. Program evaluation should be followed by another needs assessment to identify problems that should be addressed in subsequent in-service training.
7. Training that aims for long-range change needs follow-up components which focus on individual problems of participants applying what was learned to classroom settings. Follow-up sessions should be based on evaluation of the training sessions and should themselves be followed by evaluation and a needs assessment for further training.
8. In-service training should be a continuous process that is integrated with the regular activities of each school.
9. The process of in-service education should reflect the principles and practices being taught to participants.
10. Training should address individual needs to foster collective participation of the staff in a school and schoolwide adaption and change.

Specific Strategies

Several specific strategies for conducting in-service training for desegregation should be implemented within the general framework already outlined.

    1. Faculty members, administrators, and nonprofessional staff should understand the desegregation order, the desegregation plan, and

the implications of the plan's implementation to the district, individual schools, and in-service participants. Throughout the in-service process, participants should be made aware of the relationship between training and the implementation of successful desegregation of their schools.

2. The needs assessment should strive to identify problems and needs of individual teachers, administrators, and other members of school staffs that should be addressed in training programs. It should not be conducted by administrators alone nor should it reflect only one group's perceptions of problems and needs throughout the school. All members of a school's staff should be given the opportunity to express individual needs and opinions about how in-service training might be approached to best meet those needs. The assessment may be conducted in a number of ways. Surveys and group discussions frequently are successful methods to implement this strategy.

3. Participants should be included in the planning and design of in-service programs. Teachers and administrators are capable of informing the planning process with respect to specific needs and problems of individual schools.

4. Whenever possible, faculty members and administrators of host schools should be involved in the conduct of in-service training. Participants take more responsibility for training and learning if they are able to influence both the planning and implementation of in-service programs.

5. If trainers are brought in from outside the school system, they need to have knowledge of district and single-school matters. Teacher and administrator participation in planning and conducting training serves this function. Teachers and administrators often respond better to peers from their own and other schools than they do to professional consultants or university professors.

6. All members of groups targeted for training should participate in in-service programs. Ideally, training should be perceived by educators as important enough to warrant full participation. Realistically, incentives should be provided for total participation. Financial rewards, course credit, or certificate-renewal credit might be offered. After one form of inducement loses appeal, another should be tried. If strategies for voluntary participation fail, training should be mandatory. Time and resources for training should be built into participants' contractual time.

7. Teachers and administrators usually should participate in in-service programs together since they can reinforce each other to implement what is learned through training. Furthermore, teachers and administrators need to develop through training school-level norms that foster more effective desegregation-related practices.

8. Training should be designed to encourage individual participation in programs not merely attendance at them. Training incorporating dia-

logue between participants and trainers and among participants themselves is usually more effective than training through lectures or other means that preclude active participant involvement.

9. Small-group formats usually are better than larger schoolwide or multischool formats because they allow for identification of and concentration on problems of individual participants within school settings. It follows that the specific content of in-service training should be oriented toward school-level and not districtwide concerns. Problems and needs of individual schools often differ from those of other schools or of a system at large.

10. Training should be practical with a product orientation and hands-on experiences for immediate application. Abstract or theoretical presentations without practical components offer little immediate assistance to teachers and administrators and as a result, participants tend to view such programs as providing slight, if any, benefit.

11. Little attempt should be made to directly change attitudes of participants. In-service efforts to change attitudes must be long-term and, particularly in the area of interpersonal relations, should be pursued by providing educators with specific positive behavioral responses to perceived problems.

12. Programs on different topics should be coordinated and linkages between training areas should be established to provide continuity.

13. Training programs should be continuous. Simply providing workshops before schools open or infrequent training sessions is not likely to have much long-term effect.

14. In-service training should be incorporated as a component of total school or district functions. Desegregation-related training should be tied to central concerns of educators such as facilitating achievement and classroom management.

15. Whenever possible, desegregation-specific programs should be combined with general in-service training. As already asserted, the problems teachers and administrators confront in desegregated settings are usually variations of those encountered prior to desegregation. Moreover, labeling an in-service program desegregation specific may result in a loss of interest by educators who believe that desegregation is an unnecessary burden or that the goals of desegregation are not important goals of the educational process.

No one type of in-service-training format works across all school settings. In-service-training planners should be wary of adopting a program model without modification simply because that model has been thought to be effective in another school or district. Generally, effective types of in-service-training programs appear tailored to specific settings and address themselves to particular problems of those settings.

Evidence. Analyses by Nicelma King, Maureen F. Carney, and Cathleen Stasz (1980) and case studies edited by Carney (1979a, 1979b, 1979c, 1979d) of in-service-training programs in desegregated school districts provide evidence of the effectiveness of the general and specific strategies already outlined. In a survey of sixteen desegregated school districts, King and her colleagues conclude that effective training programs are based on a formal needs assessment and are well planned and evaluated. King defines a formal assessment method as one that is routinized, clearly understood by trainers and participants, and can be described by most school staff members. Most of the less effective training programs examined in this study omitted one or more of the assessment, planning, or evaluation components.

David L. Williams (1980) argues from the findings of surveys and interviews of school personnel, parents, and students in six southern states that no one strategy or set of strategies is adequate to facilitate successful training. Programs should incorporate a variety of techniques to meet individual needs of participants. Training should not be fragmented in content or short term in duration. Further, he asserts that training should involve all personnel in individual schools and foster collegiality. Leonard C. Beckum and Stephan J. Dasho (1981a) stress that provision of specific behavioral responses is essential if in-service training is to have any long-term impact. In addition, they argue from evidence presented in their case study that all training programs should be based on schoolwide needs assessments.

In a survey of schools in four states, Kenneth R. Howey (1978) found that teachers in his sample perceived job-related training more effective if conducted by colleagues than by university professors or other outside consultants. Teachers believed peers were more sensitive to individual and school-related problems and concerns than were outside trainers. In addition, surveyed teachers preferred small group formats that allowed discussion and problem solving to large lecture programs or courses held outside their schools.

Judith W. Little (1981) contends that the process and content of in-service training must focus on collegiality, experimentation, and organizational change for schools to successfully deal with the challenges posed by desegregation. In a study of elementary and secondary schools in a desegregated urban district, she found that effective in-service training fostered frequent, continuous, and concrete talk among teachers and administrators about teaching practices. Effective training also encouraged frequent peer observation and evaluation, promoted joint development of teaching materials for long-term improvements, and led to teachers and administrators teaching each other about the practice of teaching.

Example. In-service training in the Nashville-Davidson County public schools is organized around many of the strategies discussed previously. This district's teacher center has adopted a professional team (Proteam) model for training which was developed for the United States Department of Education and is described in a department publication entitled *The School Team Approach* (1980). Seven-member teacher-administrator teams from each school in the district are trained at the center to conduct school-level needs assessments and assist in planning and conducting in-service activities at the center and in their separate schools. Several Proteams conduct self-initiated activities at the school level and have become essentially independent in addressing the problems and concerns of individual teachers and administrators. School-level training needs identified by individual Proteams are fed back to the center and are used to develop additional districtwide training programs.

The emphasis of in-service training in Nashville-Davidson County has shifted since court-ordered desegregation in 1971 from human-relations training for desegregation to training that addresses instructional, curricular, and interpersonal relations needs of a desegregated school system. The desegregation-specific concerns to be addressed in training are now related to broader concerns of the school district such as increasing student achievement, promoting curricular innovation, and improving classroom management and discipline. The district requires that all school personnel, including teachers, nonprofessional staff members, and school-level and central-office administrators, participate in a specific number of training sessions. However, educators are provided latitude to choose among a variety of programs that specifically address their own professional concerns. Each training program is evaluated and findings are used to plan follow-up training. In-service programs also involve substantial numbers of parents and other adults in the community. The effectiveness of the Nashville-Davidson County's in-service-training program was noted in a 1981 federal district-court order mandating its continuance as a new desegregation plan for the district is developed and implemented.

Types of In-Service Training for Desegregation

Topics of in-service training for desegregation generally fall into five categories: (1) instructional methods; (2) curricula; (3) self-awareness, empathy, and interpersonal relations; (4) discipline techniques and classroom management strategies; and (5) parental involvement in school affairs. In some instances, training deals with the development of human-relations programs for students. Examples of these programs are discussed in chapter 7. Because efforts to improve human relations among students embody aspects of other in-service-training topics addressed in this chapter, this concern is not singled out as a unique subject of training.

Although each of the topics of in-service training for desegregation is examined separately, their contents are not mutually exclusive, nor do they differ significantly from topics addressed in general in-service training in nondesegregated schools. Evidence from the research strongly suggests that each of these topics are interrelated. One topic may be emphasized more than another, but no one content area should be stressed to the exclusion of the rest. For example, training teachers and administrators to develop and administer discipline and classroom management techniques alone may prove counterproductive without programs that deal with self-awareness of attitudes and behavior, empathy toward students, and interpersonal relations.

In addition, topics of in-service training for desegregation often relate to concerns addressed in general in-service training for improving academic achievement and interpersonal relations among students, teachers, and administrators. The components of desegregation-specific training are also similar to those of bilingual training programs and include assessment of learning needs and styles of students in heterogeneous classrooms and cultural awareness. In much the same way the processes of in-service training for desegregation are similar to general in-service training, program topics addressed in desegregation-specific training correspond to those that should be presented in training related to other areas of the educational enterprise.

In-Service Training in Instructional Methodology

Often, teachers in desegregated schools are confronted with instructional situations in which techniques that are successful with more homogeneous student groups no longer apply or at least are more difficult to implement. In-service training that centers on specific instructional strategies to assist teachers in heterogeneous classrooms can provide practical options to outmoded instructional techniques and opportunities for resolution of problems that result from the implementation of new strategies. Examples of techniques that are useful in heterogeneous classrooms include cooperative learning, small group or individual instruction, student tutors, and team teaching. These techniques are discussed in detail in chapter

7. In addition, this type of training is often linked with efforts to improve basic skills and with the development and implementation of multicultural curricula. This section deals with in-service training as it relates to instructional techniques. The following section discusses in-service training as it relates to curricula.

Classroom instruction does not take place in a vacuum. Adoption and application of new instructional techniques must be considered after assessment of the contexts in which new strategies are to be employed. For example, Miranda Braun (1977) argues that failure to successfully develop and implement new instructional strategies may be due to a lack of perception and understanding of new ethnic and cultural contexts in desegregated schools. This suggests that in-service training in instructional strategies should be combined with programs designed to assist teachers and administrators in understanding the nature and characteristics of their changed student bodies.

Although understanding the ethnic and cultural heterogeneity of desegregated schools is a precondition to the development and implementation of successful instructional strategies, in-service programs that seek to promote an understanding of cultural and ethnic differences are insufficient to adequately prepare educators to teach diverse student groups. According to Beckum and Dasho (1980), training must also provide concrete instructional techniques that address academic needs of students in desegregated settings.

Evidence. King and her colleagues (1980) conclude that in-service training for teachers in instructional methods is an effective way to improve teacher competency and teachers' approaches to diverse student populations. Teachers and administrators surveyed in the study indicate that this type of training is important, and most desire expansion of programs related to instructional techniques. The Institute for Teacher Leadership (1979) stresses that in order for teachers to meet the changing academic needs of students in desegregated schools, they should undergo training in instructional methods that relate to the different learning styles of children.

Although these studies of desegregation-specific programs do not provide definitive evidence that training of this kind leads to improvement in student achievement, it seems reasonable that this relationship exists. Several studies that examine the impact of in-service programs in non-desegregated settings suggest that training in specific instructional techniques does lead to improved student attitudes toward school and their peers, fewer disciplinary problems, and increased levels of student achievement. Paul G. Whitmore, William H. Melching, and Edward W. Frederickson (1972) found evidence that students' reading and math achievement in the second through seventh grades improved significantly after their teachers had undergone training in the development and use of instructional objectives, implementation of learning modules and mastery tests, and employment of contingency classroom-management techniques. William J. Moore and Judith A. Schaut (1976) conclude that training teachers to use instructional strategies to reduce student inattention increases student learning in the classroom. This study suggests that such in-service training positively related to improving student achievement inasmuch as increasing student attention to learning decreases opportunities for disruptive behavior and facilitates greater academic achievement. In another study, Mary L. Kruse (1976) found that students of teachers who participated in training oriented toward child-centered instructional strategies showed an average one-year gain in reading skills across pretest and posttest measures.

Several studies show that training to increase instructional capabilities of teachers increases their self-confidence in the classroom and improves their attitudes toward students. These outcomes, in turn, are found to relate to gains in students' academic performance. For example, Mercedes D. Fitzmaurice (1976) concludes that in-service training in diagnostic and prescriptive approaches to instruction not only produces higher levels of student spelling and reading achievement but improves teachers' attitudes toward students. This study suggests that a relationship exists between instructional strategies and teachers' attitudes toward improving student achievement. It further suggests that teachers' attitudes toward students may partially be determined by their ability to employ successful instructional techniques. In other words, teachers' attitudes toward students may be improved by giving them the ability to use instructional methods that are appropriate in situations where other strategies have proven ineffective. John W. Miller and Randy Ellsworth (1982) found that teachers who participated in a comprehensive program to improve their reading instruction exhibited both greater knowledge about reading instruction and more positive attitudes about teaching reading and about their students than nonparticipant teachers.

A survey of elementary school teachers in Urbana (Illinois) presents additional evidence of this relationship between instructional proficiency and the attitudes of teachers toward their students. Roger B. Marcum (1968) found that although teachers in this district generally favored desegregation, a substantial proportion expressed reluctance to work with minority students. The survey suggests that this unwillingness was due not to expressed racial prejudice but to teachers' beliefs that they were not prepared to teach minority students.

In a more recent study, Stanley H.L. Chow, Carol F. Rice, and Lynn A. Whitmore (1976) show that in-service training in tutoring skills for heterogeneous classrooms results in significant gains in teachers' attitudes toward academically disadvantaged students. Gains in student math achievement were attributed not only to the application of new instructional methods but also to improvement in the dispositions of teachers. Teachers who did not receive training in these techniques showed no significant gain on the measures of attitude, and their students exhibited no improvement in achievement.

Example. The Maureen F. Carney case studies (1979b, 1979c, 1979d) also emphasize the need for and general effectiveness of in-service training in instructional techniques. For example, Marvinia Hunter found evidence of effective training in instructional methodology conducted by a western urban school district with a student population of 13,750 that is 51 percent minority (Carney 1979d). In-service-training programs sponsored by a state-funded professional development center focus on skill training in five areas: (1) behavioral objectives, (2) diagnosis, (3) prescriptive instruction, (4) lesson analysis, and (5) application of learning theory through instructional techniques. The program is structured around five cycles that emphasize basic knowledge, understanding, and application of effective instructional skills and conclude with on-site assistance to participants in the implementation of techniques. Most teachers indicated that the in-service program helped them feel more competent about teaching, and administrators feel more competent about supervising instructional processes. Most respondents also believed that improving teaching methods leads to improved student academic achievement although test scores in this district had not substantially improved when this survey was administered.

In-Service Training Related to Curricula

Desegregation often results in increased demands for educational quality and relevance. These demands prompt many school districts to reassess instructional techniques; reexamine and alter existing curricula; and develop multiethnic, multicultural, human-relations, and perhaps alternative magnet programs to meet the educational interests and needs of heterogeneous student bodies. A greater capability for teaching from a multiethnic perspective is often required of educators regardless of the ages of the students or the courses they teach. As a result, educators frequently express a need for in-service training that helps them make curricular transitions and provides them with instructional strategies that may be used to teach new curricula.

Often, in-service training in curricula goes hand-in-hand with training in instructional techniques. Programs that stress new content areas should be accompanied by training to facilitate classroom implementation of new curricula. In other words, training to promote new instructional strategies may be necessary to ensure that new curricula are implemented success-fully. Regardless of which new types of curricula are adopted, it is particularly important that teachers and administrators be given the op-portunity to identify content areas that are appropriate to their local sit-uations and the particular needs of their students.

In-service training related to curricula should be (1) responsive to the needs assessments of teachers and administrators, (2) sufficiently prac-tical and specific so that educators can use actual practices and materials that facilitate the implementation of chosen curricula, and (3) presented so that emphases on practicality do not obscure the basic theories and propositions that underly the content of new curricula. Without this third component, educators may find themselves saddled with specific pro-grams, some of which are prepackaged without the bases to adapt and modify them to meet students' instructional needs.

Evidence. King and her colleagues (1980) indicate that in-service training for curricular change is common in newly desegregated districts. In gen-eral, training that emphasizes multiethnic and multicultural education and, to a certain extent, basic skills is considered effective in helping teachers adopt course content to the specific needs and interests of mi-nority students. This study also indicates that training in curricula may be more successful than training in interpersonal relations and discipline because curricula are often perceived to be less value laden by educators. In some districts, effective interpersonal-relations and discipline programs are given a curricular emphasis to make in-service training more value neutral (Carney 1979b, 1979c, 1979d).

John F. Greene, Francis Archambault, and William Nolen (1976) examined the impact of in-service training in curricula and instructional strategies on elementary school teachers' knowledge of and attitudes toward teaching mathematics. This study found that although significant increases in positive attitudes were related to training in both areas, the greatest determinant of improved attitudes among participant teachers was training in new approaches to curricula.

These findings, though not directly related to desegregated settings, do have implications for desegregation-specific in-service training. As suggested in the discussion of training in instructional methods, teachers need opportunities to explore different approaches to curricula that meet the educational needs of changed student bodies. Provision of new instructional strategies, though certainly helpful, may not be enough to improve teachers' capabilities and attitudes unless these methods are consistent with and facilitative of new curricula. It is reasonable to suggest, therefore, that teachers' attitudes toward their subject matter may best be improved by training that addresses both instructional strategies and curricula. The study by Greene and his colleagues (1976) supports this contention.

Example. Beth Osthimer describes multiethnic in-service training conducted through an ethnic-culture center in a midwestern school system of about fifty-eight thousand students (Carney 1979c). Approximately 26 percent of this district's student enrollment is minority. The overall purpose of the program is to train teachers in the theory, development, and implementation of multiethnic curricula. The program centers around workshops conducted by outside consultants and district resource personnel. The first sessions emphasize the philosophy of cultural pluralism, separatism, and theories of ethnic and cultural mixing. Training then shifts to developing sample lessons and using multiethnic materials. Finally, participants are assisted to develop their own lessons to use with students. Classroom teachers were observed by trainers to determine if multiethnic materials were being used and if their use had any impact on classroom activities. In order to correct perceived difficulties of integrating multiethnic emphases into general curricula, additional training sessions were conducted on the basis of an informal needs assessment. This training component involves formulating lesson plans, implementing them in the classroom, reporting back to the training group, and disseminating successful plans to other teachers.

In-Service Training in Interpersonal Relations

There is general agreement that in-service training for teachers and administrators to improve relations with and among students is a necessary component of desegregation. Most experts believe that increasing teachers' self-awareness of their race-related attitudes and behavior is vital for improving student-teacher relations in desegregated schools (see Broh and Trent 1981). Furthermore, it is thought that increasing teacher empathy for and sensitivity to individual student's attitudes, behavior, and instructional and psychological needs facilitates the development and implementation of more effective and less challenging techniques in instruction, classroom management, and student discipline. Ideally, interpersonal relations and related training should enable teachers and administrators to better respond not only to the needs and behaviors of ethnically and racially different students but also to ethnically and racially different colleagues.

A variety of approaches to interpersonal-relations training exists in terms of both format and content, and there is little agreement about which prove most effective. In general, however, three aspects of this type of training seem important:

1. Training should concern itself with specific needs of individual schools and participants and with characteristics of student bodies.
2. The effectiveness of training that seeks to change teacher attitudes and behavior appears to be directly related to a certain degree of preliminary self-awareness that interpersonal-relations problems either exist or could exist in their particular schools and to participant receptivity to training programs. This receptivity is influenced by the degree to which participants believe training programs are potentially effective (see Winecoff and Kelly 1971).
3. Attempts to directly change attitudes are much less effective than training in behavioral responses to particular sources of interpersonal conflict or prejudice. These behavioral changes often are followed by changes in attitudes.

This last point should be emphasized. Few people are willing to acknowledge that they are insensitive to or prejudiced toward others, especially children of another race. Thus, working in a direct way to change attitudes or increase sensitivity may seem unnecessary and even insulting to educators. Interpersonal-relations training should emphasize, therefore, the identification of positive behaviors in much the same way that training in instructional methods focuses on theory and technique.

Evidence. Henry Acland (1975) identifies positive results of interpersonal-relations training to improve teachers' attitudes and increase teachers' expectancies of minority students. The United States Commission on Civil Rights (1976) reports that interpersonal-relations training is an effective way to alter teachers' and administrators' attitudes and behavior that lead to differential treatment of students by race. Also, William J. Doherty and his colleagues (1981) conclude that interpersonal-relations training is related to positive student attitudes toward school, particularly among minority students. In addition, this study finds that the percentage of minority nonprofessional staff receiving interpersonal-relations training is related to improving interracial attitudes of all students and interracial behavior of minority students.

Examples. Several studies of local in-service programs indicate that training in interpersonal relations improves teachers' attitudes and student-teacher interactions. Data from an assessment of federally supported in-service-training project in Los Angeles (1974) suggest that providing teachers with supportive and motivating techniques for all students improves their attitudes toward low achievers and accelerates the academic growth of those students. Stephen B. Hillman and G. Gregory Davenport (1977) found that interpersonal-relations training in Detroit increased cross-race student-teacher interactions in the classroom. Before training, these types of interactions occurred infrequently. It was noted in this study, however, that although cross-race interactions increased as a result of training, in certain instances minority students began to receive a disproportionate amount of attention from teachers. Although this study deems increased frequency of cross-race interaction beneficial, it may be that too frequent interaction and too much attention are dysfunctional to improving student-teacher relations.

In other studies of local in-service programs, George L. Redman (1977) discovered significant increases in teacher empathy toward minority students as a result of interpersonal-relations training in the Minnesota public schools. In an earlier study of this program, Michael E. Carl and Larry W. Jones (1972) found that participation in training increased teacher flexibility, self-awareness of attitudes and behavior, and sensitivity to colleagues and students.

Nancy Schniedewind (1975) evaluated an in-service-training program in classroom strategies for dealing with racism and sexism. The program, implemented in St. Mary's County and Prince George's County Maryland school districts, focused on analysis of modification of teaching behavior, on interpersonal relations, and on microteaching. When compared with a control group, teachers who participated in the training exhibited significant increases in self-awareness and self-confidence that they could change their attitudes and behavior and make a positive impact on the learning environment. Participants showed signs of growing trust in colleagues. Finally, participants exhibited increased awareness of racism and sexism while the control group of nonparticipating teachers regressed slightly on this measure.

In-Service Training to Improve Discipline Techniques and Classroom Management

Training for dealing with disruptive classroom behavior, ranging from lessened respect for authority to personal threat, is a need increasingly expressed by educators. Improving capacities in these areas may reduce the use of unnecessary suspensions or felt needs for grouping techniques that may address discipline problems but foster resegregation within schools. This type of training seems particularly important for schools that are undergoing the initial period of desegregation.

Classroom discipline techniques are generally of two types: first, preventive techniques, and second, punitive techniques. Desegregation experts generally agree that effective techniques to prevent or correct discipline problems involve components of effective classroom management, empathy, sensitivity, and concepts of fairness, equal treatment of students, and due process (see Broh and Trent 1981). In-service training in interpersonal relations, classroom management, and instructional strategies helps create positive and more comfortable classroom environments. This, in turn, reduces antagonistic relations which might lead to discipline problems. Furthermore, training in these areas may facilitate positive teacher attitudes and behavior that better assist them to deal with occurrences of discipline in an equitable and nonresegregative manner.

Although in-service training in instructional techniques and interpersonal relations relates to ways in which teachers approach discipline in their classrooms, teachers often express a need for programs that equip them with specific discipline techniques for immediate application. Often, in-service programs that provide such techniques are effective in helping teachers develop methods for preventing and reprimanding disruptive student behavior. It should be stressed, however, that this type of training may be ineffective in the long run without the provision of programs in interpersonal relations and instructional strategies that help teachers improve their attitudes about and relations with students and create positive learning and social environments to avoid situations that result in disciplinary problems.

Evidence. King and her colleagues (1980) found evidence that teacher requests for conflict- and discipline-management training differ considerably between desegregated and nondesegregated school districts. Teachers in recently desegregated districts request this type of training far more frequently than teachers in nondesegregated districts or districts that have been desegregated for some time. King reports that in-service training in discipline techniques contributes to successful desegregation because staff members believe it helps prevent desegregation-related student-behavior problems. In addition, teachers and administrators tend to believe that this type of training improves morale and promotes feelings of competence because it provides specific methods for dealing with behavioral problems of students.

Carney (1979b, 1979c, 1979d) also indicates that there is a great demand for in-service training in classroom-discipline techniques among teachers in recently desegregated school systems. In exemplary programs, discipline-specific training is but one part of a more comprehensive training agenda that, in most instances, places primary emphasis on interpersonal relations. Although the relative effectiveness of training in discipline techniques cannot be evaluated apart from other aspects of inservice programs, the success of discipline-specific programs appears directly related to effective interpersonal-relations training.

The available evidence does not suggest that interpersonal-relations training can take the place of training related to classroom management. As Walter R. Borg (1977) found, training designed solely to improve teacher and student self-concepts and student-teacher interactions has little impact on reducing mildly and seriously deviant student behavior. However, training in classroom management techniques was shown to reduce incidences of these types of behavior.

Programs on discipline techniques and classroom management and training in interpersonal relations are mutually reinforcing. Data presented by Jeannette A. Brown, Mary A. MacDougall, and Charles A. Jenkins (1972) suggest that although the solution to many disciplinary problems lies in the development and implementation of classroom-management techniques, avoidance of disciplinary practices detrimental to positive classroom environments and learning seems to rest with providing teachers with training opportunities to assess their behavior in the classroom and improve their general interactions with students. This study found that teacher assessments of students' ability to perform school-related tasks and of students' propensity for good behavior in the classroom are related to student self-assessment on these measures. The findings suggest that if teachers develop favorable concepts of students and those concepts are communicated to them, student self-concepts will improve and discipline problems will decrease.

In a survey of research assessing the effectiveness of staffing practices and in-service training to help schools manage student conflict and alienation, Irwin A. Hyman (1979) found scattered evidence that in-service programs help reduce student-discipline problems. Hyman suggests that training in discipline techniques and interpersonal relations has a positive effect on changing teachers' attitudes toward students and that these changes in attitude tend to improve student self-image, reduce punitive teacher behavior, and lower incidences of disruptive student behavior. When these changes occur on a schoolwide basis, Hyman concludes that the total learning climate is improved.

Example. The Positive Alternatives to Student Suspension Program of the St. Petersburg public schools, for example, effectively combines interpersonal-relations programs with training in school and classroom-discipline techniques (Bailey 1978). This program offers participants strategies for crisis and remedial intervention that include use of a time-out room to which students are sent to talk out their problems and devise plans to resolve their difficulties with the assistance of a facilitative listener. Another focus of the program is the development of a student school-survival course. Students with recurrent behavioral problems are referred to this course that meets once a week. Under the guidance of a skilled leader, students having problems are taught that it is possible to survive in school and to receive positive feedback from teachers, administrators, and other students. Training in these crisis and remedial intervention strategies is accompanied by extensive interpersonal-relations programs designed to prevent discipline problems. These programs focus on increasing teacher sensitivity to students' behavior and needs and on helping teachers devise means by which classroom environments and student-teacher relations may be improved. The central purpose of the interpersonal-relations components of training is to promote more effective communication systems among teachers and students, teacher and administrators, and teachers themselves through participation in non-threatening activities that emphasize positive verbal expression.

Comment. It seems likely that instances of disruptive behavior may be reduced if teachers are trained to implement instructional strategies and alter curricula to increase students' interest in learning and their academic success. Many of the instructional strategies described in chapter 7 seek to promote achievement and student involvement in learning activities within a management framework that may improve student discipline. Therefore, in-service programs aimed at improving student conduct should include training in discipline techniques as well as training in interpersonal relations, instructional strategies, and curricular innovation.

In-Service Training for Parent Involvement in Schools

Almost all experts on school desegregation stress the importance of various ways of involving parents in the schools and, more particularly, in the education of their children (see Broh and Trent 1981). At the same time, teachers and administrators appear to receive very little training in how to relate to parents and involve them more effectively in school affairs.

Desegregation can lead to special problems in parent-school relations, and in-service training might focus on means by which these relations can be improved. Because desegregation invariably increases the heterogeneity of a school's student body, educators must relate to a different and more diverse group of parents. This suggests a need for teachers and administrators to understand differences in the behavior and values of parents with varied cultural and socioeconomic backgrounds. In other words, the lessons that educators need to learn about students, they also need to learn about parents. Specifically, training should help educators develop communication skills, awareness of power and status differences, and techniques parents can use to help their children learn at school and at home.

Because parents often have to travel further to schools after desegregation and into neighborhoods in which they may not feel comfortable, educators need to consider ways to involve parents other than those traditionally used. For example, parent-teacher conferences and PTA meetings might be held in different neighborhoods, and teachers may want to visit homes rather than waiting for parents to come to school. Activities designed to include parents should be scheduled at times that minimally conflict with parents' work and teachers' after-hours time.

School desegregation may establish an adversarial relationship between some parents and the schools. For example, parents who oppose desegregation may resist participating in school activities or be angry at the changes that result from desegregation. Other parents, through advisory councils and monitoring groups, may be perceived as threatening by educators. These possibilities should be discussed, and ways of relating to parents who take a skeptical view of schools or who share in the traditional authority of educators should be developed.

Evidence. The importance of promoting parent support for desegregation and involvement in schools is identified by Doherty and his colleagues (1981). Their study finds that parent support for desegregation promotes positive interracial attitudes among minority students and positive attitudes toward school among white students. Furthermore, activities that involve parents in schools were found to improve interracial behavior among minority students. Other research, already discussed in chapters 5 and 7, identifies a positive relationship between parent involvement in schools and student achievement (Armor et al. 1976; Coulson et al. 1976; Wellisch et al. 1976). These findings emphasize the need to train educators to develop and implement strategies that increase parent support of an involvement in desegregated schools.

Virtually no literature exists on the impact of in-service training for educators on increasing parent involvement in desegregating and desegregated schools. The suggestions given here are based on inferences made by considering both the changes in educator-parent relationships that might result from desegregation and the literature and perspectives on other aspects of in-service training.

Examples. The literature provides only few examples of in-service-training programs for school personnel designed to encourage parent involvement in schools. The Institute for Teacher Leadership (1979) describes two such programs. In 1973 the New Brunswick Education Association (New Jersey) began a three-year training program that involved both school and community participants. One component of this program trained teachers and local education-association leaders to plan and implement parent-student activities to increase parent involvement in school affairs. The Denver school system instituted a number of in-service training programs that included sessions designed to improve parent-teacher communication and to train teachers in methods to stimulate parent interest in school curricula, parent-teacher organizations, and other school activities.

In-Service Training for Administrators

Principals play an extremely important role in influencing the course of student race relations, achievement, and the nature of student behavior in schools. Partly, this is because of explicit actions that principals must take to resolve matters that involve race. Examples of such actions are student discipline and assignment of students to classrooms. In addition, principals' racial attitudes and behavior become modest for teachers and students in schools. The importance of the principal in setting a school-wide tone for race relations implies that there should be more in-service training for these and other administrators than is presently offered. Although virtually all desegregation experts agree that principals are very important to effective desegregation (see Beckum and Dasho 1981b; Broh and Trent 1981), little such training occurs and little has been written about how to prepare principals and other administrators for desegregation. It seems likely that the same general strategies that apply to both the content and the character of teaching training discussed above should be applied to the training of administrators.

In particular, Ronald G. Davison (1973) proposes the following strategies for in-service training of principals and other administrators:

1. Planning of in-service programs for administrators should include selected participants who might later serve as leaders of training sessions.
2. Incentives should be provided to facilitate full participation. It should not be assumed that administrators are more eager to participate in training than teachers.
3. Program content should be designed to ensure balance and associ-

ation between theoretical understandings of training topics and their
practical application in specific situations.

4. In-service training for administrators will be more successful if it is
    designed to address specific needs of participants.
5. Training should emphasize concrete ways that administrators can
    consider, develop, and implement new administrative practices. Pro-
    grams should not be critical of existing practices but should provide
    means by which those practices may be examined and perhaps
    amended.
6. In-service training for administrators should engender commitment
    to educational change and provide a knowledge base for such com-
    mitment.

In addition, school administrators in desegregating systems probably
need special training to help teachers deal with stress, organize the system
of public transportation (which is more than a logistical problem), deal
with the media, identify sources of funding, and, at the district level,
coordinate external financial resources. In more general terms, Beckum
and Dasho (1981b) argue the importance of preparing principals and
district-level officials to plan and implement both short-term and long-
term desegregation strategies, promote and coordinate community involvement in schools, and educate community and monitoring groups
about school and district characteristics and the dynamics of organizational change in schools. Of course, other members of administrative
staffs influence school climates. Assistant principals, deans, and guidance
counselors should also participate in in-service training related to desegregation.

Evidence. Martha Turnage (1972), Crain, Mahard, and Narot (1982),
Forehand and Ragosta (1976), and St. John (1975) all stress the importance of principals' behavior in influencing school climate. The Safe
School Study (National Institute of Education 1978b) found that differences among secondary schools in levels of student crime, misbehavior,
and violence are strongly related to the degree of school-level coordination
of discipline policy by the principal. This study concludes that a school's
overall climate will be safer and teachers will express more positive
attitudes toward and perform better in school if principals see that all staff
members follow the same general set of rules and that those rules are
clearly communicated to students. In addition, principals must promote
mutual reinforcement of teacher and administrator behavior and help
teachers maintain discipline within their classrooms.

The importance of the principal's role in shaping school climate is
emphasized in a recent reanalysis of the Safe Schools data. Gottfredson

and Daiger (1979) identify the following factors as important to mini-mizing interpersonal conflict with desegregated schools:

1. Principals should stress the importance of desegregation and of im-proving race relations publicly and with conviction.
2. They should support teachers in their efforts to alter their behavior and manage their classrooms and prohibit teacher practice that dis-courages good race relations.
3. They should help draft and fairly administer rules of conduct for students and staff.

Development of principals' capabilities to achieve these conditions seems to be an important goal of training programs for school administrators.

Doherty and his colleagues (1981) find that in-service training for principals in interpersonal relations has a positive relationship to im-proving overall school climate and to improving student attitudes toward school. These findings suggest that such training promotes a harmonious and cooperative school environment that may lead to positive interactions not only among students but among students and teachers, teachers them-selves, and among administrators and teachers.

Some evidence from case studies suggests that principals indirectly influence the climate of their schools by the emphases they place on the in-service training of teachers (Carney 1979b, 1979c, 1979d). Principals who express strong support of teacher training in interpersonal relations, instructional methods, and discipline, and who themselves participate in such training, promote the improvement of school climate. In addition, involvement of principals in teacher training creates an atmosphere of cohesion and administrative support of teachers. Beckum and Dasho (1981a) support these findings in their case studies and argue that ad-ministrative leadership and participation in in-service training is essential to the adoption of schoolwide improvement. Further, they contend that principals must be informed and committed to training if desired outcomes are to occur.

Example. Carney (1979c) found evidence that comprehensive in-service training involving principals, administrative staff, and teachers effectively reduced problems in the desegregation of a midwestern unified school district of approximately twenty-six thousand students. Retreats were held for principals and other administrators that concentrated on crisis man-agement and interpersonal relations. In addition, administrators attended in-service training for teachers that emphasized multicultural and bilingual education, instructional methods, and interpersonal relations. Much of the effectiveness of this program was attributed to the comprehensive training of both administrators and teachers, separately and together.

Summary

Despite the problems inherent in research on in-service training in general and desegregation-specific training in particular, there emerges a rather clear set of strategies for effectively planning and conducting in-service training for educators in desegregated schools. In addition, the literature identifies a number of relationships between types of training and promotion of educator and student outcomes. The most useful and successful in-service training programs appear to be those that educators themselves plan and implement to address specific needs of teachers and administrators in single-school settings and to foster collegiality and schoolwide change. Participant involvement in the development and conduct of training seems to enhance the impact of programs on both teachers and administrators. In addition, training of both teachers and administrators should include development of practical skills and behavioral responses that may be immediately applied in classrooms and throughout schools.

The practical aspects of training should be based on theory and principles to explain the appropriateness of adopting and implementing specific techniques in desegregated settings and to provide a basis upon which techniques may be amended as changes occur in schools. In-service programs for desegregation, like general in-service training programs, should include a variety of content areas and coordinate topics to provide continuity throughout the training process. Training should be continuous and incorporated as a component of total school or district functions. Desegregation-specific programs should be related to the central concerns of educators such as increasing student achievement, improving interpersonal relations, enhancing discipline and classroom-management techniques, and stimulating curricular innovation.

9 Conclusion: Myths, False Promises, and Possibilities

Myth and Reality in Desegregation

How one views the evidence on the social and educational consequences of desegregation will depend on one's predispositions and priorities. It seems safe to say that the available empirical evidence is substantially more positive than most of the public believes it to be and conflicts dramatically with the justifications for abandoning nonvoluntary desegregation that are offered by many state and national political leaders. How can this gap between evidence and belief be so great? One possibility is, of course, that the available data do not capture important aspects of the national experience. This is probably true, but it could be that more and better data would provide a better report card for desegregation. Indeed, it does appear—for understandably scientific reasons—that methodologically weaker studies have been less positive in their findings than more sophisticated studies. The following are six other reasons why the nation has an inaccurate impression of what desegregation has wrought and of what the prospects are for more positive outcomes in the future.

1. People are more aware of what is going on in schools as a result of desegregation. Normally, most parents know very little about the educational experiences their children have at school. To allow oneself to be uninvolved may require the assumption that the school one's child attends is a good school. When desegregation occurs, parents ask questions that they did not ask before, and they compare the answers to the fantasies that they held about how school was before desegregation. Thus, even if a school improved after desegregation, it would probably not meet the standards parents thought existed before desegregation.

2. Desegregation raises expectations. Not only do parents pay more attention to what goes on in desegregating schools; they probably also expect more than they did before desegregation. Desegregation requires change, and change presents risks, potential gains, and potential losses. Some whites, for example, may assume that the education minorities usually receive is inadequate. They may insist, therefore, that schools be better after desegregation than before because they expect that the effects of minority peers on the curriculum and on learning will be negative.

3. Some persons assume that minority schools are unlikely to be good schools. A related belief is that minority students, in general, are

161

unlikely to be good students. These assumptions lead to conclusions that desegregation must inevitably reduce the quality of education in the public schools.

4. If the evidence about school quality is mixed, parents may see it as negative. Parents concerned about their children's welfare can be very cautious. Bad evidence is believed; positive evidence is discounted. That is a responsible parental predisposition. Isolated incidents of disruption or weaknesses of individual teachers are risks that parents may not want their children to have any probability of experiencing. Thus, negative stories dominate parental consciousness.

5. The media often focus on problems and thus distort reality. Problems are news; achievements are at best human-interest stories. Analyses of media coverage during the initial stages of desegregation show that the press and television generally focus on difficulties rather than on positive developments. The story is conflict. Good news is no news.

6. The problems of schools may be generalized to desegregation rather than to other events. Schools have been at the cutting edge of social change for the last decade. Hosts of new demands have been placed on them resulting in overloads in many cases. School desegregation is a lightening rod for other concerns. When one sees complexity, one wants simple answers. The idea that the perceived problems of public education can be cured by backing away from desegregation is understandably attractive.

Disappointments and False Promises

To make the case, as this book has, that school desegregation has been more successful than is popularly believed does not mean that desegregation has been a big success. Clearly, its achievements have fallen far short of the hopes of its advocates. As the old mythology has lost believers, a new mythology has risen to justify new directions. Like the convictions and assumptions it seeks to replace, the new mythology holds forth a bold promise. By placing the blame for many of the problems of public education squarely on desegregation, particularly mandatory desegregation, advocates of the new mythology imply that if busing were eliminated, the problems of public education would largely disappear or at least be substantially easier to resolve. This assertion, like the claim that desegregation was the path to racial, social, and educational equity, is a false promise. This promise, and the beliefs that sustain it, leads people away from the complicated task of meeting the educational needs of children who, although differing greatly in their achievement and interests, need to understand people different from themselves and to find that learning is not a contest in which some must lose so that others can realize their full potential. Inequality is no more essential to learning than it is to economic prosperity.

The United States has been in a funk about its public schools. It is ironic that the demonstrable extension of equal educational opportunity this nation has witnessed over the last fifteen to twenty years has brought about the realization that social inequality will not yield to education alone. Equality of opportunity is a condition that can never be fully secured in the context of inequality rooted deep in this country's history, culture, and social institutions.

Desegregation and other social policies aimed at fostering social change force one to recognize that this country's commitments to equality have always been partial and contingent on and in conflict with other values. The principles expressed in Fourth of July speeches cannot be secured by policies that go no further than guaranteeing persons an equal chance to compete.

Not surprisingly, those who have opposed government efforts to foster social change, and especially those who have consistently opposed desegregation, have seized upon frustrations derived from unrealized high hopes to launch a new and powerful attack on desegregation. This attack focuses its attention on forced busing rather than on interracial schooling. Despite abundant evidence to the contrary, the antibusing forces boldly assert that desegregation can be achieved voluntarily. Thus opponents of desegregation are allowed to be supportive of integration. The school bus has become a symbol that triggers images of government intervention. The antibusing movement, therefore, has attracted not only those who oppose desegregation but those who call for general retreat from educational and other policies concerned with the disadvantaged and the handicapped. In order for the antibusing movement to succeed, there must be another way to achieve the goals of justice and equality. That way is supposedly quality education for all.

Antibusing advocates advise that it is time to turn attention from equity to quality. Moreover, they insist that the search for equity diminishes quality and that educational excellence for all is the best way to eliminate inequities. The myth of education as the remedy to inequality has been turned on its head. And what an attractive argument: emphasizing equality diminishes excellence in education, and without excellence in education, one cannot have equality. Once one accepts the first assumption, that is, that both equity and excellence cannot be achieved simultaneously, the choice is easy.

Plessy Redux

The policy that follows from conclusions that busing is the problem and that the pursuit of quality schools must proceed to lead to equality is nothing less than that schools should be racially separate but equal. One of the contentions that makes the separate-but-equal argument salable to those one would expect to dismiss it as a disproven doctrine is the assertion that a belief that blacks or Hispanics must go to school with whites to learn is a new form of racism.

There can be little doubt that the idea of racially separate but equal schools, though ways of talking about it may be indirect and subtle, has a large number of advocates. It is also true that many of these advocates are minority parents and community leaders. What can be said in response to the charge that desegregation detracts from both the attention and resources that should be invested in the higher goal of quality education for all and thus retards rather than advances the pursuit of social equality?

There are four reasons to believe that it would be a mistake to return to the time when innocence and racism combined to produce the Supreme Court's decision in *Plessy* v. *Ferguson*. First, improving minority schools and desegregation are not mutually exclusive objectives. Although it is clear that all minority schools that employ appropriate instructional methods and have teachers and administrators who want minority children to learn, and believe that they can learn, can be effective in fostering academic achievement (Bloom 1976; MacQueen and Coulson 1978; Edmonds 1979; Brookover and Lezotte 1979), it is also true that these conditions can be and often are achieved in desegregated schools.

Second, even if it is true that the academic achievement of minorities can be as great in segregated as in desegregated schools, racially isolated schools cannot be as effective as desegregated ones in fostering greater postschool income and occupational status or in developing among minorities a sense of confidence that they can be effective in a society which is, and is likely to be for the foreseeable future, dominated by whites (see McPartland 1981; McPartland and Braddock 1981). Also, it is surely the case that racially identifiable schools will be less effective in promoting racial tolerance among both whites and minorities than desegregated ones. Those who lack first-hand experience with persons of other races and who are racially prejudiced are handicapped. Other attributes being equal, those who are not burdened by racial stereotypes will have a greater chance of achieving their own goals.

Third, as the evidence cited on the academic benefits of desegregation suggests, it appears that teachers are generally less demanding of and responsive to minority children in segregated than in desegregated classrooms. Presumably, this situation can be corrected without desegregation, but this cannot be shown by looking at evidence from studies of exemplary minority schools or research on educational innovations.

Finally, the case can be made that desegregation, in general, increases the equity with which educational resources necessary to foster minority achievement are allocated. This case for the benefits of desegregation is based on three basic assumptions:

1. Resources, particularly physical facilities, and quality of teaching make a difference to the quality of education and opportunities minority students have.
2. Economic resources and control over their allocation are usually in the hands of whites. This is true even when communities are politically controlled by minorities because a significant proportion of the resources available derive from an economic system and from state and federal agencies dominated by whites.
3. Whites will discriminate against racially isolated minority schools in the allocation of resources.

There is growing evidence that financial resources applied intelligently to the needs of students will bring about improved learning (see, for example, Coulson et al. 1977; Glass and Sanders 1978; Hawley 1982). This does not mean, of course, that spending more money on schools will necessarily have positive effects.

It is also clear that in most cases whites control the economic resources available to public education. It can reasonably be argued, and many minority leaders believe it to be the case, that whites generally will discriminate against minorities in the allocation of funds and that this propensity is held in check when whites go to school with minority students. If this resource-allocation theory is correct, its negative consequences might be remedied either by school desegregation or by school-finance laws that assign resources to public schools according to learning needs that are tied to objective indicators to reduce the opportunities whites have to discriminate against minorities. (It is not surprising that minorities have sought increased federal and state support for public schools since such support is invariably tied to funding formulas which if they had negative consequences for minorities would be subject to constitutional challenge.)

One response to the idea that whites will discriminate against minorities in the allocation of resources if schools are segregated is that whites will be willing to pay the bill for minority schools as long as doing so reduces the contact whites must have with minorities. Surprisingly, there appears to be little evidence that speaks clearly to this possibility. However, contrary evidence is found in a recent study by Noboa (1980) which finds that Hispanics are more likely to have access to a broad range of special programs—including bilingual instruction—in racially mixed than in segregated school districts. In addition, David L. Colton (1979) found that desegregation serves as a catalyst for extensive redistribution of school resources that might not have occurred had desegregation not been ordered.

It is important to reemphasize that quality minority schools can be pursued at the same time as desegregation occurs. In many big cities, where most minorities live, almost all desegregated schools will have more minority students than white students. They will be, in effect, minority schools. Moreover, judges have been willing to tolerate, in the context of a desegregation plan, the existence of some schools where almost all students are nonwhite. It seems reasonable, as the minority plaintiffs argued in the Los Angeles desegregation case, that more effective minority schools should be preserved when the logistics and demography of desegregation place limits on the elimination of racially identifiable schools.

In short, before the United States returns to the days of *Plessy* v. *Ferguson* when separate but equal was a legal fiction, it is necessary to be sure that the racism that sustained that doctrine and increased its costs no longer plays a central role in current intergroup relationships. There is little doubt that racial prejudice has declined. It remains true, however, that the race and ethnicity of the possible beneficiaries of public policies and private choices are important determinants of the decisions that are made.

Possibilities

What then can be expected to result from school desegregation? It is certain that desegregation promises challenges to school systems, administrators, teachers, parents, and communities. School desegregation invariably requires changes in the things schools do and the ways in which parents and communities view and participate in the education of children. The evidence indicates that simply mixing students of different races and ethnic backgrounds and heading off conflict produce no magical results and may lead to more problems than benefits. It seems quite evident that the ultimate success or failure of desegregation depends on the manner and the degree to which schools meet the challenges and seize the opportunities for change that are posed by desegregation. Some school systems have been more successful than others in meeting these challenges, and no one school system is doing all it can to make desegregation work most effectively.

Regardless of one's perceptions of past experiences, the research and the work of numerous school systems throughout the country indicate that a variety of things can be done to increase the effectiveness of school desegregation in terms of educational equity, educational quality, and community response. The strategies identified here carry no guarantees. School desegregation, like any other educational policy, depends fundamentally for its success on the commitment and capabilities of school personnel and the support of those on whom schools depend most, the community and especially parents.

Appendix: Methodology for Interviews with Local and National Desegregation Experts

A major task of the project *Assessment of Current Knowledge about the Effectiveness of School Desegregation Strategies* called for interviews to be conducted in twenty local school districts which were generally representative of the sites in which future desegregation would occur or in which various desegregation strategies had been implemented. Initially, a list of districts was prepared using data from Karl E. Taeuber and Franklin D. Wilson's (1979) survey. These data provided information on school-district size, type of desegregation plan (mandatory or voluntary), and the agency governing the desegregation plan (federal, state, or local). In addition, the data contained the racial and ethnic composition of each local system.

The primary criteria for site selection were: (1) prior significant desegregation activity, (2) occurrence of successful or significant practices or changes in desegregation strategies, and (3) potential generalizability of lessons learned at an individual site to other systems. After consultation with the project's advisory board, a final list of school-system sites was developed.

1. Tucson, Arizona
2. Riverside, California
3. Stockton, California
4. Denver, Colorado
5. New Castle Consolidated (Wilmington), Delaware
6. Hillsborough County (Tampa), Florida
7. Atlanta, Georgia
8. Evanston, Illinois
9. Jefferson County (Louisville), Kentucky
10. Prince George's County, Maryland
11. Boston, Massachusetts
12. Minneapolis, Minnesota
13. Omaha, Nebraska
14. Montclair, New Jersey
15. Charlotte-Mecklenburg County, North Carolina
16. Shaker Heights, Ohio
17. Nashville-Davidson County, Tennessee
18. Seattle, Washington
19. Milwaukee, Wisconsin
20. Racine, Wisconsin

Because Prince George's County and Nashville-Davidson County were engaged in legal action related to desegregation during the interview period, these sites were omitted from the list even though one interview

169

was eventually conducted in Prince George's County. Deletion of these districts was based on a rationale that these court actions or reviews might affect or limit the responses of local officials. Omaha was also excluded based on preliminary inquiries about that city. In each of the remaining sites, from four to eight individuals who held key positions with each school system were interviewed. In total, ninety-four interviews were conducted with local experts.

The research plan placed special emphasis on gathering information from those individuals most involved in and informed about the desegregation process in their districts. For each school system, members of the study team who were to conduct interviews were instructed to choose from the following list of local officials and citizens:

1. Superintendent or senior system staff member(s) involved in desegregation
2. School-board members
3. Teachers
4. Curriculum specialists
5. Court appointed plan masters
6. Journalists
7. Monitoring/citizen-committee members
8. Plaintiff's/defendant's attorney.

Table A–1 identifies the positions of persons interviewed in each site along with the total number of persons interviewed there.

In addition, interviews were conducted with forty national experts who because of their unique types of involvement or position were especially qualified to respond to issues of school desegregation. Table A–2 identifies the roles or positions of these respondents. Careful attention was given to identifying those persons whose professional roles provided valuable insights into school-desegregation issues. To select these national experts the authors first solicited names from the advisory board and the entire project team and, second, identified authors with multiple publications in the field of school-desegregation research. Heads of federally sponsored Desegregation Assistance Centers were polled for nominees.

The questionnaires used for local and national experts were developed and prepared by the project staff. No formal pretest of the instrument was conducted. The types of interview items were discussed with the advisory board and were then assessed by the entire project team. The open-ended items used in the instruments allowed the interviewers to follow their

Table A–1
Positions Held by Local Experts Interviewed for Each School Site

	Super-intendent	Other System Administrator	Teacher	Principal	Minority Spokesperson	School-Board Member	Judge	Journalist
Tuscon, Arizona		4				1		
Riverside, California	2	3	1					1
Stockton, California		4	1			1		
Denver, Colorado		2				1		
New Castle, Delaware		2				1		
Hillsborough County, Florida	2	5						1
Atlanta, Georgia	1							
Evanston, Illinois	1	2	1			1		
Jefferson County, Kentucky	1	2						
Boston, Massachusetts		1			1			
Minneapolis, Minnesota		1			1	1		
Montclair, New Jersey								
Charlotte, North Carolina	2							
Shaker Heights, Ohio		2	1	1		1		
Seattle, Washington		2				2		2
Milwaukee, Wisconsin		1			1	1		
Racine, Wisconsin	1					1		1
Total	10	31	4	1	3	11		5

Table A–1 Continued

	Researcher	Civil Leader	Monitoring-Committee Member	State or Federal Official	Consultant	Attorney for Plaintiffs	Attorney for School Board	Total for Site
Tuscon, Arizona		1				2		8
Riverside, California	1							7
Stockton, California		1		1				7
Denver, Colorado			1					6
New Castle, Delaware		2						5
Hillsborough County, Florida								8
Atlanta, Georgia				1	1			4
Evanston, Illinois	1							5
Jefferson County, Kentucky				1				4
Boston, Massachusetts		1			2			4
Minneapolis, Minnesota								4
Montclair, New Jersey				2				2
Charlotte, North Carolina	1			1				4
Shaker Heights, Ohio								5
Seattle, Washington	1						1	8
Milwaukee, Wisconsin		2		1	2			8
Racine, Wisconsin				2				5
Total	4	7	1	9	5	2	1	94

Table A–2
Positions Held by National Experts Interviewed

Position of National Expert	Number Interviewed
Academician/researcher/consultant	19
Director of policy/research center	7
Federal Education Administrator	4
Desegregation planner	1
Civil-rights attorney	1
Superintendent of schools	1
Head of federal desegregation-assistance center	7
Total	40

own instincts about which issues or questions to pursue. This departure from the format provided considerable richness on certain topics. The local interview instrument contained thirty-one items and included an identification of the characteristics of the local school system, position of the respondent, and length and type of interview (personal or telephone). The national-expert questionnaire was somewhat longer, containing fifty-nine items. Local and national-expert interviews averaged one hour and thirty minutes and two hours respectively.

Items in both instruments focus on the five goals or outcomes of desegregation identified in chapter 2 of this book: (1) reducing racial isolation among and within schools, (2) avoiding resegregation among and within schools, (3) improving race relations among students, (4) improving educational quality and student academic performance, and (5) improving public response to desegregation. The open-ended questions generally required respondents to identify strategies that would be beneficial in achieving one of these outcomes. In many instances, probes were used to elicit responses about particular practices about which there has been considerable debate.

Eight senior researchers from the project team conducted the interviews between July and December 1980. The interviewers were Robert L. Crain, Ricardo R. Fernández, Willis D. Hawley, Christine H. Rossell, William Sampson, Rachel Tompkins, William T. Trent, and Ben Williams. Each interviewer was responsible for from one to five sites; only one researcher was assigned a single site. Each interviewer has published on or consulted in various areas of school desegregation. Indeed, some had the unique advantage of having conducted research or provided expert testimony in the school system where their interviews were conducted. Their experience made training unnecessary and also expedited access to key personnel in most systems. For each local site, however, the interviewers were provided with available background material on that system. This information was provided by the Horace Mann Bond Center for Equal Education and the files of its director, Meyer Weinberg. Interviews with the national experts were conducted by the same researchers.

The completed instruments were returned to the project staff by December 1980. Upon receipt of the interviews, responses were coded by the project coordinator and a research assistant. Following the coding of the responses, the local and national interview data were put into machine-readable form. The simple frequencies from the local and national interviews were somewhat less informative than the full responses from the actual instruments themselves. This is primarily because the range of responses to many items was broad and because of a substantial number of nonresponses to items about which respondents thought they were inadequately informed. In some instances, as many as 65 percent of the questions posed to local experts were unanswered.

Despite varying rates of response, the local and national interview data provide expert insight into particular desegregation strategies, many of which are identified as successful in facilitating effective school desegregation. The interview data identify perceptions and opinions of persons uniquely situated in the field of school desegregation. Although they provide valuable and unique insight, they are not objective measures of effective strategies and should not be taken as such. Samples of interview schedules and lists of local and national experts interviewed are available upon written request from the authors of this book.

Bibliography

Abney, Glenn. "Legislative Morality: Attitude Change and Desegregation in Mississippi." *Urban Education* 11 (October 1976):333–338.

Acland, Henry. *Secondary Analysis of the Emergency School Assistance Program*. Santa Monica, Calif.: The Rand Corporation, 1975.

Ahmadjian-Baer, Janis. "Producing More Active Learning Behavior from Poor Readers: The Multiple Ability Classroom." Paper presented at the annual meeting of the American Educational Research Association, April 1981, at Los Angeles.

Alexander, Dorothy L. "An Investigation into the Absence of Black Parental Involvement in the Administration of Desegregated Schools." Paper presented at the annual meeting of the American Educational Research Association, April 1979, at San Francisco.

Alexander, Kelly M. "Is Boston Burning?" *The Crisis* 82 (March 1975):90–92.

Allen, H.M., and Séars, David O. "White Opposition to Busing in Los Angeles: Is Self-Interest Rejuvenated?" Paper presented at the annual meeting of the American Psychological Association, August 1978, at Toronto.

Allport, Gordon W. *The Nature of Prejudice*. Reading, Mass.: Addison-Wesley Publishing Co., 1954.

Armor, David J. "White Flight and the Future of School Desegregation." In *School Desegregation: Past, Present, and Future,* edited by Walter G. Stephan and Joe R. Feagin. New York: Plenum Press, 1980.

Armor, David J.; Conry-Oseguera, Patricia; Cox, Millicent; King, Nicelma; McDonnell, Lorraine; Pascal, Anthony; Pauly, Edward; and Zellman, Gail. *Analysis of the School Preferred Reading Program in Selected Los Angeles Minority Schools*. Santa Monica, Calif.: The Rand Corporation, August 1976.

Arnez, Nancy L. "Implementation of Desegregation as a Discriminatory Process." *Journal of Negro Education* 47 (Winter 1978):28–45.

Arnove, Robert F., and Strout, Toby. "Alternative Schools for Disruptive Youth." *Educational Forum* 44 (May 1980):453–471.

Arthur v. Nyquist, 473 F. Supp. 830 (1979).

Bailey, Ralph. "Staff, Student and Parent Training as Positive Alternatives to Suspensions." In *Student Rights and Discipline: Policies, Programs, and Procedures,* edited by Charles D. Moody, Sr., Junious Williams, and Charles B. Vergon. Ann Arbor: The University of Michigan, School of Education, Program for Educational Opportunity, 1978.

Banks, James A. "The Emerging States of Ethnicity: Implications for Staff Development." *Educational Leadership* 34 (1976):190–193.

———. "Shaping the Future of Multi-Ethnic Education." *Journal of Negro Education* 45 (1979):237–252.

Banks, William H., Jr. "What to Do Until the Court Order Comes." *Phi Delta Kappan* 58 (1977):557–561.

Bardwell, George. Testimony before U.S. District Court for the District of Colorado in *Keyes* v. *School District No. 1,* March 1982.

Barker, Roger G., and Gump, Paul V. *Big School—Small School.* Palo Alto, Calif.: Stanford University Press, 1964.

Beady, Charles H., Jr., and Hansell, Stephen. "Teacher Race and Expectations for Student Achievement." *American Educational Research Journal* 18 (1981):191–206.

Beckum, Leonard C., and Dasho, Stephan J. "Confronting Diversity: A Multi-Disciplinary Study of Teacher Training Needs in Newly Desegregated Schools." Paper presented at the annual meeting of the American Educational Research Association, April 1980, at Boston.

———. *Accommodating Diversity: An Assessment of Teacher Training Needs in Newly Desegregated Schools.* San Francisco: Far West Laboratory for Educational Research and Development, April 1981a.

———. "Managing Social Change: Administrative Decision-Making in Desegregated Schools." Paper presented at the annual meeting of the American Educational Research Association, April 1981b, at Los Angeles.

Berman, Paul, and McLaughlin, Milbrey W. *Factors Affecting Implementation and Continuation.* Federal Programs Supporting Educational Change, vol. 7. Santa Monica, Calif.: The Rand Corporation, April 1977.

Billington, Monroe. "Public School Integration in Missouri, 1954–1964." *Journal of Negro Education* 35 (1966):252–262.

Blanchard, Fletcher A.; Weigel, Russell; and Cook, Stuart W. "The Effect of Relative Competence of Group Members Upon Interpersonal Attraction in Cooperating Interracial Groups." *Journal of Personality and Social Psychology* 32 (September 1975):519–530.

Blom, Gaston; Waite, Richard; and Zimet, Sara. "Ethnic Integration and Urbanization of a First-Grade Reading Textbook: A Research Study." *Psychology in the Schools* 4 (1967):176–181.

Bloom, Benjamin S. *Human Characteristics and School Learning.* New York: McGraw-Hill, 1976.

Boardman, Anthony E., and Lloyd, Anne S. "The Process of Education for Twelfth Grade Asian American Students." *Cross Reference: A Journal of Public Policy and Multicultural Education* 1 (1978):338–353.

Borg, Walter R. "Changing Teacher and Pupil Performance with Protocols." *Journal of Experimental Education* 45 (1977):9–18.

Bosma, Boyd. "The Role of Teachers in School Desegregation." *Integrated Education* 15 (November-December 1977):106–111.

Braddock, Jomills H., II, and McPartland, James M. "The Perpetuation of Segregation from Elementary-Secondary Schools to Higher Education." Paper presented at the annual meeting of the American Educational Research Association, April 1979, at San Francisco.

Braun, Miranda. "Toward Teacher Training for 'Desegregated' Schools: Organization, Content and Sociocultural Context." *Education and Urban Society* 9 (1977):353–368.

Bridge, R. Gary; Judd, Charles; and Moock, Peter R. *The Determinants of Educational Outcomes: The Effects of Families, Peers, Teachers, and Schools.* New York: Teachers College Press, 1979.

Broh, C. Anthony, and Trent, William T. "Qualitative Literature and Expert Opinion on School Desegregation." In *Assessment of Current Knowledge about the Effectiveness of School Desegregation Strategies,* vol. 6, edited by Willis D. Hawley. Nashville, Tenn.: Vanderbilt University, Institute for Public Policy Studies, Center for Education and Human Development Policy, April 1981.

Brookover, Wilbur B., and Lezotte, Lawrence W. *Changes in School Characteristics Coincident with Changes in Student Achievement.* East Lansing: Michigan State University, The Institute for Research on Teaching, May 1979.

Brown, Jeannette A.; MacDougall, Mary A.; and Jenkins, Charles A. *Changing Culture Perceptions of Elementary School Teachers.* Charlottesville: The University of Virginia, School of Education, April 1972.

Budoff, Milton. "Learning Potential: A Supplementary Procedure for Assessing the Ability to Reason." *Seminars in Psychiatry* 1 (August 1969):278–290.

Bullock, Charles S., III. *School Desegregation, Interracial Contact, and Prejudice.* Washington, D.C.: National Institute of Education, 1976.

Bullock, Charles S., III, and Rodgers, Harrell R. "Coercion to Compliance: Southern School Districts and School Desegregation Guidelines." *Journal of Politics* 38 (1976):987–1011.

Burrello, Leonard C., and Orbaugh, Tim. "Reducing the Discrepancy

Between the Known and the Unknown in Inservice Education." *Phi Delta Kappan* 63 (1982):385–388.

Burton, Nancy W., and Jones, Lyle V. *Recent Trends in Achievement Levels of Black and White Youth*. Chapel Hill: The University of North Carolina, 1982.

Campbell, Bruce A. "The Impact of School Desegregation: An Investigation of Three Mediating Variables." *Youth and Society* 9 (September 1977):79–111.

Carl, Michael E., and Jones, Larry W. *Some Preliminary Observations Regarding the Minnesota State Human Relations Requirement and Its Effect on In-Service Teachers*. Moorhead, Minn.: Moorhead State College, 1972.

Carney, Maureen F. *Inservice Education for Desegregation: A Review of the Literature*. Santa Monica, Calif.: The Rand Corporation, November 1979a.

————, ed. *Inservice Training in Desegregated School Districts: Eastern Region Case Studies*. Santa Monica, Calif.: The Rand Corporation, August 1979b.

————, ed. *Inservice Training in Desegregated School Districts: Midwestern Region Case Studies*. Santa Monica, Calif.: The Rand Corporation, August 1979c.

————, ed. *Inservice Training in Desegregated School Districts: Western Region Case Studies*. Santa Monica, Calif.: The Rand Corporation, August 1979d.

Carter, Thomas P. "Interface between Bilingual Education and Desegregation: A Study of Arizona and California." Mimeographed. Sacramento: California State University, 1979.

Chow, Stanley H.L.; Rice, Carol F.; and Whitmore, Lynn A. "Effects of a Mediated Training Course on Teachers and Students in Mainstreaming Programs." Paper presented at the annual meeting of the American Educational Research Association, April 1976, at San Francisco.

Clotfelter, Charles. *Analyses of Measures of Segregation and Desegregation*. Nashville, Tenn.: Vanderbilt University, Institute for Public Policy Studies, Education Policy Development Center for Desegregation, March 1982.

Cohen, Elizabeth G. "The Desegregated School: Problems in Status Power and Interracial Climate." Paper presented at the annual meeting of the American Psychological Association, September 1979, at New York.

————. "A Multi-Ability Approach to the Integrated Classroom." Paper presented at the annual meeting of the American Psychological Association, September 1980, at Montreal.

Cohen, Peter A.; Kulik, James A.; and Kulik, Chen-Lin C. "Educational Outcomes of Tutoring: A Meta-Analysis of Findings." *American Educational Research Journal* 19 (1982):237–248.

Coleman, James S. "Population Stability and Equal Opportunity." *Society* 14 (1977):34–36.

Coleman, James S.; Campbell, Ernest Q.; Hobson, Carol J.; McPartland, James; Mood, Alexander M.; Weinfeld, Frederic D.; and York, Robert L. *Equality of Educational Opportunity*. Washington, D.C.: U.S. Government Printing Office, 1966.

Coleman, James S.; Kelly, Sara R.; and Moore, John A. *Trends in School Segregation, 1968–1973*. Washington, D.C.: The Urban Institute, 1975.

Colton, David L. "Urban School Desegregation Costs." Paper presented at the annual meeting of the American Educational Research Association, April 1979, at San Francisco.

Colton, David L., and Berg, M.W. *Budgeting for Desegregation in Large Cities, Final Report*. St. Louis: Washington University, Center for the Study of Law in Education, January 1981.

Columbus Board of Education v. Penick, 443 U.S. 449 (1979).

Columbus Public Schools. Report to the Federal District Court on the Status of Desegregation, *Penick et al.* v. *Columbus Board of Education et al.*, 20 November 1980.

Cook, Valerie, J. "Psychometric Critique of School Testing Litigation." Paper presented at the annual meeting of the American Psychological Association, September 1979, at New York.

Cook, Valerie; Eyler, Janet; and Ward, Leslie. *Effective Strategies for Avoiding within School Resegregation*. Nashville, Tenn.: Vanderbilt University, Institute for Public Policy Studies, Education Policy Development Center for Desegregation, 1981.

Coulson, John E.; Ozenne, Dan G.; Bradford, Clarence; Doherty, William J.; Duck, Gary A.; Hemenway, Judith A.; and Van Gelder, Nancy C. *The Second Year of Emergency School Aid Act (ESAA) Implementation*. Santa Monica, Calif.: System Development Corporation, July 1976.

Coulson, John E.; Ozenne, Dan G.; Hanes, Sally; Bradford, Clarence; Doherty, William; Duck, Gary A.; and Hemenway, Judith. *The Third Year of Emergency School Aid Act (ESAA) Implementation*. Santa Monica, Calif.: System Development Corporation, 1977.

Crain, Robert L. "Racial Tension in High Schools: Pushing the Survey Method Closer to Reality." *Anthropology and Education Quarterly* 8 (May 1977):142–151.

———. "Making Desegregation Work: Extracurricular Activities." *The Urban Review* 13 (1981):121–127.

Crain, Robert L., and Mahard, Rita E. "Desegregation and Black Achievement: A Review of the Research." *Law and Contemporary Problems* 42 (Summer 1978a):17–56.

———. "School Racial Composition and Black College Attendance and Achievement Test Performance." *Sociology of Education* 51 (April 1978b):81–101.

———. "The Influence of High School Racial Composition on the Academic Achievement and College Attendance of Hispanics." Paper presented at the annual meeting of the American Sociological Association, August 1980, at Montreal.

———. "Minority Achievement: Policy Implications of Research." In *Effective School Desegregation: Equity, Quality, and Feasibility*, edited by Willis D. Hawley. Beverly Hills, Calif.: SAGE Publications, 1981.

Crain, Robert L.; Mahard, Rita E.; and Narot, Ruth E. *Making Desegregation Work: How Schools Create Social Climate*. Cambridge, Mass.: Ballinger Press, 1982.

Criscuolo, Nicholas P. "Parent Involvement in the Reading Program." *Phi Delta Kappan* 63 (1982):345–346.

Cunningham, George K., and Husk, William L. *The Impact of Court-Ordered Desegregation on Student Enrollment and Residential Patterns in the Jefferson County Kentucky Public School District, Final Report*. Louisville: Jefferson County Education Consortium, June 1979a.

———. "A Metropolitan Desegregation Plan: Where the White Students Went." Paper presented at the annual meeting of the American Educational Research Association, April 1979b, at San Francisco.

Cunningham, George K.; Husk, William L.; and Johnson, James, Jr. "The Impact of Court-Ordered Desegregation on Student Enrollment and Residential Patterns (White Flight)." Paper presented at the annual meeting of the American Educational Research Association, March 1978, at Toronto.

Damico, Sandra B.; Bell-Nathaniel, Afesa; and Green, Charles. "Effects of School Organizational Structure on Interracial Friendships in Middle Schools." *Journal of Education Research* 74 (1981):388–393.

Damico, Sandra B.; Green, Charles; and Bell-Nathaniel, Afesa. "Facilitating Interracial Contact: Let the Structure Do It for You." Paper presented at the annual meeting of the American Educational Research Association, April 1981, at Los Angeles.

Davis, J. "Busing." In *Southern Schools: An Evaluation of the Emergency School Assistance Program and of Desegregation*. Chicago: National Opinion Research Center, 1973.

Davison, Ronald G. "Better In-Service Programs for School Administrators." *The Clearinghouse*, April 1973, pp. 498–501.

Demarest, Sylvia, and Jordan, John F. "*Hawkins* v. *Coleman:* Discriminatory Suspensions and the Effect of Institutional Racism on School Discipline.'' *Inequality in Education* 20 (July 1975):25–41.

Devin-Sheehan, Linda; Feldman, Robert S.; and Allen, Vernon L. ''Research on Children Tutoring Children: A Critical Review.'' *Review of Educational Research* 46 (Summer 1976):355–385.

Diana v. State Board of Education, C.A. No. C–70 37 RFP (ND Cal., filed February 3, 1970).

Doherty, William J.; Cadwell, Joel; Russo, Nancy A.; Mandel, Vicki; and Longshore, Douglas. *Human Relations Study: Investigations of Effective Human Relations Strategies,* vol. 2. Santa Monica, Calif.: System Development Corporation, April 1981.

Dornbush, Sanford M., and Fernandez, Celestino. ''The Effects of Teacher Praise and Warmth on Student Effort: A Socio-Cultural Comparative Analysis of Chicano and Anglo High School Students.'' *California Sociologist* 2 (Winter 1979):1–28.

Drewry, Galen N. ''The Principal Faces Desegregation.'' *Educational Leadership* 13 (October 1955):14–17.

Dziuban, Charles D. ''A Comparison of the Relationship among Indices of School Desegregation.'' Paper presented at the annual meeting of the American Educational Research Association, April 1980, at Boston.

Edmonds, Ronald. ''Effective Schools for the Urban Poor.'' *Educational Leadership,* October 1979, pp. 15–24.

Egerton, John. *Promise of Progress: Memphis School Desegregation, 1972–1973.* Atlanta: Southern Regional Council, June 1973.

Emmer, Edmund T. ''The First Weeks . . . and the Rest of the Year.'' Paper presented at the annual meeting of the American Educational Research Association, April 1979, at San Francisco.

Epstein, Joyce. ''After the Bus Arrives: Resegregation in Desegregated Schools.'' Paper presented at the annual meeting of the American Educational Research Association, April 1980, at Boston.

Erbe, Brigette M. ''Student Attitudes and Behavior in a Desegregated School System.'' *Integrated Education* 15 (November-December 1977):123–125.

ESEA Title III Project: Equal Opportunity in the Classroom, 1973–1974. Downey, Calif.: Office of the Los Angeles County Superintendent of Schools, 1974.

Evans v. Buchanan, 416 F. Supp. 328 (1976).

Evertson, Carolyn M.; Sanford, Julie P.; and Emmer, Edmund T. ''Effects of Class Heterogeneity in Junior High School.'' *American Educational Research Journal* 18 (Summer 1981):219–232.

Fantini, Mario D., ed. *Alternative Education: A Source Book for Parents, Teachers, Students, and Administrators.* Garden City, N.Y.: Anchor Books, Doubleday and Company, 1976.

Farley, Reynolds; Bianchi, Suzanne; and Colasanto, Diane. ''Barriers to the Racial Integration of Neighborhoods.'' *Annals of the American Academy of Political and Social Quarterly* 441 (January 1979):97–113.

Farley, Reynolds; Richards, Toni; and Wurdock, Clarence. "School Desegregation and White Flight: An Investigation of Competing Models and Their Discrepant Findings.'' *Sociology of Education* 53 (July 1980):123–139.

Felkner, Donald W.; Goering, Jacob; and Linden, Kathryn W. "Teacher Rigidity and Continuing Education.'' *The Journal of Teacher Education* 22 (1971):460–463.

Fernández, Ricardo R., and Guskin, Judith T. "Hispanic Students and School Desegregation.'' In *Effective School Desegregation: Equity, Quality, and Feasibility,* edited by Willis D. Hawley. Beverly Hills, Calif.: SAGE Publications, 1981.

Feuerstein, Re'uven. *The Dynamic Assessment of Retarded Performers.* Baltimore: University Park Press, 1979.

Findley, Warren G., and Bryan, Miriam M. *Ability Grouping, 1970: Status, Impact, and Alternatives.* Athens: The University of Georgia, Center for Educational Improvement, 1971.

First, Joan, and Mizell, M. Hayes, eds. *Everybody's Business: A Book About School Discipline.* Columbia, S.C.: Southeastern Public Education Program, 1980.

Fitzmaurice, Mercedes D. "Learning Institute In-Service Results.'' Paper presented at the annual meeting of the International Reading Association, May 1976, at Anaheim, California.

Forbes, Roy H. "Test Score Advances among Southeastern Students: A Possible Bonus of Government Intervention?'' *Phi Delta Kappan* 62 (January 1981):332–335.

Forehand, Garlie A., and Ragosta, Marjorie. *A Handbook for Integrated Schooling.* Princeton, N.J.: Educational Testing Service, 1976.

Foster, Gordon. "Desegregating Urban Schools: A Review of Techniques.'' *Harvard Educational Review* 43 (February 1973):5–36.

————. *Discipline Practices in the Hillsborough County Public Schools.* Coral Gables, Fla.: University of Miami, School Desegregation Consulting Center, April 1977.

Froman, Robin D. "Ability Grouping: Why Do We Persist and Should We?'' Paper presented at the annual meeting of the American Educational Research Association, April 1981, at Los Angeles.

Furtwengler, Willis J., and Konnert, William. *Improving School Discipline: An Administrator's Guide.* Boston: Allyn and Bacon, 1982.

Gartner, Alan; Kohler, Mary C.; and Riessman, Frank. *Children Teach Children.* New York: Harper and Row, 1971.

Genova, William J., and Walberg, Herbert J. *A Practitioner's Guide for*

Achieving Student Integration in City High Schools. Washington, D.C.: U.S. Government Printing Office, November 1980.

Gerard, Harold B., and Miller, Norman, eds. *School Desegregation: A Long-Range Study.* New York: Plenum Press, 1975.

Giles, Michael W.; Gatlin, Douglas S.; and Cataldo, Everett F. "Racial and Class Prejudice: Their Relative Effects on Protest against School Desegregation." *American Sociological Review* 41 (1976):280–288.

Glass, Gene V.; Cahen, Leonard S.; Smith, Mary Lee; and Filby, Nikola, N. *School Class Size: Research and Policy.* Beverly Hills, Calif.: SAGE Publications, 1982.

Glass, Gene V., and Smith, Mary L. *Meta-Analysis of Research on the Relationship of Class Size and Achievement.* Boulder: The University of Colorado, Laboratory of Educational Research, 1978.

Glass, Thomas E., and Sanders, William. *Community Control in Education: Study in Power Transition.* Midland, Mich.: Pendell Publishing Co., 1978.

Gottfredson, Gary D., and Daiger, Denise C. *Disruption in Six Hundred Schools, Report No. 289.* Baltimore: The Johns Hopkins University, Center for the Social Organization of Schools, November 1979.

Grant, William R. "The Media and School Desegregation." *Integrated Education* 14 (November-December 1976):12–13.

Green, Robert L., and Griffore, Robert J. "School Desegregation, Testing, and the Urgent Need for Equity in Education." *Education* 99 (Fall 1978):16–19.

Green v. New Kent County, 391 U.S. 430 (1968).

Greene, John F.; Archambault, Francis; and Nolen, William. "The Effect of Extended In-Service Training Curricula upon the Mathematics Achievement and Attitudes of Elementary Teachers." Paper presented at the annual meeting of the American Educational Research Association, April 1976, at San Francisco.

Guthrie, James W. "Organizational Scale and School Success." In *Education Finance and Organization: Research Perspective for the Future.* Washington, D.C.: National Institute of Education, January 1980.

Gwaltney, Meg. "Mercer School District: Eastern Region." In *Inservice Training in Desegregated School Districts: Eastern Regional Case Studies,* edited by Maureen F. Carney. Santa Monica, Calif.: The Rand Corporation, August 1979.

Hall, Leon. "Pushouts: The Implementors Revenge." *Southern Exposure* 7 (May 1979):122–125.

Hargrove, Erwin, C.; Graham, Scarlett G.; Ward, Leslie E.; Abernethy, Virginia; Cunningham, Joseph; and Vaughn, William K. *Regulation and Schools: The Implementation of Equal Education for Handi-*

capped Children. Nashville, Tenn.: Vanderbilt University, Institute
for Public Policy Studies, March 1981.

Harnischfeger, Annegret, and Wiley, David E. "A Merit Assessment of
Vocational Education Programs in Secondary Schools." Statement
to the Subcommittee on Elementary, Secondary, and Vocational Education, U.S. House of Representatives, September 1980.

Harris, Louis. *Majority of Parents Report School Busing Has Been Satisfactory Experience.* Chicago: Chicago Tribune-N.Y. News Syndicate, Inc., 26 March 1981.

————. *Big Shift in Single-Issue Voting Expected this Fall.* Chicago:
Chicago Tribune-N.Y. News Syndicate, Inc., 11 March 1982a.

————. *Majorities Oppose Many "Moral Majority" Positions.* Chicago:
Chicago Tribune-N.Y. News Syndicate, Inc., 15 March 1982b.

Hawley, Willis D. *Increasing the Effectiveness of School Desegregation:
Lessons from the Research.* Durham, N.C.: Duke University, Institute
of Policy Sciences and Public Affairs, Center for Educational Policy,
July 1980.

————, ed. "Effective Educational Strategies for Children at Risk."
Peabody Journal of Education 59 (July 1982).

Hayes, Edward J. *Busing and Desegregation: The Real Truth.* Springfield, Ill.: Charles C. Thomas, Publisher, 1981.

Hayes, J.G. "Anti-busing Protest." Paper presented at the annual meeting
of the North Carolina Education Association, November 1977, at
Charlotte.

Haywood, H. Carl. "Alternative to Normative Assessment." In *Research
to Practice in Mental Retardation: Education and Training,* vol. 2,
edited by Peter Mittler. Baltimore: University Park Press, 1977.

————. "Compensatory Education." *Peabody Journal of Education* 59
(July 1982):272–300.

"Helping Children Learn: A Guide for Parents." *The News from the
Pittsburgh Public Schools,* February 1982.

Hillman, Stephen B., and Davenport, G. Gregory. "Teacher Behavior
in Desegregated Schools." Paper presented at the annual meeting of
the American Educational Research Association, April 1977, at New
York.

Hochschild, Jennifer L., and Hadrick, Valerie. *The Character and Effectiveness of Citizen Monitoring Groups in Implementing Civil Rights
in Public Schools.* Washington, D.C.: National Institute of Education,
January 1981.

Howey, Kenneth R. "Inservice Teacher Education: A Study of the Perceptions of Teachers, Professors, and Parents about Current and Projected Practice." Paper prepared for the annual meeting of the
American Educational Research Association, March 1978, at Toronto.

Howey, Kenneth R.; Bents, Richard; and Corrigan, Dean. *School-Fo-*

cused Inservice: Descriptions and Discussions. Reston, Va.: Association of Teacher Educators, April 1981.

Hughes, Larry W.; Gordon, William M.; and Hillman, Larry W. *Desegregating America's Schools.* New York: Longman, Inc., 1980.

Hyman, Irwin A. *An Analysis of Studies on Effectiveness of Training and Staffing to Help Schools Manage Student Conflict and Alienation: A Report.* Philadelphia: Temple University, National Center for the Study of Corporal Punishment and Alternatives in the Schools, January 1979.

Inger, Morton, and Stout, Robert T. "School Desegregation: The Need to Govern." *The Urban Review* 3 (November 1968):35–38.

Institute for Teacher Leadership. *The Prevention of Resegregation: Strategies for Teachers.* Fullerton: California State University, Institute for Teacher Leadership, 1979.

Jaynes, Gregory. "Little Rock Schools, Trailblazers in Integration, Now Drawing Whites Back." *The New York Times,* 13 September 1981, p. 30.

Johnson, David W., and Johnson, Roger T. "Effects of Cooperative and Individualistic Learning Experiences on Interethnic Interaction." *Journal of Educational Psychology* 73 (1981):444–449.

Johnson, Richard A. "Renewal of School Placement Systems for the Handicapped." In *Public Policy and the Education of Exceptional Children,* edited by Frederick Weintraub. Reston, Va.: Council for Exceptional Children, 1976.

Kaeser, Susan C. *Orderly Schools That Serve All Children: A Review of Successful Schools in Ohio.* Cleveland: Citizens' Council for Ohio Schools, 1979a.

———. "Suspensions in School Discipline." *Education and Urban Society* 11 (1979b):465–484.

Katz, Phyllis A. *Modification of Children's Racial Attitudes.* New York: City University of New York, 1976.

Kentucky Commission on Human Rights. *Housing Desegregation Increases as Schools Desegregate in Jefferson County.* Louisville: Kentucky Commission on Human Rights, May 1977.

———. *Housing and School Desegregation Increased by Section 8 Moves: Under Public Housing Program Most Black Families Chose Jefferson County Suburbs,* staff report 80–1. Louisville: Kentucky Commission on Human Rights, April 1980.

King, Nicelma J. *The Los Angeles Experience in Monitoring Desegregation: Progress and Prospects.* Santa Monica, Calif.: The Rand Corporation, September 1980.

King, Nicelma J.; Carney, Maureen F.; and Stasz, Cathleen. *Staff Development Programs in Desegregated Settings.* Santa Monica, Calif.: The Rand Corporation, February 1980.

Kluger, Richard. *Simple Justice: The History of Brown v. Board of Ed-*

ucation and Black America's Struggle for Equality. New York: Vintage Books, 1977.

Koslin, Sandra; Koslin, Bertram; and Pargament, Richard. *Efficacy of School Integration Policies in Reducing Racial Polarization*. New York: Riverside Research Institute, 1972.

Krol, Ronald A. "A Meta Analysis of Comparative Research on the Effects of Desegregation on Academic Achievement." Ph.D. dissertation, Western Michigan University, 1978.

Kruse, Mary L. "The Effects of Increasing Teacher Competencies as Related to Improved Secondary Student Reading Scores." Paper presented at the meeting of the International Reading Association, May 1976, at Anaheim, California.

Larkins, A. Guy, and Oldham, Sally E. "Patterns of Racial Separation in a Desegregated High School." *Theory and Research in Social Education* 4 (December 1976):23–28.

Larson, John C. *Takoma Park Magnet School Evaluation: 1977–1979*. Rockville, Md.: Montgomery County Public Schools, Department of Educational Accountability, January 1980.

Levine, Daniel U., and Eubanks, Eugene F. "Attracting Nonminority Students to Magnet Schools in Minority Neighborhoods." *Integrated Education* 18 (Spring 1981):52–58.

Levinsohn, Florence H. "TV's Deadly Inadvertant Bias." In *School Desegregation: Shadow and Substance*, edited by Florence H. Levinsohn and Benjamin D. Wright. Chicago: The University of Chicago Press, 1976.

Litcher, John H., and Johnson, David W. "Changes in Attitudes toward Negroes of White Elementary School Students after Use of Multiethnic Readers." *Journal of Educational Psychology* 60 (1969):148–152.

Little, Judith W. *School Success and Staff Development: The Role of Staff Development in Urban Desegregated Schools*. Boulder, Colo.: Center for Action Research, January 1981.

Longshore, Douglas. *The Control Threat in Desegregated Schools: Exploring the Relationship between School Racial Composition and Intergroup Hostility*. Santa Monica, Calif.: System Development Corporation, 1981.

Lord, J. Dennis. "School Busing and White Abandonment of Public Schools." *Southeastern Geographer* 15 (November 1975):81–92.

Los Angeles Unified School District. *Racial Ethnic Survey, Fall 1981—Preliminary Tabulations*. Los Angeles: Los Angeles Unified School District, October 1981.

McConahay, John B. "Reducing Racial Prejudice in Desegregated Schools." In *Effective School Desegregation: Equity, Quality, and Feasibility*, edited by Willis D. Hawley. Beverly Hills, Calif.: SAGE Publications, 1981.

McConahay, John B., and Hawley, Willis D. *Reactions to Busing in Louisville: Summary of Adult Opinions in 1976 and 1977*. Durham, N.C.: Duke University, Institute of Policy Sciences and Public Affairs, 1978.

McDonnell, Lorraine M., and Zellman, Gail L. "The Role of Community Groups Facilitating School Desegregation." Paper presented at the annual meeting of the American Political Science Association, August-September 1978, at New York.

McPartland, James M. Testimony before the Subcommittee on Separation of Powers of the Committee on the Judiciary, U.S. Senate, 97th Cong., 1st sess. on Court-Ordered School Busing, 30 September 1981. Washington, D.C.: U.S. Government Printing Office, 1982.

McPartland, James M., and Braddock, Jomills H., II. "Going to College and Getting a Good Job: The Impact of Desegregation." In *Effective School Desegregation: Equity, Quality, and Feasibility*, edited by Willis D. Hawley. Beverly Hills, Calif.: SAGE Publications, 1981.

Mackler, Bernard. "Children Have Rights Too!" *The Crisis* 81 (August-September 1974):235–238.

MacQueen, Anne H., and Coulson, John E. *Emergency School Aid Act (ESAA) Evaluation: Overview of Findings from Supplemental Analyses*. Santa Monica, Calif.: System Development Corporation, 1978.

Mahard, Rita E., and Crain, Robert L. "The Influence of High School Racial Composition on the Academic Achievement and College Attendance of Hispanics." Paper presented at the annual meeting of the American Sociological Association, August 1980, at Montreal.

Marcum, Roger B. "An Exploration of the First Year Effects of Racial Integration of the Elementary Schools in a Unit District." Ph.D. dissertation, University of Illinois, 1968.

Marshall, Kim. "The Desegregation of a Boston Classroom." *Learning* 4 (August-September 1975):33–40.

Massachusetts Research Center. *Education and Enrollments: Boston During Phase II*. Boston: Massachusetts Research Center, 1976.

Mayeske, George W., and Beaton, Albert F., Jr. *Special Studies of Our Nation's Students*. Washington, D.C.: U.S. Government Printing Office, 1975.

Mayo, Samuel T. *Measurement in Education: Mastery Learning and Mastery Testing*. East Lansing, Mich.: National Council on Measurement in Education, March 1970.

Mercer, Jane R. *Labelling the Mentally Retarded*. Berkeley: The University of California Press, 1973.

Mercer, Jane R., and Lewis, June F. *System of Multicultural Pluralistic Assessment*. New York: Psychological Corporation, 1978.

Metz, Mary H. *Classrooms and Corridors: The Crisis of Authority in Desegregated Secondary Schools*. Berkeley: The University of California Press, 1978.

————. "Questioning the Centipede: Analysis of a Successful Desegregated School." Paper presented at the annual meeting of the American Educational Research Association, April 1980, at Boston.

Miller, John W., and Ellsworth, Randy. "The Evaluation of a Longitudinal Program to Improve Teacher Effectiveness in Reading Instruction." Paper presented at the annual meeting of the American Educational Research Association, March 1982, at New York.

Miller, Joyce D. "Student Suspensions in Boston: Derailing Desegregation." *Inequality in Education,* no. 20 (1975), pp. 16–24.

Milliken v. Bradley, 433 U.S. 282 (1977).

Mills, Roger, and Bryan, Miriam M. *Testing . . . Grouping: The New Segregation in Southern Schools?* Atlanta: Southern Regional Council, 1976.

Mizell, M. Hayes. "School Desegregation in South Carolina." *Integrated Education* 4 (December-January 1966–1967):30–50.

Mohlman, Georgea G. "Assessing the Impact of Three Inservice Teacher Training Models." Paper presented at the annual meeting of the American Educational Research Association, March 1982, at New York.

Monti, Daniel J. "Government Abandonment of Desegregation in Missouri." *Integrated Education* 17 (January-April 1979):2–8.

Moody, Charles D., Sr., and Ross, Jeffrey D. *Costs of Implementing Court-Ordered Desegregation.* Ann Arbor: The University of Michigan, School of Education, Program for Educational Opportunity, Fall 1980.

Moody, Charles D., Sr.; Williams, Junious; and Vergon, Charles B., eds. *Student Rights and Discipline: Policies, Programs, and Procedures.* Ann Arbor: The University of Michigan, School of Education, Program for Educational Opportunity, 1978.

Moore, J. William, and Schaut, Judith A. "Stability of Teaching Behavior, Responsiveness to Training and Teaching Effectiveness." *Journal of Educational Research* 69 (1976):360–363.

Morgan, David R., and England, Robert E. *Assessing the Progress of Large City School Desegregation: A Case Survey Approach.* Norman: The University of Oklahoma, Bureau of Government Research, November 1981.

Murphy, Hardy R. "District and Community Characteristics Influencing Desegregation Strategy Choice and Effectiveness." Paper presented at the annual meeting of the American Educational Research Association, April 1980, at Boston.

National Assessment of Educational Progress. Three National Assessments of Reading: Changes in Performance, 1970–80, Report No. 11–R–01. Denver, Colo.: Education Commission of the States, 1981.

National Institute of Education. *Compensatory Education Study: A Final Report*. Washington, D.C.: U.S. Government Printing Office, 1978a.

————. *Violent Schools—Safe Schools: The Safe School Study Report to the Congress*, vol. 1. Washington, D.C.: U.S. Government Printing Office, 1978b.

————. *In-School Alternatives to Suspension, Conference Report*. Washington, D.C.: U.S. Government Printing Office, April 1979.

National School Public Relations Association. *Suspensions and Expulsions: Current Trends in School Policies and Programs*. Arlington, Va.: National School Public Relations Association, 1976.

Natkin, Gerald L. "The Effects of Busing on Second Grade Students' Achievement Test Scores (Jefferson County, Kentucky)." Paper presented at the annual meeting of the American Educational Research Association, April 1980, at Boston.

Nitko, Anthony J., and Hsu, Tse-Chi. "Using Domain-Referenced Tests for Student Placement Diagnosis and Attainment in a System of Adaptive Individualized Instruction." *Education Technology* (June 1974):48–54.

Noboa, Abdin. *An Overview of Trends in Segregation of Hispanic Students in Major School Districts Having Large Hispanic Enrollments, Final Report*. Washington, D.C.: National Institute of Education, January 1980.

Oakes, Jeannie. "Tracking and Educational Inequality within Schools: Findings from a Study of Schooling." Paper presented at the annual meeting of the American Educational Research Association, April 1980, at Boston.

Orfield, Gary. *Toward a Strategy for Urban Integration: Lessons in School and Housing Policy from Twelve Cities*. New York: The Ford Foundation, December 1981.

————. *Desegregation of Black and Hispanic Students from 1968 to 1980*. Washington, D.C.: Joint Center for Political Studies, 1982.

Pearce, Diana M. *Breaking Down the Barriers: New Evidence on the Impact of Metropolitan School Desegregation on Housing Patterns*. Washington, D.C.: National Institute of Education, November 1980.

————. "Deciphering the Dynamics of Segregation: The Role of Schools in the Housing Choice Process." *The Urban Review* 13 (Summer 1981):85–102.

Peretti, Peter O. "Effects of Teachers' Attitudes on Discipline Problems in Schools Recently Desegregated." *Education* 97 (Winter 1976):136–140.

Plisko, Valena W., and Noell, Jay. "Elementary and Secondary Education." In *The Condition of Education: Statistical Report*. Washington, D.C.: U.S. Government Printing Office, 1978.

Ragosta, Marjorie; Holland, Paul W.; and Jamison, Dean T. *Computer Assisted Instruction and Compensatory Education, Final Implementation Reports, 1978–1979 School Year.* Princeton, N.J.: Educational Testing Service, 1980.

Redman, George L. "Study of the Relationship of Teacher Empathy for Minority Persons and Inservice Relations Training." *Journal of Educational Research* 70 (1977):205–210.

Regens, James L., and Bullock, Charles S., III. "Congruity of Racial Attitudes among Black and White Students." *Social Science Quarterly* 60 (1979):511–522.

Rist, Ray C. "Student Social Class and Teacher Expectations: The Self-Fulfilling Prophecy in Ghetto Education." *Harvard Educational Review* 40 (August 1970):411–451.

————, ed. *Desegregated Schools: Appraisals of an American Experiment.* New York: Academic Press, 1979.

[Robertson] v. Perk, Civil Action C 72–115, 2 May 1972 (USDC, ED).

Rogers, Everette. *Diffusion of Innovations.* New York: The Free Press, 1962.

Rogers, Marian; Miller, Norman; and Hennigan, Karen. "Cooperative Games as an Intervention to Promote Cross-Racial Acceptance." *American Educational Research Journal* 18 (1981):513–516.

Rosenholtz, Susan J. "The Multiple Abilities Curriculum: An Intervention against the Self-Fulfilling Prophecy." Ph.D. dissertation, Stanford University, 1977.

————. "Modifying a Status-Organizing Process of the Traditional Classroom." In *Status Attributions and Justice,* edited by Joseph Berger and Morris Zelditch, Jr. San Francisco: Jossey-Bass Publishers, 1982.

Ross, John Michael. Prepared testimony before the Subcommittee on Separation of Powers of the Committee on the Judiciary of the U.S. Senate, 97th Cong., 1st sess. on Court-Ordered School Busing, 1 October 1981. Washington, D.C.: Government Printing Office, 1982.

Ross, John Michael; Gratton, B.; and Clarke, R.C. *School Desegregation and "White Flight" Re-examined: Is the Issue Different Statistical Models?* Boston: Boston University, October 1981.

Rossell, Christine H. *District Council Liaison Committee Monitoring Report.* Boston: Citywide Coordinating Council, August 1977.

————. *Assessing the Unintended Impacts of Public Policy: School Desegregation and Resegregation.* Washington, D.C.: National Institute of Education, 1978a.

————. "The Effect of Community Leadership and the Mass Media on Public Behavior." *Theory into Practice* 17 (April 1978b):131–139.

————. "School Desegregation and Community Social Change." *Law and Contemporary Problems* 42 (Summer 1978c):133–183.

————. ''Magnet Schools as a Desegregation Tool: The Importance of Contextual Factors in Explaining Their Success.'' *Urban Education* 14 (1979):303–320.

————. ''The Effectiveness of Desegregation Plans in Reducing Racial Isolation, White Flight, and Achieving a Positive Community Response.'' In *Assessment of Current Knowledge about the Effectiveness of School Desegregation Strategies,* vol. 5, edited by Willis D. Hawley. Nashville, Tenn.: Vanderbilt University, Institute for Public Policy Studies, Center for Education and Human Development Policy, April 1981a.

————. *Is It the Distance or the Blacks?* Boston: Boston University, Department of Political Science, 1981b.

Rossell, Christine H., and Hawley, Willis D. ''Understanding White Flight and Doing Something about It.'' In *Effective School Desegregation: Equity, Quality, and Feasibility,* edited by Willis D. Hawley. Beverly Hills, Calif.: SAGE Publications, 1981.

————. ''Policy Alternatives for Minimizing White Flight.'' *Educational Evaluation and Policy Analysis* 4 (Summer 1982):205–222.

Rossell, Christine H., and Ross, John Michael. *The Long-Term Effect of Court-Ordered Desegregation on Student Enrollment in Central City Public School Systems: The Case of Boston, 1974–1979* (report prepared for the Boston School Department). Boston: Boston University, 1979.

Royster, Eugene C.; Blatzell, Catherine; and Simmons, Fran C. *Study of the Emergency School Aid Magnet School Program.* Cambridge, Mass.: ABT Associates, Inc., February 1979.

St. John, Nancy. *School Desegregation: Outcomes for Children.* New York: Wiley and Sons, 1975.

Schniedewind, Nancy. *Integrating Personal and Social Change in Teacher Training: A Project Report.* New Paltz, N.Y.: State University College, 1975.

Schofield, Janet W. ''Desegregation School Practices and Student Race Relations Outcome.'' In *Assessment of Current Knowledge about the Effectiveness of School Desegregation Strategies,* vol. 5, edited by Willis D. Hawley. Nashville, Tenn.: Vanderbilt University, Institute for Public Policy Studies, Center for Education and Human Development Policy, April 1981.

Schweitzer, John H., and Griffore, Robert J. ''A Longitudinal Study of Attitudes of Students and Parents Coincident with Court-Ordered School Desegregation.'' *The Urban Review* 13 (1981):111–119.

Serow, Robert C., and Solomon, Daniel. ''The Proximity Hypothesis of Parents' Support for Desegregation.'' Paper presented at the annual meeting of the American Educational Research Association, April 1979, at San Francisco.

Sharan, Shlomo. "Cooperative Learning in Small Groups: Research Methods and Effects on Achievement, Attitudes and Ethnic Relations." *Review of Educational Research* 50 (1980):241–272.

Sherif, Muzafer. "Superordinate Goals in the Reduction of Intergroup Conflict." *American Journal of Sociology* 68 (January 1958):349–356.

Shipman, Virginia; Boroson, Melinda; Bridgeman, Brent; Gant, Joyce; and Mikovsky, Michaele. *Notable Early Characteristics of High and Low Achieving Black Low-SES Children.* Princeton, N.J.: Educational Testing Service, December 1976.

Slavin, Robert E. "Multicultural Student Team Instructional Programs and Race Relations in Desegregated Schools." Paper presented at the annual meeting of the American Educational Research Association, March 1978, at Toronto.

———. "Cooperative Learning in Teams: State of the Art." *Educational Psychologist* 15 (Summer 1980):93–111.

Slavin, Robert E., and Madden, Nancy. "School Practices That Improve Race Relations." *American Educational Research Journal* 16 (1979):169–180.

Slavin, Robert E., and Oickle, Eileen. "Effects of Cooperative Learning Teams on Student Achievement and Race Relations: Treatment by Race Interactions." *Sociology of Education* 54 (July 1981):174–198.

Smith, Al D.; Downs, Anthony; and Lachman, M. Leanne. *Achieving Effective Desegregation.* Lexington, Mass.: Lexington Books, D.C. Heath, 1973.

Smylie, Mark A. *Reducing Racial Isolation in Large School Districts: The Comparative Effectiveness of Mandatory and Voluntary Desegregation Strategies.* Nashville, Tenn.: Vanderbilt University, Institute for Public Policy Studies, Center for Education Policy, February 1982.

Smylie, Mark A., and Hawley, Willis D. *Increasing the Effectiveness of Inservice Training for Desegregation: A Synthesis of Current Research.* Washington, D.C.: National Education Association, 1982.

Southern Regional Council. *The Student Pushout: Victim of Continued Resistance to Desegregation.* Atlanta: Southern Regional Council, 1973.

———. "A Conflict of Cultures." *Southern Exposure* 7 (May 1979):126–128.

Southern Schools: An Evaluation of the Emergency School Assistance Program and of Desegregation, vol. 1. Chicago: National Opinion Research Center, 1973.

Spangler v. Pasadena City Board of Education, 375 F. Supp. 1304 (1974).

Stuart, Reginald. "Busing and the Media in Nashville." *New South* 28 (Spring 1973):79–87.

Study Group on Racial Isolation in the Public Schools. *School Participation and School Quality: Attendance, Suspension and Dropouts in the Cleveland Public Schools.* Cleveland: Study Group on Racial Isolation in the Public Schools, 1978.

Stulac, Julie T. "The Self-Fulfilling Prophecy: Modifying the Effects of a Unidimensional Perception of Academic Competence in Task-Oriented Groups." Ph.D. dissertation, Stanford University, 1975.

Swann v. Charlotte-Mecklenburg County Board of Education, 243 F. Supp. 667 (1965); 369 F. 2d 29 (1965).

Swann v. Charlotte-Mecklenburg County Board of Education, 300 F. Supp. 1358 (1968).

Swann v. Charlotte-Mecklenburg County Board of Education, 402 U.S. 1 (1971).

Taeuber, Karl E., and Wilson, Franklin D. *A Study to Determine the Impact of School Desegregation Policy on the Racial and Socioeconomic Characteristics of the Nation's Schools and Residential Communities.* Madison: The University of Wisconsin, Institute for Research on Poverty, 1979.

Taylor, Garth, and Stinchcombe, Arthur. *The Boston School Desegregation Controversy.* Chicago: National Opinion Research Center, 1977.

Thomas, Charles B. "Race Relations in Desegregated Schools of Different Racial and Social Class Compositions." Paper presented at the annual meeting of the American Educational Research Association, April 1979, at San Francisco.

Thomas, Gail E. *The Impact of College Racial Composition on the Prompt Four-Year College Graduation of Black Students.* Baltimore: The Johns Hopkins University, Center for the Social Organization of Schools, 1980.

Turnage, Martha. *The Principal as Change-Agent in Desegregation.* Chicago: Integrated Educational Association, 1972.

U.S. Bureau of the Census. *Travel to School: October 1978.* Current Population Reports, Series P–20, no. 342. Washington, D.C.: U.S. Government Printing Office, 1979.

U.S. Commission on Civil Rights. *School Desegregation in Ten Communities.* Washington, D.C.: U.S. Government Printing Office, 1973.

————. *Fulfilling the Letter and Spirit of the Law: Desegregation of the*

Nation's Public Schools. Washington, D.C.: U.S. Government Printing Office, August 1976.

————. *Desegregation of the Nation's Public Schools: A Status Report.* Washington, D.C.: U.S. Government Printing Office, February 1979.

U.S. Department of Education. *The School Team Approach.* Washington, D.C.: U.S. Government Printing Office, 1980.

Vergon, Charles B. "The Courts and Desegregation Strategies: Ten Key Decisions." In *Assessment of Current Knowledge about the Effectiveness of School Desegregation Strategies,* vol. 7, edited by Willis D. Hawley. Nashville, Tenn.: Vanderbilt University, Institute for Public Policy Studies, Center for Education and Human Development Policy, April 1981.

Walberg, Herbert. Prepared testimony before the Subcommittee on Separation of Powers of the Committee on the Judiciary of the U.S. Senate, 97th Cong. 1st sess. on Court-Ordered School Busing, 30 September 1981. Washington, D.C.: U.S. Government Printing Office, 1982.

Weatherly, Richard L. *Reforming Special Education: Policy Implementation from State Level to Street Level.* Cambridge: Massachusetts Institute of Technology Press, 1979.

Weinberg, Meyer. *Minority Students: A Research Appraisal.* Washington, D.C.: U.S. Government Printing Office, March 1977.

————. "Housing and School Desegregation: Citizen Initiatives and Government Responses." *Integrated Education* 18 (January-August 1980):2–11.

Weinberg, Meyer, and Martin, Gertrude, eds. *Covering the Desegregation Story: Current Experiences and Issues.* Evanston, Ill.: Center for Equal Education, 1976.

Wellisch, Jean B.; Marcus, Alfred C.; MacQueen, Anne H.; and Duck, Gary A. *An In-Depth Study of Emergency School Aid Act Schools: 1974–1975.* Santa Monica, Calif.: System Development Corporation, July 1976.

Whitmore, Paul G.; Melching, William H.; and Frederickson, Edward W. *Gain in Student Achievement as a Function of Inservice Teacher Training in Classroom Management Techniques, Report No. 72–26.* Alexandria, Va.: Human Resources Research Organization, October 1972.

Williams, David L., Jr. "Validation of Effective Staff Development/Inservice Education Strategies." Paper presented at the annual meeting of the American Educational Research Association, April 1980, at Boston.

Williams, Robin, and Ryan, Margaret. *Schools in Transition.* Chapel Hill: The University of North Carolina Press, 1954.

Willie, Charles V., and Greenblatt, Susan. *Community Politics and Educational Change: Ten School Systems under Court-Order*. New York: Longman Press, 1981.

Winecoff, Larry, and Kelly, Eugene W., Jr. "Problems in School Desegregation: Real or Imaginary?" *Integrated Education* 9 (January-February 1971):3–10.

Wortman, Paul. Personal correspondence to Willis D. Hawley, 14 October 1981.

Wright, Lawrence. "The New Word is PUSHOUT." *Race Relations Reporter* 4 (May 1973):8–13.

Yudof, Mark G. "Implementing Desegregation Decrees." In *Effective School Desegregation: Equity, Quality, and Feasibility*, edited by Willis D. Hawley. Beverly Hills, Calif.: SAGE Publications, 1981.

Zoloth, Barbara. "Alternative Measures of School Segregation." *Land Economics* 52 (1976a):278–298.

———. "The Impact of Busing on Student Achievement: A Reanalysis." *Growth and Change* 7 (July 1976b):43–52.

Index

About the Authors

Robert L. Crain is senior social scientist for The Rand Corporation and principal research investigator at the Center for the Social Organization of Schools of The Johns Hopkins University. He has coauthored four books on the politics of school desegregation and effective desegregation strategies and has published a number of articles on desegregation and minority academic achievement. He holds the Ph.D. in sociology from the University of Chicago.

Ricardo R. Fernández is associate professor in the Department of Cultural Foundations of Education of the University of Wisconsin at Milwaukee and is director of the Midwest National Origin Desegregation Assistance Center. He is past president of the National Association for Bilingual Education and is a member of the Monitoring Board of Directors for the Puerto Rican Legal Defense and Education Fund. His research and writing emphasize the status of education for Hispanic students and desegregation and Hispanics. He received the Ph.D. in Romance languages and literatures from Princeton University.

Willis D. Hawley is dean of Peabody College, Vanderbilt University's School of Education and Human Development, and professor of education and political science at Vanderbilt. Before coming to Vanderbilt, he was director of the Center for Education Policy at Duke University. He served as director of the education study of the President's Reorganization Project from 1977 to 1978. He has been a consultant to the Office of Management and Budget, the U.S. Department of Education, and numerous state and local agencies. From 1979 to 1981 he was director of the U.S. Department of Education's Education Policy Development Center for Desegregation. His research and writings deal with desegregation, education policy, education research and development, organizational change, and the learning of political and social values. He received the Ph.D. in political science from the University of California at Berkeley.

Christine H. Rossell is associate professor of political science at Boston University. She has served as consultant to The Rand Corporation, the U.S. Office of Education, and the U.S. Department of Justice. Her primary research areas include white flight and school desegregation, community social change, and the use of social-science research in education-equity cases. She received the Ph.D. in political science from the University of Southern California.

209

Janet W. Schofield is associate professor of psychology at the University of Pittsburgh. She has also held policy-research positions with the federal government and has served as a consultant to both federal and local agencies. Her research and publications focus primarily on the development of students' racial attitudes and behavior. She holds the Ph.D. in social psychology from Harvard University.

Mark A. Smylie serves as coordinator of the Education Equity Project of the Center for Education Policy in Vanderbilt University's Institute for Public Policy Studies and is a doctoral candidate in education policy at Vanderbilt. His research and writing focus on the progress and status of desegregation in public schools and in higher education, and on in-service training for desegregation. He received the M.Ed. from Duke University and worked in public schools for six years.

Rachel Tompkins is director of the Children's Defense Fund and served as director of the Citizen's Council of Ohio Schools. She has supervised the development of materials for citizens and legislators in Ohio on the topic of school desegregation. She was editor of *Desegregation Update,* a periodical on current social-science research and legal developments in school desegregation. She received the Ed.D. from Harvard University.

William T. Trent is a research Fellow at The Johns Hopkins University Center for the Social Organization of Schools. Before going to Johns Hopkins, he was research associate at the Center for Education Policy, Institute for Policy Sciences and Public Affairs, Duke University. His research focuses on the education of minorities. He received the Ph.D. in sociology from the University of North Carolina at Chapel Hill.

Marilyn S. Zlotnik served at the Center for Education and Human Development Policy of Vanderbilt University's Institute for Public Policy Studies as grant and project coordinator for the *Assessment of Current Knowledge about the Effectiveness of School Desegregation Strategies.* She received the M.A. from Vanderbilt University and was awarded a Fulbright teaching assistantship in France.